Hope,
Interrupted

Hope, Interrupted

America Lost & Found In Letters

Byron McCauley and Jennifer Mooney

10/21/2021

Keep Hope Alive

Jenny Mooney

ORANGE *frazer* PRESS
Wilmington, Ohio

ISBN 978-1949248-418

Published for the copyright holders by:
Orange Frazer Press
37½ West Main St.
P.O. Box 214
Wilmington, OH 45177

Authors' Note: Following announcements made by both *The New York Times* and *The Washington Post* in July of 2020, we, too, began capitalizing the "B" in black, the "W" in white, and the "B" in brown whenever these words were used as racial or ethnic identifiers in our subsequent correspondence.

For price and shipping information, call: 937.382.3196
Or visit: www.orangefrazer.com

Book and cover design by:
Kelly Schutte and Orange Frazer Press

Library of Congress Control Number: 2021904218

First Printing

To the loves of our lives:
Don and Jill

And to our seven daughters:

Caroline

Laila

Loren

Nora

Maureen

Ryan

Simone

All our love,
Byron and Jennifer

"My country, 'tis of thee, sweet land of liberty, of thee I sing. Land where my fathers died, land of the pilgrim's pride, from every mountainside, let freedom ring. And if America is to be a great nation this must become true."

—*The Reverend Martin Luther King, Jr., 1962*

"Never doubt that a small group of thoughtful, committed, citizens can change the world. Indeed, it is the only thing that ever has."

—*Margaret Mead, Anthropologist, 1978*

Kudos for *Hope, Interrupted*

"The trusting friendship created in these beautiful letters is the cure for the cascade of crises that was 2020. You will believe again—that the future will be righteous and bright."

—*Buck Niehoff*, author of *Something Funny at the Library, Jammu Mail, Breathing in Africa, Walking the Thames*

"I have known Jennifer and Byron for almost twenty years. Byron was my first hire on the editorial page when I arrived as Editor of *The Cincinnati Enquirer* and in my first weeks I met Jennifer, who was an influential public relations expert in the community. Over the years they both became good friends and I thought I knew them well, but reading their touching and thoughtful letters introduced me to a new dimension of their character and caring.

Hope, Interrupted is a powerful story of hope, optimism and perseverance, told well by two superb writers. Thank you Byron and Jennifer for this gift to the world, and for your continued friendship."

—*Tom Callinan*, retired in 2010 after a 35-year career as an editor, including *The Arizona Republic, Cincinnati Enquirer,* Rochester (NY) *Democrat and Chronicle.*

"*Hope, Interrupted* is a tale told through a series of letters between two people from disparate backgrounds. At a time when people are being forced to isolate, these two scribes seek a deeper bond. The politics of racism are examined against the backdrop of a pandemic, while the two principles share experiences while always looking toward hope and understanding. This sharing of thoughts while engaging in communication, real communication, helps both make sense of a senseless time. Jennifer and Byron are different from one another in race, religion and upbringing, but these differences, instead of driving a wedge between them, acts as an opening to stronger understanding. Walk a mile in their shoes. I did and found the walk worth taking."

—*Craig Dirgo,* author of *The Einstein Papers* and other novels

"If *Hope, Interrupted* crystalizes the anxiety, disbelief, rage, and grief so many of us experienced in 2020, it also reminds us how foundational—how utterly vital—our friendships are in such times. These pages are filled with a wise interrogation of history (both personal and political) but above all else they are filled with trust, and the knowledge that openness and honesty and a ceaseless, unflinching look into the past has always been the only human way forward."

—*Daniel Anderson,* Creative Writing Professor University of Oregon, American Poet, author of *Drunk In Sunlight*

"As May turned to June 2020, most of us knew we were truly living in a year unlike any we'd seen or would see. It was perhaps, for us, our 1968. A three-headed crisis grew that combined pandemic, economic collapse and racial tensions. Many of us thought of journaling, wanting to write down and record our observations and experiences. Jennifer Mooney and Byron McCauley actually did. And when they decided to play their journal entries off each other in the form of almost daily email correspondence, their collective perspectives gained richness and depth. Here, a Southern Black Christian and a White Northern Jew shared secrets, fears, hopes and chatted electronically like two neighbors sitting on a porch. What emerges is a map forward, a path that our divided nation and its people might follow, one of civility and thoughtful conversation recognizing their shared love of country despite its flaws and their own differences of opinion. McCauley has the newspaper columnist's chops, but Mooney proves his equal in this format. You could say that's the idea.

There's a lot happening here at once. A retelling of a pivotal six months in our national life. Two smart people sharing their observations on race, public health, the economy, their families, and the common good. The reader also becomes privy to watching a friendship bloom into fuller blossom. On their own, McCauley and Mooney's journals are worth a read. Together, they become something even better."

—*Mark Curnutte,* visiting instructor of social justice, Miami
University; author of *Across the Color Line* and *A Promise in Haiti*

"While the beautiful and searching letters of *Hope, Interrupted* take place between two very different but deeply connected people, there is a third participant as well: each reader, like this one, who enters into the dialogues with intrigue and delight, moved and inspired by the probing, often poignant, conversations. Whether the topics be family or faith, Black or Jewish identity, or a pandemic and political upheaval, McCauley and Mooney practice an ancient art that gives fresh meaning to the turbulence of the day and shores up hope for the future—what McCauley calls 'the healing power of communication.'"

—*Roy Hoffman,* author of the essay collection *Alabama Afternoons,*
and the novels *Chicken Dreaming Corn* and *Come Landfall*

Table of Contents

Prologue

November, 2020

A spotlight literally shone on Jennifer Mooney, a respected communications executive in a town admired by seasoned and aspiring marketers, as she delivered a keynote address at a local university ballroom.

"She glowed like a celebrity behind a podium. I didn't know her that well, but I had the nerve to ask her if she would share her presentation with me," said Byron, one of 500 people who heard her. "She said 'she wasn't sure,' but she said it in a very kind way. I liked her immediately. Later, a 'clean' version of her PowerPoint showed up in my inbox."

Byron was a columnist for the local paper and Jennifer liked his work. One day, they met for coffee, and a deep and lasting friendship was born.

Hope, Interrupted is a cautionary story of hope and fear. It is a story of optimism and existential dread. It is a story of choosing to live fully in a country enduring unprecedented challenges.

Byron is a Black man who was born and raised in the South. Jennifer is a Jewish woman who grew up in the North. They are friends who wrote to each other daily over six months of COVID, a failing economy, challenged social justice and political unrest. They are average Americans, born two years apart who jointly experience family, working lives, marriage, health and the future of a fractured nation.

Written from the Midwest, Mountain West and South, they explore the mood that traverses our country. Byron, an award-winning columnist and business executive and Jennifer, an award-winning communications executive with scholarship in psychology, lean into hope and ask if there is or ever truly was, an American Dream.

We picked up our pens and told our own stories of life during COVID in a fractured nation. We are two regular people who developed a deep friendship that intensified along with deepening life challenges. To be sure, to some we might be unlikely allies, born into what may appear vastly different circumstances, miles from one another with contrasting life stories.

Yet, ultimately our stories are similar and they are an American story.

We have the love of strong and supportive families, the gift of good mothering, solid educational opportunities, Midwestern sensibilities and place high value on that thing called hope. These attributes bless us with the ability to see beyond the here and now to better times.

We also know that once individuals connect personally, bigotry and hate become less possible.

While it is often easy to malign a group, it is much more difficult to malign a person. An editor laughed at us and said that he didn't imagine that our mutual exercise could result in disparate people suddenly writing to one another, the old-fashioned way.

We disagree.

We believe that we might encourage people to really know one another.

To learn what is in one another's hearts.

To understand one other's minds.

To value one another's differences.

To respect one another's lives.

We are optimists who believe in the best of humanity.

We invite you to explore *Hope, Interrupted*.

We agree with the young Anne Frank who wrote the following a short time before her life abruptly ended:

"It's difficult in times like these: ideals, dreams and cherished hopes rise within us, only to be crushed by grim reality. It's a wonder I haven't abandoned all my ideals, they seem so absurd and impractical. Yet I cling to them because I still believe, in spite of everything, that people are truly good at heart."

Byron and Jennifer
Cincinnati and Arroyo Seco-Taos, USA

Hope,
Interrupted

Burying a Friend

Saturday, June 6, 2020
Taos, New Mexico

Dear Byron,

A weird day here in Taos, New Mexico. It is the third anniversary of the death of my friend Karen (thankfully she doesn't know what's become of her name, Karen...that a "Karen" is now a moniker for an annoying white woman who complains.)

Today is the anniversary of the day that we spread her ashes to her favorite place. It is called La Junta and where the Rio Grande meets the Red River. It is untamed with a rapid current, a steep canyon and history carved into the hillsides. There are rarely many people on the trail. I am sad and miss her and am mutually thinking of the poor folks who are not able to have funerals or gatherings due to threatening COVID.

I can't get my head around it. Is it better to have died with public tributes or to have lived until now through the madness? Welcome to the times that COVID wrought. I know she would have been an asset to life today.

She was a professor in Texas and would have been involved with COVID solutions. Her major study areas were both cancer and AIDS. She also knew national infectious disease expert Dr. Fauci and called him "Tony."

To the rest of us, he is Dr. Fauci.

She was my first friend in Taos. During her life, we both lived here part time. We met in a bar. (A since closed place called The Old Blinking Light, located at mile marker one on the Ski Valley Road.) She thought (with my brownish skin) that I was a Pueblo Indian. Turned out we were both just American Jews.

So, get this. I was called a Nazi today—in the grocery store. We went to the farmer's market first. All good. Everyone was in masks and peaceful. Going to the big store always feels "risky" even though masks are required by law here.

We were in the checkout and I looked over and saw a woman gesturing in the face of a store employee. She was not wearing a mask—the only a person (whom I observed) in a crowded store without one. She was about my age, hippie wear, and looked like a peace-loving type. He was a young, tall black man monitoring people at the self-checkout.

I noticed that she was yelling, and finger-pointing. I approached and said, "please move back, you do not have on a mask and are less than six feet away from him." She yelled at me and said, "You are the problem, you believe the hoax and you are being violent." He looked at me and said "thanks" and stared straight ahead. I went back to my lane. Don looked as if he thought that I might get in a fistfight (never been in one). I kept track of her.

I noted she was in his face again yelling about the self-serve checkout. Again, I approached, and she yelled, "You are a Nazi." And I yelled back "No, I am a Jew." Our checker said, "That lady always causes problems here and never wears a mask."

That's a first; my being called a Nazi.

Then I am thinking, should I have gotten involved? I don't know how to sit back now.

I also had that article on my mind that I sent you this morning about Black Lives Matter; "I don't need love texts from my white friends (*NY Times*, today) in which the writer (Chad Sanders) said that the "thinking of you, etc" texts are pretty much vapid. When I sent it to you…you said that you didn't feel that way at all.

Since it seems I text daily about all of the injustice out there—wondered if I am, in fact, one of those annoying white people?

It continues to be the question.

Maybe this was all on my mind when I viewed this woman. Don't think I can continue to just be polite. Ugh.

Love,

Jennifer

Our Neighbor's Daughter Died

Sunday, June 7, 2020
Cincinnati, Ohio

Jen,

No, you are not one of those "annoying white people."

I'm writing at the end of a very long day. I wanted to write earlier, but I also really wanted to be done with everything that was going on today to put things in perspective.

I hardly watched any news today (yay, me!). But as I was riding in the car, I had Sirius/XM Radio on CNN and heard Gen. Colin Powell say he will not be voting for Trump in 2020. He didn't support him in 2016, either. And just now, I saw where Sen. Mitt Romney, never a friend of Trump, is not supporting him in his run for president. I have always liked Colin Powell. I was enamored with his role in government in the 1980s and 1990s because he was one of the few African-American Republicans who could provide an example for those of us who fancied ourselves conservatives as well.

Romney's dad was an integrationist in Michigan, which I appreciated, but the Mormon Church once considered African Americans inferior and would not allow them to become church leaders. Life—it's full of contradictions. Lord knows the Mormons haven't cornered the religious bigotry market.

I feel like we are embarking on significant social change, the kind that I have not seen in my lifetime—even when Americans elected President Obama in 2008.

So, let me tell you about today. We canceled services at our church, Compass Community Church in Sharonville, and partnered with the Red Door Church in Forest Park to walk to honor George Floyd and other African Americans who have died at the hands of police. Our church is fully integrated, peppered with blended and mixed-race families. I would say inclusion is one of our core values. Our pastor is Bahamian. Most worshippers at the Red Door Church would probably self-identify white. And when we got together and walked 4.8 miles from our church to theirs, it was quite a sight. It was hot and many people could not make the entire route.

But here we were in suburban Cincinnati with our little protest with a large dose of unity. The police chiefs of Forest Park and Springdale walked with us, too, along with some of their deputies. Springdale police walked with a heavy heart because they had just lost a promising African-American officer in a tragic automobile accident on the loop around the city. The blue lights of more than forty police cars lit up the night. Jill was out and passed by the scene. We all knew a tragedy had occurred.

I told you that I had not been able to weep since Mr. Floyd's death nearly two weeks ago, but reading how you were called a Nazi for wearing a mask and standing up for a young black man in New Mexico brought tears. I really don't know why. It could have been a feeling of hopelessness that there will always be jerks around. Or maybe the fact that I saw myself in that young man once upon a time.

I would like to talk more later about how I—as a black man—always have to navigate two worlds. I'm the same person in both worlds, but I realize I become more magnanimous and exaggerated when I'm meeting a white person for the first time (argh!). That's what I found myself doing today when I met three police officers for the first time. I really felt good about them being there. Any time we get to have an interpersonal experience with police, that is an opportunity to connect and see the other as human. I love my children. They love their children.

Finally, our former neighbor, Lizzie, died Wednesday in Florida. We met Lizzie when she was eight and we moved two doors down from them in a great neighborhood in the northern suburbs of Cincinnati. Our Loren was eight as well, and they became fast friends. We still don't know how Lizzie died. Her dad is a member of the Republican Central Committee out there and a terrific human being. We were always good to each other. I sent the family two large pizzas for dinner tonight.

He texted me: "Perfect touch. Thanks so much. We were hungry, too. Love to you." MJM

I love MJM, too, Jen.

For the second time in two days, I shed tears. Lizzie, like members of my own family, struggled with mental health, we have learned. To me, she will forever be the skinny, tow-headed girl who rode her bike down the hill, rang our doorbell and came to play with Loren. I read her posts on Facebook. The last was made three days before she died. She was a furious supporter of Black Lives Matter. She was furious about George Floyd's killing. She told her friends her choices did not mean she was not a good, moral person. They didn't get her. She told them to get over themselves.

This made me smile.

Goodnight, Jen. I'm sleepy.

Byron

Life Lessons from Gretchen

Monday, June 8, 2020
Taos, New Mexico

Good Morning my friend,

Wow. What a day you had. It is truly sad about Loren's friend. And yet so heartening to see a young person who stood up for justice. Our youngest, Nora (in Berlin), attended a 15K (people) protest on Saturday. We are proud of her. Maybe I should be concerned about her being close to people with COVID, but more than anything, I am glad for her actions. Having her so far away now is hard. It never occurred to me that my daughter, living in the seat of the Reich, would be safer than we Americans.

She is doing what young people are meant to do—on their own terms.

Don and I took to the trail. A client (on a Sunday morning) decided to bug me about needless stuff. I tried to shut her down. I needed a day off and the work is not life changing. Not even close. From the trail I texted her—severing the agreement. We all work for $$$, but at times we make choices. My priorities have changed for sure.

I grew up in Wyoming, Ohio. I was raised to understand discrimination, by both my family and, as you know, Gretchen, who took care of my sister and me, along with my mother. I am not proud that I was in a family with a black housekeeper, helper, friend, but that was my reality.

Gretchen taught me more than anyone could about what it was like living as Gretchen. When she gave us baths, she told us stories. She taught me to sew, to knit, to crochet. She made clothing for my dolls. I remember watching "The Ten Commandments" with her on the small black and white Sony TV (that was in her room.) She was a sweet woman with her own children and a son who died.

Her other two (daughters) turned out well. I feel her impact today.

She was small in stature and wore the cat-eye eyeglasses that were the style in the 1960s. She was mighty and she loved us. She often spoke of her church. Years later she died. My mother and I went to her funeral. We were the only white people and it was the first time that I witnessed an uplifting religious service. It was filled with joy about Gretchen being called home.

I was a privileged white girl. Yes, it was kind of like the book, *The Help* (Kathryn Stockett). While I am embarrassed to have grown up like this, I am pretty sure that my view of equality and humanity was molded by the learnings taught by Gretchen.

Today, I ended up getting into a heated FB exchange that was launched by the Wyoming (Ohio) High (WHS) School 1981 head cheerleader and most popular girl. I have learned that many of my classmates are not only pro-Trump but feel deep sympathy for cops.

In my younger years, I just wanted these people to like me.

I maintained what I thought was a group of diverse and forward-thinking friends. I had my share of antisemitic tropes thrown at me. I understood feeling different and not being invited to join the local country club or to participate in the Young Life Christian Group. I sang along with the other Girl Scouts to the song "you know that we are Christian by our love." I felt like an imposter, but I am certain, never like the small group of black students felt.

Today on FB, the cheerleader posted … and an old friend, yes, a Black girlfriend. Both she and her husband went to WHS. We challenged the cheerleader about racism in this country. About people who are not classic American white people. I then had some sidebar chats with my girlfriend. She said, "They make me sick." She thanked me for stepping out. I let her know that her experience is much different than mine. That I have been able to navigate discreetly, something that she has not been able to (due to my complexion). She said, "she thinks of Jews as her brothers and sisters."

Me too. Like the '60s.

I am bothered by the really wealthy Jews who ignore all of this; some voted for Trump. And then there is Malcolm X and that he and Farrakhan espoused some antisemitism.

Our American experience has been much more fair than yours. But we also know what it means to be maligned, hated and not welcome.

We need each other now more than ever—regardless of what any of our own leaders have said. And when they "come for one of us," they "come for all of us."

Hope your day is good. The sun is shining here. We have work. Our kids are well. Onward, right? You and I have never talked about some of this. Love to know what you think.

Jennifer

Too Many Gretchens

Tuesday, June 9, 2020
Cincinnati, Ohio

Dear Jennifer,

Thank you for sharing, especially the part about Gretchen and Wyoming Miss Congeniality (ha!). It's amazing how the older we get, the less some of us change. Frankly, I cannot see how folks can still support the current president. He simply has no feelings and no rock bottom.

There are so many Gretchens in this world, and thank God for them, because for so many non-black children, the Gretchens represented love and protection. I had a friend in Louisiana who was originally from Mississippi. He still kept the "farmland" that had been in his family for generations. He used to tell me how he was practically raised by their housekeeper, and I think it made him a better adult. However, our relationship did not get a chance to progress much because of who he was in the community and who I was in the community. I guess what I'm getting at is we all have a role to play to move the world forward, and we don't have much time left to get it right.

That's why I feel so fortunate to have you as a friend and confidante.

Today, I published a column titled "Are you black first, or are you a journalist first?" You might have read it. I received a ton of feedback from friends and strangers. The most surprising feedback came from the editor of the paper, who called my reversing the races of the subject "brilliant" and copied my immediate supervisor, his second in command, who is reserved (I'm being kind) about encouragement. That is unfortunate.

Something else unusual. My neighbor came over and stood in the front yard while I was on the porch (which is what our families were going to do before you returned to NM). They moved here a year ago. He told me his parents and grandparents were racists, and they will be on the losing side of history.

Everyday, something like that has happened since all the unrest surrounding George Floyd's death, whether online or in-person. I sense a huge change is afoot, but I also feel uncertainty because our sitting president is a divider, not a unifier.

Good night, my friend.

Byron

Life on the Continent

Wednesday, June 10, 2020
Taos, New Mexico

Dear Byron,

Today was a day of mostly hope. It sounds like yours was yesterday. Hope for humanity and hope for learning. Candidly, it is easy to hope in Taos, NM. Yep, this is a bubble of mostly like-minded people. Yet we all know that "off the grid" and in the hills are people running from things, hiding and yes, haters. Compounds of "no good activity" are found here every few years. So, we live in the sun dappled spaces, work remotely and pretend that things will be OK.

It says something to me—that your neighbor came over—and put himself out there. I am also glad that your column was so well-received. People are starting to finally talk. For hundreds of years our country has simply tried to get on with things. What is happening now is humans doing the one-to-one thing, not commissions or studies.

At the same time, COVID does not seem to be abating, and yet people are getting out to connect with one another. Who would have thought that it took a medieval virus to possibly bring us together?

And while you and I have been friends for a while, writing to each other has taken our raw thoughts to a deeper place. After a lifetime in communications—I now know that honest and straightforward talk might actually work.

We talked to Nora via FaceTime in Berlin today—more about the "protest." She explains that it wasn't a protest, but people coming together for "Black Lives Matter." She also told us that she fears that the behavior in the U.S. (racism) will mimic itself around the world.

There is something powerful about 15,000 people congregating together in Berlin to stand up for social justice. She also went to a major government building today for some paperwork. She noted the "Hitler" eagle still on the building with the Swastika covered by a number.

All of these symbols in the same city at the same time. Truth, power, frightening and real.

Later on, we were in a part of town with a famous church. And yes, all towns in NM have major churches. They are old, Spanish and rustic. This one is the St. Francis Assisi that Georgia O'Keeffe painted (1930) and has been widely photographed.

The original structure was built in the 1700s. This is a place that has been through something. The straw bale structure is failing, maybe to be repaired someday. I am not a Christian and not religious, but that it still stands while possibly losing the heft to its structure speaks loudly.

And while I am writing and listening to music John Lennon's "Imagine" comes on…

This gives me hope.

Look forward to hearing from you.

Love,

Jennifer

Are You Black First?

Thursday, June 11, 2020
Cincinnati, Ohio

Dear Jennifer,

I felt a range of emotions when you described Nora's experience in Berlin, the Hitler Eagle, all the evil that came out of the country, and also the good that's happening today. It makes me feel sad that Nora sees the exportation of racism on the horizon. The president's actions are not being helpful.

I also chuckled about the way you talked about Taos—"compounds of no good activity." The churches, as I mentioned earlier, fascinate me. I will visit someday. I feel like New Mexico holds my heart song.

Meanwhile, what a day!

This morning, I appeared on the Lincoln Ware radio show on WDBZ "The Buzz," which, to the uninitiated, is the radio station that has a largely Black audience in Cincinnati.

He wanted to discuss the column that appeared in the *Enquirer* Thursday titled "Are you black first, or are you a journalist first?" which has been making the rounds throughout the country. Lincoln is a professional agitator (some might say "pot stirrer") and a very good person. He asked the question again on the radio as if to say, "well, what ARE you," initially choosing not to address the intent of the column, which was to question why I was even asked such a question thirty years ago by my managing editor.

Then, an hour later, I appeared on WVXU's (Cincinnati Public Radio) *Cincinnati Edition* with Michael Monks, who wanted to talk about the issue as well as something I wrote the other day about reaching back to police officers (referencing our church walk). There is great irony in both approaches to the subject. The Black host was mildly antagonistic; Monks, who is white, spent the first half of the show (thirty minutes) expressing compassion and empathy. Two different broadcast styles, both effective.

And then my editor shared this and these words with the staff today as part of his Friday memo. For context, in the previous paragraph, he talked about having courageous conversations in his Leadership Cincinnati class as a precursor to a meeting we will have next week. I predict a lot of uncomfortable situations that we have swept under the rug heretofore, but that we really need to discuss.

OK, here goes:

"Speaking of courageous voices, I want to thank Byron McCauley for sharing his this week. His column about an experience early in his career, 'Are you black first or are you a journalist first?' struck a chord with our readers. Here's one response:"

I have always appreciated your even-handed yet passionate journalism, Byron. You bring so much to the Enquirer *and to the city. This white, 66-year-old woman hopes you'll stay a long time, making a difference. I have begun praying that God will grant racial reconciliation in my lifetime. Why not ask? Only God can change hearts, including mine.*

Until next time,

Repeating History

Friday, June 12, 2020
Taos, New Mexico

Hey Friend,

An interesting day of contradictions. I pitched media while heading to a Santa Fe outing. We have had a few out-of-towners in (I know, poor form during the time of COVID) and took them to see the old city. We were very masked up (as was all of town).

I was heartened to hear that your work is being given long-overdue credit. You are one of the best writers (of our time) and I'm glad that the brass sees your value. I also hope that you are able to take your talents to a place in which you are appreciated daily.

You and I texted back and forth about adventure. It has been in my DNA since I was a young girl and the oldest grandchild. My grandfather (Gramps), a lifelong West Virginian, was raised poor by immigrants and became a pediatrician.

He believed in the outdoors, solitude and adventure. I was his sidekick while fishing, riding horses and walking in nature. He viewed these adventures as an important luxury. Long term, it has stuck with me and continues to be an elemental part of life—especially now. He knew the world (as a doc) prior to vaccines and penicillin. He is truly turning in his Charleston, West Virginia grave re: what is happening today.

Much adventure is on hold, but I contend that it can be found when least expected.

Our generation has been fortunate. We have lived in the times of modern medicine and relative peace (or so we gathered). The past months have articulated the fragile and flimsy nature of our country. We have lived with false American bravado.

Our land of the free and home of the brave.

Santa Fe is a scenic and historic town. It boasts the oldest government building in the nation and is the second oldest city in the USA. New Mexico became a state in 1912. The square is surrounded by buildings of brown mud bricks and massive vigas.

Santa Fe is ground zero of convergence between Spanish settlers, Indians and gringo traders. I am always stunned at how folks crossed the country and claimed land that was never "ours-theirs" to begin with. This is a land in which the white man has "learned his place."

Up the road in Los Alamos, the atomic bomb was invented (The Manhattan Project, 1945). Our government ultimately imported German (Nazi) scientists to teach us about their own technology. As we look back (which we almost never do) we witness the same patterns, century after century: war, disease, bigotry, money winning and values in question. This collision is stark in New Mexico.

Yet, I love it here, with all of its challenges and hypocrisy. And I love that, statewide, gringos are not, in fact, in charge. And yes, that Nixon gave the Taos Indians back their land (Taos Pueblo, Blue Lake, 1970).

They say that those who ignore history are doomed to repeat it. Here we go again.

Look forward to hearing from you.

Love,

Jennifer

Sweet Home, New Mexico

Saturday, June 13, 2020
Cincinnati, Ohio

Dear Jen,

Today was a terrific day. The temperature was sixty-eight degrees at 4 p.m., and there was no humidity to speak of. I mowed the lawn, then I drove out to see my friend who lives in the suburbs. He is a terrific guy. He has two boys, each of whom attended/or are currently attending a great public school. His oldest is doing well at a big public university. The younger child is an honor student and a pretty good basketball player.

I mentioned this friend in our texts. He works at one of our region's traditionally conservative companies and is doing well. Sadly, it looks like he has reached a glass ceiling of sorts, which is unfortunate. He's a Black man who has done well and knows he can do so much more; yet, he may not fulfill the potential both he and I believe he has if he does not unlock the golden handcuffs. He also noted that it took company leadership ten days to issue a statement in the aftermath of the George Floyd tragedy. I felt that was about par for the course. I have believed in this company. Today, I feel like it has regressed, from a cultural standpoint at least.

Moving on, I have always been fascinated by the Southwest, specifically New Mexico. Twenty years ago in New York, I met a doctor named Diane Alaimo, who was moving to an Indian Reservation to practice medicine. She is still there. I have been to Albuquerque to visit one of the New Tech Network schools developed by KnowledgeWorks, my former company. Just something about the air and the sky and the soil and the food. Oh, the food! We went to El Pinto, made more famous by President Clinton when he visited. Have you guys ever eaten there? And we stayed at the Hotel Andaluz. I know Taos and Santa Fe and Albuquerque have different vibes, but my heart and soul felt freer during the days I visited.

Perhaps oddly, when I think of New Mexico and the Southwest, I only think of the food, the architecture and the topography. So, I find the conflagration of gringo, Native peoples, and Mexico super interesting. Tell me more? Why did you guys choose Taos? Is it pricey? Are there other options? And, finally, how do the cultures mix? How would we be welcomed? I hate to have to ask that.

Love,

Byron

P.S. I love "Imagine." That's so apropos right now.

When It's Okay to Shoot a Black Man

Sunday, June 14, 2020
Taos, New Mexico

Dear Friend,

Your letters always teach me. For what it's worth, I don't trust most people in the "C-suite" either. Having worked in one for two decades, I saw first-hand the machinations, drama and intentions. Although, the president for whom I worked for fifteen of those twenty years was a stellar and fair man. As with anything, there are some decent folks. Business places have their own competitions and political aura which often "gets in the way" of the work.

Regarding New Mexico, our journey to finally land here was cosmic as with many things New Mexico. We started to come to Taos for vacation in the 90s. We fell pretty hard for the place. The confluence of cultures, the deep history and the rugged land. To be sure, this is certainly a state with both far left and far right elements. And everyone has a story. Go into a bar any night and you learn history of both this place and the people.

One is as likely to run into actor Dennis Hopper (when he lived) as the former governor and presidential candidate Libertarian Gary Johnson.

Confession: I did vote for Johnson when he ran for president.

All these years later and this rough-hewn place still has a hold on me.

Prior to 9/11, we had been traveling quite a bit internationally. The world collapsed and we sought a place to go that we could reach by car, grab the kids, grow our own vegetables and hide out. Little did we know that nineteen years later, we would do just that, but this time due to a microscopic element.

It is a privilege that we are able to work remotely. Our governor is strict and prudent.

There is an odd sense that we are amidst epic beauty with the world crumbling around us. My mom said to me, "It seems that you and Don are hiking lots." I said, "We will until (for some reason) we can no longer."

My goal (from age ten) was to become a full-time Westerner. I did a two-year stint in the mountains of Colorado after college. My gramps used to say, "the people are different out West, more open." It certainly feels that way.

Your own family would embrace life here. No, there are not many black people, but it is most certainly a brown state. We (both you and me) are minorities here.

Honest truth. I am really having trouble determining whether I am a decent white person or not. Trolling the news, social media and reading, I know that I am fair-minded. I know that I have always had friends who are black, brown, yellow, red and white. I know that I am appalled at how black America has been treated. I know that I get it—to know that some people are simply going to loathe me due to the "race" or religion to which I was born.

I also know that as painful as it is at times, I have often hidden it. Again, a privilege.

The hiding has offered a periscope into what people really think. And I come from a people who have been systematically hated and destroyed.

The place in which I grew up has what is sometimes the number one school district in the state and usually in the top tier in the nation. People live in Wyoming for the schools. I also recently learned that our school district was the last to integrate in the state. I am embarrassed about this. The black children with whom I went to school were not permitted to enter the swim club. How did I not know this?

I recently learned that there is a "plaque" (placed in 1993) that says:

"Site of the Oak Avenue School.
Established 1873-1956
For the Education of African American Students of Wyoming."

My family moved to Wyoming in the 1960s. An instant later.

This hurts my heart. While my family was progressive—we were part of the white community, the lesser white community though since we were "Jews."

So, to today…

My friend who lives in another Cincinnati neighborhood (in which we lived for a time) showed me a note that someone placed on the "on-line next-door publication." It is a flow chart that indicates when it is OK to "shoot a black man" and reviews different scenarios that relate to everything from someone minding their own business, to someone breaking and entering, to someone performing bodily harm on another.

This was this past week. Now. Today.

I remember a Spielberg interview in which he said that "the Holocaust was yesterday." It has taken me years to understand what this meant. What I know for sure is that bigotry is today.

Look forward to your next letter,

Jennifer

An Ordinary Day

Monday, June 15, 2020
Cincinnati, Ohio

Dear Jen,

Is it OK to have just an ordinary day?

Because that's what today was. Ordinary. And, given the circumstances, that's OK. One thing I realized is that I am spent. Tired of answering the question, "What can I do?" Because I'm in the public eye, everyone asks. Or at least it feels like everyone. And so when I got a breathless request today from a friend working in Kenya who was told "go home and put out your own fire," that felt like the straw that broke the camel's back.

He wants to paint the letters BLACK LIVES MATTER in the Central Business District like the one in DC. Did I have some people in place who can help get this done?! Pronto!

Lord.

I truly feel like we don't need any more grand gestures. We just need earnest listeners. If anything, I think we should register people to vote. I would bet half the people protesting are not registered to vote.

Let me tell you about my diet. I've been eating 1,500 calories a day for three weeks. I have lost nine pounds and one inch. I have yo-yoed. It has to do with stress, poor eating habits, exercise and, I believe, trauma. On Wednesday, I'm entering into a guided medical weight-loss program that reduces calories even more drastically while increasing nutrients.

Two newspaper colleagues completed the program. One lost 100 pounds in twelve months. He is a new man! For me, I feel like it is a matter of life and death. So I'm getting on with it.

Funny thing, I finished the column I was telling you about. No one from the restaurant called me back. I left messages with three people, including on the Frenchman's cell phone.

Oddly enough, the Frenchman's wife followed me on LinkedIn after poking about. I asked if she wanted to chat.

Crickets.

To be clear, I admire the chef and owner who has added unmatched culinary value to our town. It is because of him that others have come here and expanded our culinary tastes far beyond cheesy, cinnamon chili and sausage with oats.

Meanwhile, I think the problem is that they have one employee who is not practicing great customer success habits. There is some kind of loyalty connection there. But a friend told me he stopped going there because this person, the general manager, was an Ajole and was not enthusiastic about making customers happy.

What a fantastic web we weave.

Talk soon!

Byron

It's Happening Again

Tuesday, June 16, 2020
Taos, New Mexico

Dear Byron,

It is exactly OK to have an ordinary day. I, too, had one yesterday. Most of our days connect to COVID or bigotry. My mind seems to not want to break free from any of it.

The soundtrack of the day is a governor (any governor) reading stats in a disembodied voice.

And then there are weird intense dreams. They say that everyone is having them. It seems like our brains are on overtime. Again, I am fortunate to be in what seems a peaceful place.

I woke up today and learned of a bad situation here in the Land of Enchantment. Like in many places, monuments are being removed. This time Albuquerque and a monument of a Spanish conquistador with one group tearing it down and the other in militia wear trying to stop the first. No police in sight. And a man is shot. Violence in The Land of Enchantment.

NM is the land of historic warring factions. The issues were generally land and freedom. People here are angry just like everywhere else. We are no different. This news made it in *The Washington Post* and *The New York Times*—big time for a little state that Trump thought wasn't part of the USA.

The other night we had our guide from our 2017 Kilimanjaro summit over for socially distant cocktails. Both he and Don are "liberals" and peace-loving men. Both talked about getting guns. My mouth dropped. I imagine that many people are considering the same.

I don't think either has ever fired a gun.

My reading is 50% about WWII, Nazis and Europe. In my current read, *When Time Stopped* (Neumann), a woman travels back to learn about what really happened to her family in WWII Europe. Some themes are emerging about what feels a little too much like today:

1. Loss of Freedom
2. Poor economy, loss of jobs
3. Families spread across different borders and not able to see one another

Different times. Maybe.

Maybe nothing has changed.

The underlying reasons appear to be unique, but not so much.

I have always asked (since I was young) if what happened in Europe could happen again? I attest that it can and it is. Maybe the group of people to whom it is happening to is a different group—but once bigotry and hatred are activated, they come for all of us. No one is spared.

You and I exchanged texts about the column that I wrote for the paper (two years ago) that started by saying "I am a Jewess" and explained my own fears and growing up afraid and a goal for blacks and Jews to stick together.

The American Jewish Community has benefited from prosperity and relative acceptance in the USA, while the black community most certainly has not. We do each live as "others." I also think that it is NOT the time for Jews to make any of this about us. It is the time for us to stand with you as your allies.

Bigotry ultimately is about all of us … and none of us can stand idly by.

Yet in the madness, a bright moment is the Supreme Court ruling that says workplaces cannot discriminate based on LGBTQA. So maybe there is hope. And scribed by a conservative justice. This is most certainly a good thing.

While reading, Don had Bruce Springsteen on, and some lyrics popped out that feel so on point.

"What you do to survive, kills the things you love."

Let's continue to pray for peace and love. It is all that we truly have.

Love,

Jennifer

Aunt Jemima, Interrupted

Wednesday, June 17, 2020
Cincinnati, Ohio

Dear Jen,

Your most recent letter was profound, sad, and hopeful: it does seem like our freedom is being undermined on all fronts.

Bolton's book says the president encourages China's placing Uighur Muslims in concentration camps. And this evening he hastily signed a bill condemning the camps.

Tonight, I served as moderator for a panel discussion with journalists about "allyship." I was so encouraged by the folks on the panel, including TV journalists and UC professors. All expressed difficulty and fatigue covering our current state of affairs, but their wisdom and perspective was impressive.

Earlier today I took an EKG and had some preliminary blood work performed at the hospital as I prep for my Great Weight Loss Adventure. I want to lose sixty pounds by Christmas; 100 by July 1, which would mark a year anniversary on the program. I view it as a matter of life and death. I have to do it.

Oddly, I wondered if I encountered a "Karen." Two women in hospital scrubs were stationed at the front door. One of the women asked me if I was going to see a doctor. I showed her the appointment and location on my app. She said, "Who's your doctor?" I said maybe it's just screenings as I spot a sign pointing me to room 1700, the same number on my app. She is still standing in front of me asking who my doctor is.

And I point: "There is the sign pointing to Room 1700."

"Well, there are no doctors back there," she said.

Then I'm wondering why she is making a scene?

I stop talking to her and walk to my appointment. And I'm angry the whole time. And my blood pressure is high when they take it.

Why? Why?!

She is still there when I exit. Both of us avoid eye contact.

So senseless. And unnecessary. Was she just doing her job? Were my sensibilities heightened? Likely, the answer to both is "yes."

Finally, PepsiCo decided to take Aunt Jemima pancakes off the market today. That's a big deal. But if it's racist yesterday, hasn't it been for, like 140 years?

The world is changing at warp speed. No one wants to be caught on the wrong side of history.

Except for, perhaps, the president. He seems soulless sometimes.

Perturbed,

Byron

Kicked to the Curb in a Black Suit

Thursday, June 18, 2020
Taos, New Mexico

Good Afternoon my friend,

Some days it seems like a lot happens. Others, like not much at all. I spent most of the day working remotely and on Zoom calls. I really am tired of Zoom calls. (Yea, one at 6 a.m. tomorrow since that is 8 a.m. EST.) Still early in either time zone. Clients have gone from being grateful and decent to panicked and ridiculous. I am weary of it. Yet I keep slogging along.

I am most proud of your weight loss plans. Just take it one step at a time. We cut way back on carbs ten months ago and it has made a vital difference. Mostly, we just feel better. I have always exercised lots; but know from life and my daughter Caroline (expert in nutrition and fitness) that you simply can't out-exercise problematic eating. She says that we are the only people (she knows) who lose weight while drinking vodka-sodas. Ha-ha.

Time of COVID calls for stiff drinks. With a father who was an alcoholic, I have generally been leery of "drinks." I have learned that I am able to have a nightly cocktail and be healthy.

We went out to eat last night—a local fave spot to hear a friend of ours play music. All distant. All in masks. The restaurant team was glad to be back at work. And there is that moment when one looks around and thinks, "Wow, this is life now." It seems dystopian. The madness and all that comes with it. And I plan my outfits around my masks. Maybe, when this all ends, (the optimist) I will have them made into a mini quilt.

This is the world in which we inhabit.

We stay busy. I hear people saying that they are bored. I am never bored.

I have been thinking back over life and decisions that I have made. I was this hard-charging Midwest-based VP-Officer-Corporate Comm, etc. I was being paid well, the girls were thriving and our marriage was good. I then had an "opportunity" to jump up about three levels, manage a large national team, make more $$$, with fancy trappings. I signed on the "line," determined that Don and I would commute and within a year the girls and I lived in Florida and Don in the Midwest.

It made sense on paper.

At the time Don said, "Aren't the girls and I enough for you?"

My mom was furious. Don constantly told me that I was worth so much more than I was being compensated, and my mom pushed me toward total independence. I heard them—loudly. Never their faults—but it was this tape in my head playing over and over.

For one year, I commuted and then it was Don's turn. The airline's ground crews came to know us by name. For the first few times, it seemed glamorous.

He was on a plane every Thursday and Monday. We maintained this lifestyle for five years. While this was no way to be a family, we experienced life in a twisted place (like only Florida can be) and made lifelong friends.

Florida is everything that one has heard. It is also historic, deep, problematic and intensely diverse. My daughters often spoke Spanglish.

This worked for our family; until it didn't.

Ultimately, I found myself in my boss' office—breaking my work agreement (at the end of 2008 and the financial meltdown and the kids were well-settled). I realized that if I continued on this path, my marriage might not survive. We owned three homes and I had no plan. I just knew that it was time to go home.

My life has included a bittersweet connection to Cincinnati with stints in Michigan, Colorado and Florida—with always a return to Cincinnati.

After our return and for three months, the kids barely spoke to me. We drove two cars north over the Smoky Mountains (in snow, wearing sandals). Mom and Don were glad that my charade had ended and that we returned. I interviewed in Cincinnati—but while well-connected, had been too senior and no one really wanted to touch me. My career screeched to a halt. And, as you know, I figured that out, too.

I often think back over those days—the decisions that I have made. The regrets that I have. The turmoil. The wasted money. And yes, I wonder. This is a first-world challenge.

How do we ever know if we are doing the right thing? Do we ever?

I sit back today and think of how I miss the girls—of faulty former priorities—of what matters.

At the moment, things seem to have worked out.

I guess that this is just life.

Love,

Jennifer

Jennifer, Caroline, Don, and Nora Mooney

Seeking Fatherhood

Friday, June 19, 2020
Cincinnati, Ohio

Dear Jen,

This is Father's Day weekend. It is awkward for me. I did not grow up with my bio dad. Mom became pregnant with me during her third year at Grambling College in September 1964.

When she wrote my bio dad a letter informing him she was with child, she said he wrote her back with what was essentially a "Dear John" letter that she would not finish reading. She burned it. She was too proud. She would raise me on her own with a lot of help from her mom and her siblings. I lived with my grandparents for the first six years of my life until my mom married Herman "Buddy" McCauley, a small business owner and a school bus driver.

Buddy died in 1988, but he was gone years earlier after a second stroke left him an invalid for the final six years of his life. He was blind, paralyzed and in the final year he ate only because of the feeding tube in his abdomen. My robust, happy surrogate dad died wearing an adult diaper at 120 pounds.

Today, I have a relationship with my bio dad. It's like having a big brother, honestly. We make small talk and one tells the other "I love you" at the end of most conversations, and we really mean it. I mean, this person shares my DNA. It's just that there is so much confusion and unanswered questions because it's hard to fill in fifty years with essentially no communication and knowing the way mom felt about my establishing a relationship with him. She was not in favor of it. I struck an awkward balance during major life events—my marriage to Jill, the birth of our children, the deaths of close relatives. Out of respect for my mother's wishes, I did not invite him to our wedding, which broke my heart.

When people post photos of their dads on social media I am always left with mixed emotions. No one in my hometown knows my paternal relatives, even though the rumors going around my small town burned like wildfire when I was a boy. Kids teased me a lot, saying that the elementary school principal was my dad. Nothing could have been further from the truth. I even tried to date his daughter, my main motivation being to snuff out the filthy rumors.

If they read our book, they will learn my truth on this very page today.

There is a picture of my bio dad, Wilson Pete Jr., of Lake Charles, La., on his wedding day. I have shown it to you. He was married to Etta for fifty-two years. She died two months ago from complications of COVID-19.

I have great empathy for him. And I wish we had been able to have a father-son relationship. I once was angry about it often, imagining that I missed out on the strength and wisdom fathers get to impart on their sons. I'm not angry anymore. It turned out well, and I have children of my own to try to figure out how to be the best father I can be. I had Buddy for ten years. He was a good man and a decent father to a child who wasn't biologically his. That's huge.

Parents sometimes wound their children and don't know how to acknowledge their child's pain. I have tried not to do that to my own children, but I'm sure I have without knowing it.

My lack of having a father in my childhood is one source of childhood trauma for me, which leads to my rarely feeling completely safe or supported as an adult. A bit of insecurity comes with that. I never really admitted this publicly until now. It's nice to release it.

Love,

Byron

A Somber Father's Day

Saturday, June 20, 2020
Taos, New Mexico

Good Morning,

Usually, I wait until later in the day to write—until something has happened. It turns out that something has happened. I, too, have been dreading the run up to Father's Day. I am fortunate to be married to a man who has been an excellent father. Mine was not. He had challenges, problems, alcoholism, likely bipolar—and it made for a strange childhood as well as the things that go along with "girls" not raised by a good father figure.

My dad, Leon, was the son of poor immigrants (Russia-Poland) and reared in Canton, Ohio. I, too, was born in Canton. Many of my dad's family stayed in the old country and became lost. Lost to the hell that took so much of the world's Jewish population. My mom, from a prosperous West Virginia family, married him, in spite of her parent's disapproval. They met at Ohio State. Dad was handsome, had a winning personality and was likely a bad boy. They were young. They moved to his hometown and she was a schoolteacher. He was starting out in the business world—and would ultimately do very well—in Cincinnati.

I often walk by the buildings in which he had offices (in Cincinnati)—Carew Tower and a historic structure on Fourth Street. I remember going to his offices with my mom. At the time, she was a stay-at-home mom, and meeting one's husband for lunch with the "kids in tow" was a typical outing. When Dad was successful, our lives seemed idyllic. He had offices in other places, and we spent summers in places like Malibu and Hyannis Port.

This was the veneer.

At the same time, he was a serial cheater, had a terrible temper, was abusive, and a raging alcoholic. He tended to "yell" and act out when I had friends over. It was difficult. I remember many yelling scenes with my mother crying.

My grandparents were understandably concerned. They often spoke ill of him with both my sister and me in the room. Ultimately, when I was thirteen, my mother left him. And he left us with nothing. He moved to Arizona and remarried, but never rebounded in the business world. My mother's parents stepped in and (with my mom) offered the semblance of a solid life.

On the face of it, one might say, good riddance, we dodged a bad thing—now get on with life. Not so simple, he still was our father—and we shared half of his DNA. Our loyalty was to our mother.

Yes, we did travel to Arizona and visited Dad and his new wife. There were some good memories made, but he was still drinking lots and depressed. And while this may be a first world challenge, the "abandonment and insecurity issues" that both my sister and I grapple with, to this day, are real.

Over time, I distanced myself from him. I knew that spending time with him hurt my mother. I went to counseling. I married (twice) and had the kids. And then I heard from him. He had bad cancer and wanted to visit. He came to Cincinnati and spent the weekend drinking every drop of alcohol in the house. I felt that seeing him would again destroy me and that my priority must be my own children. I never spoke to him again. He died some years later at age sixty-two.

As I age, I see simply a broken man with undiagnosed issues. I still remember the "good" days and a seemingly idyllic childhood. He often enters my dreams. And yes, I feel guilt.

I share his DNA. And I (to some extent) am him. My mother was/is a wonderful mother but being a girl without a "good" male role model does things to a person. Yes, I had my Gramps, but he was not my dad. Mom has been remarried for thirty-six years to a good man, who was never my dad either.

I am a grown-up. I have had a good life. I am married to a fine man. I am fortunate, but on Father's Day, I am also sad.

Peace and love to you tomorrow—a great Dad of three wonderful daughters.

Love,

Jennifer

The Most Painful Moment

Sunday, June 21, 2020
Cincinnati, Ohio

Jennifer,

Thank you for opening up about your father. I have had more than twenty-four hours to digest your letter, and I decided that we both owe it to ourselves to be honest and candid. I have much more to say on this, my twenty-second year as a father.

I want to be able to like Father's Day. But I never can. Never have. If I think about all the friends in my little town when I was growing up, the majority of them had fathers and mothers in the home. They defied the stereotype, or so I imagined. But things are never, ever as one imagines them. We idealize the thing that we think we lack. I had a father in my life for precisely nine years.

As I noted earlier, my mother became pregnant with me while she was a junior at Grambling State University. She went home to Plain Dealing, La., and taught elementary school on a provisional teacher's license. She wore a rubber girdle to conceal her pregnancy until she couldn't wear it anymore. I was born during the summertime at Confederate Memorial Hospital, weighing four pounds, six ounces. It's a wonder I lived, considering her lack of prenatal care and the fact that I was a little black boy born in a "charity" hospital in a dangerously racist and segregated town.

I didn't see my biological dad until I was sixteen years old when I demanded that my mother tell me who my biological father was. Imagine never knowing that for sixteen years. I would not be satisfied and I knew something was amiss. Nothing about me matched the people I lived with.

My face, my body type, my feet, my eyes. It was like I always knew a part of me was definitely missing.

Mom had been engaged to a man named J.C. in college. They broke up. Then she met Wilson. Apparently, J.C. died thinking he was my bio dad. Mom died with her secret. (It hurts to reveal this today and some of my relatives will be hurt, too.) But when I was sixteen, she pulled out the 1966 Grambling yearbook. There I was, staring back at myself. It was like my soul opened up. I must've looked at that picture for hours, going over his cheekbones, his eyes, his lips! I looked just like this man, and I had the affirmation I sought.

"How many boyfriends did you have, Mama," I asked her, realizing that my perfect mother had become flawed in my eyes. There was an unspoken accusation in the tone of my voice.

"I WAS A WHORE, BYRON. I WAS A SLUT!" she yelled and sobbed. That was the worst day of my life. I had hurt my beloved mother, the best person on Earth. The unexpected response was guttural and revealed a deep hurt.

When she settled down she clarified some things. Her mother had been accusing her of having sex, but she had not—until she was twenty, and with J.C. Then, heartbroken, she met Wilson.

That was that. Sexual encounters with two men at twenty years old. And pregnant with the child of one of them in the unforgiving 1960s, poor, in rural Northwest Louisiana.

Herman "Buddy" McCauley adopted me during the summer of 1976, five years into his marriage to my mother, and three years before he had the catastrophic stroke. He gave me his name and made me feel like I was his child until I reached my fourteenth birthday. Then, he became much less tolerant. It was probably from the stress of the stroke and the loss of mobility and faculties.

Even though I am a father of three daughters, and have been married for a quarter century, there remains a hole in my heart. I am a child whose father never acknowledged him, never sought to find him (to my knowledge) or tried to maintain any sort of relationship.

Behind all of my success, I suffer from abandonment issues, which, I believe, is the genesis of the depression I have suffered for as long as I can remember. I overachieve in public. I am the epitome of professionalism. In private I sometimes feel like someone places a millstone around my neck. I sometimes feel like a poser.

This year, I finally acknowledged all my feelings to my therapist, and I am working through it—more than four decades later. I am healing and thriving.

Thanks for listening,

Byron

Broken Parents

Monday, June 22, 2020
Taos, New Mexico

Hi and Good Morning,

Your letter is heavy, and I feel for you. I also get it. While my situation is different than yours, it also is about things that happened (to us) across the course of our lives and the impact. When I have conversed with my mom about my own life, she essentially indicates that I should get over it, that I am almost fifty-seven, and that it is time.

And she is right.

It is difficult for me to write anything about my own family that does not portray us in a certain light. And, I am a lifelong "PR" person, so there is that. There is also the part about "airing" family laundry outside. The truth is though that my sister and I chose a parent. My mom was/is an amazing parent. Yet, she could only be one, the mom, not the dad. And we are fortunate people—never went hungry, had privileges, were safe, educated and yes, white and free.

Yet choosing one parent and discarding the other parent inflicts permanent scars.

It is also true that all families have challenges and ours are minor. This is all accurate—however, the very real "sense of abandonment" and "intense personal insecurity" is something that has impacted me across time and circumstance, Don says that I am easy to live with, yet I know that the reassurance that I often "need" can be troubling.

For both of us, living "without" a father and trying to "forget" or "not bother" is something that is tied to our tails (as they say in psychological sessions). It creates a sense of our not being worthy of love—since a parent chose to abandon us. It also has a long-term cumulative effect with our relationship with the remaining parent. And we both know that our "mothers" did what they thought was best.

Being "abandoned" by a dad, who was also an alcoholic, leads to all of those complicated challenges like insecurity and not ever being "enough." And then sometimes far too much.

And I cannot imagine how tough this was for my father, as broken as he was. To this day, I am sad for him.

It has taken years, but what I feel most is sadness and guilt.

It honestly has been more difficult for my sister than for me. She was named after him, looked more like him and he (in our young lives) was kinder to me.

My own focus has been on my own children and not repeating blood history. It's hard to see the world paying tribute to their own fathers.

My driving sense in life has been to make others happy and to be responsible. And to feel intense guilt when I prioritize myself. I know that it is all bound together.

So, another Father's Day comes to pass.

On another note I am reading *The Warmth of Other Suns* about black migration from the South to the North and West throughout 1970. It is an amazing and fascinating read. It is also shocking. While, like many, I knew about Jim Crow, mass segregation and all of the major court cases (separate, but equal; Brown vs. the Board of Education, etc.) from school—I don't think that I ever quite realized how truly bad things were post-slavery through the 1960s. This book is raw—and clearly the end of slavery meant the beginning of something else.

Something that seemed almost as brutal.

What is happening in America is long overdue. And you, struggling with challenges relating to your own paternity, as well as being black in America is deep. While I have believed myself to be an enlightened person, Byron, I am not certain that it was until now, in this moment—that I began to understand the depth and the horror wrought on your people. The stories that we have shared delivered an epiphany.

And it was not only the being ripped initially from other countries to serve white people, or the systematic hatred and brutality that occurred for centuries, but the residual impact that stays with a person—or a people.

I feel my own version—the collective DNA—that occurs when one is part of a tribe that has been loathed for centuries.

While neither of us can solve these challenges, we can certainly relate to one another's plight.

From Father's Day to the sins and troubles of the past, we both have turned out well.

Heavy for a Monday. Be well, my friend. At least that clown who calls himself a president fell on his face this weekend at the Tulsa rally (Saturday, June 20.) At least there is that.

I recently learned that the Beatles' tune "Blackbird" was written about race relations in the United States. Have always loved the song.

"You were only waiting for this moment to be free."

Maybe there is hope or as Jesse Jackson says, "Keep Hope Alive."

Love,

Jennifer

The Train Engineer,
My Father-in-Law

Tuesday, June 23, 2020
Cincinnati, Ohio

Dear Jen,

This may not be the final father-oriented letter but I, personally, want to get off this subject for a while after I write this. This is to say I do not mind if you write more on the subject. Truth is, I don't know any child whose life was idyllic. All seem to have some kind of weird thing with their parents. This is true with children of means or the poorest of the poor. Anywhere in the world.

I feel as if I got a quadruple dose. I lived with my grandmother until I was six years old, along with my mom and her six siblings, ages ten to eighteen. One sibling, her older brother, had moved out and started his own family. Mom's younger brother, Raymond, was fighting in that unpopular war in the steamy Far East jungles.

My earliest childhood memory was me convulsing in tears on my grandmother's vinyl pastel flower patterned couch. Mom was leaving to live with Buddy. They were already married. I had no idea. And she was giving me the choice of who I wanted to live with: her or Mama? Mama was her mother and my grandmother. But Mama felt like my mother, and my own mother was more like an aunt. I did not go the first night, nor the second. When I did go, my world opened up—but slowly. I had my own room and my own things for the first time. Eventually, I got used to it and embraced life as an only child.

There was one thing I never could get used to.

A freight train ran in front of our house twice each night. Every time it rumbled over the tracks, it literally felt like the world was coming to an end. No one warned me about this. But, then, how do you remember to tell a kid how loud something would be when it had probably become white noise to you? The first time I heard it, it scared the hell out of me. I did not know if the house was falling or the world was ending.

Today, when I go home and sleep in the same room I slept in forty-eight years ago, the train has become white noise.

Oddly enough, my ex-wife's father, who was a railroad engineer based in Little Rock, Arkansas, had traveled that route hundreds of times and knew exactly where I lived. My future father-in-law, one degree of separation apart and a whole world away all that time.

In 2008, I took a job as Director of Communications for Grambling State University, their alma mater. I stayed nine months, something I may talk about later. Grambling, Louisiana, was twenty-one miles away from Homer, Louisiana, J.C.'s "Jay" (Mom's college boyfriend) hometown. He was a fine man with a great reputation. He worked in funeral home sales and handled burials. He was awarded two Purple Hearts for valor in Vietnam. He was a deacon in his church. And, even at seventy, his clothes looked as great on him as David Bowie's suits looked on him. Both were lean and angular.

Jill and the girls remained in Cincinnati. J.C. had arranged to rent me a three-bedroom house in Homer. I was grateful. He was proud that I had come home. I rarely saw him, as I worked ungodly hours at the university. But I lived in his town for three months, leaving before the sun rose and getting home just to shower, eat, sleep and do it all over again the next day.

Mom once remembered that J.C. visited us at my grandmother's house when I was a toddler and I stepped on his black, shiny shoes. It upset him. Funny, she remembered that. J.C. and Mom married other people and he and his wife had twin boys, one of whom grew up to serve time in the state penitentiary. She had two daughters from a previous marriage. They divorced eventually. Mom and J.C. rekindled their romance that never died and married in 1993. It felt like the best day of her life. They lived in their own homes in towns thirty miles apart and he visited my mother on weekends, Fridays and Saturdays, anyway. Mom could not live with him because she often saw the irrefutable spirit of his mother there, especially at bedtime.

It was early March. Mom was crying when she called me at my office. Jay had been found slumped over his desk that afternoon. He had vomited. He was taken to the VA hospital in Shreveport, Louisiana I left work and met mom there. He was on life support. I spent the night at Mom's house. The doctors called everyone to his room, meaning one of his twin boys, his two stepdaughters, me, and my mother. Jill and the girls remained outside the room, as did my sister, Lanny. Everyone knew what had to be done, though I could feel negative energy from sisters, whom I had never met. "Who is this man?" The twin boy did not speak.

There was nothing more to do than to take him off life support. I was asked to approve the DNR order. My signature, *Byron McCauley*, set in motion the beginning of the end of a man's earthly life. We left the hospital as Jay labored to breathe. But before that, we all prayed together. The hospital called three hours later to tell us Jay was gone.

His military funeral was solemn and reverential. J.C. was revered as a town leader and an honorable man. Mom and I walked slowly to and from his casket. I loved him because he loved Mom, and she had loved him forever. His Masonic Lodge brothers, many of whom worked at Grambling and had seen me on campus and approached me with expressions of sympathy on their brow.

Surprisingly, the other twin was there, too. I didn't recognize him. He was thinner than his brother, and looked older. He was allowed to see his father one last time, in shackles, escorted by the state police.

Thanks for reading,

Byron

What Tolstoy Said

Wednesday, June 24, 2020
Taos, New Mexico

Good Morning my Friend,

This is way off topic and out of sequence, but I am finding that our letters are a good outlet. It is truly a kind of therapy. I have endeavored to better understand my birth family. It seems that all families are a mess. Some are just better at "posing." Mine is dark. There is that famous Tolstoy quote:

"All happy families are alike; each unhappy family is unhappy in its own way." —*Anna Karenina*

The family into which I was born had its challenges. My own little family (Don, me, daughters, stepdaughters) is happy. We both had our own family strife and were determined to foster stability.

The clan (passed down from the ancestors of my mom and dad) netted a pretty complex gang. My parents were not the optimal match. I know lots more about my mom's family than my dad's. I do know that we are fortunate and privileged people. We are free and have not had to worry about where we would get our next meal. We attended good schools in safe communities.

Sure, we experienced the "Jewish" thing, but in America since the 60s (when my sister and I were born) we were accepted as people. We have been able to make contacts and get good jobs because of it. Most of us have been healthy. No one has died young.

It has been the American Dream.

Sure, our parents divorced, and we weren't the smartest in the class and not always liked or respected, but we had nice wardrobes and decent genes, and we traveled; but that is window dressing.

We have had the benefit of freedom and making our own choices.

Our parents (yes, both of them) are/were broken people—but who's parents are not? We are broken people. We were trained to dress well, have good manners and behave—so that no one could see the cracks. And that has worked outwardly.

My younger sister's life has been different than my own. We were raised in the same home by the same parents and our lives headed in different directions. Much like my own children. We all made our choices. Today, the world seems to be tilted on its axis. Yep, falling apart some might say.

And, at the same time we humans seem to tear relationships apart. It is important to me that somehow we find a way to connect, even if it's only in agreeing to the most superficial terms.

My relationship with my sister is at odds. It gives me great pause.

She doesn't seem to like me much. This makes me sad.

It may go back to when our father was dying. She wanted to see him. I was afraid. Instead I flew to Chicago so that we could be together. We were told that "we were never close to him, so it would be OK." It wasn't. It isn't.

She is a well-to-do white girl living in one of the most prosperous zip codes in the USA. I know that overall things have been tough (for her), but years of anger directed at me is not OK. I often lose my patience.

I am hoping that we find our way.

So, on to today. Not a great one thus far.

Don is not feeling well (the hernia thing is acting up). I am concerned and also guilty that I didn't even notice for a few hours as I was consumed with my family-of-birth challenges.

I did catch up on the phone with a friend from young childhood with whom I have not spoken in years. She is one of those people whom I have always known. Our lives stayed close and sometimes conflicted. She is from a WASP family and never understood my reality. In talking as women past middle age today, I saw how she has evolved. And her eighty-three-year-old mom is an organizer against Trump—so there is that.

People do grow up. Some even surprise us. This makes me smile.

We sit here now, at these later ages, with our history, baggage, regrets, still hopes, some dreams and wish for the best. We know that the years ahead are shorter than the years behind. We live in a difficult time; but others (before us) had it much worse.

I know one thing: I am not squandering time or my life.

Let me know how your medical appointment went.

Love,

Jennifer

Red Pepper, Squash, Zucchini

Thursday, June 25, 2020
Cincinnati, Ohio

Dear Jennifer,

How are you today? Man, being a sibling is hard, especially when you are the responsible one and the other harbors ill feelings.

I want to thank you for listening to me talk about my family situation. This has been so therapeutic for me. I didn't expect to delve into these feelings, but they are always raw and top of mind. Kids really don't know what they are missing. It's like that saying, "Be careful what you wish for." Truth is, I don't know what I missed not growing up with my bio father. Buddy provided a fine life for a kid desperately in need of a father figure. He taught me how to fertilize the land "organically," plant and harvest purple-hulled peas, watermelons, tomatoes, peanuts, sweet potatoes, corn, and okra. I also learned to fish, ride horses, and raise cows for food and for profit.

Most important, he taught me how to be self-sufficient, which I'm sure led to my conservative predisposition.

So, I mentioned offline that I was going to see a urologist. I completed that visit. The last time I visited my urologist was twelve years ago after Laila was born. Jill demanded that I get the "snippy snip" after we became pregnant three months after Laila was born. It would have been child number four. It's not like we were seeing each other with great frequency, but we hit home runs.

"Our families are going to think we have lost our minds," Jill said. This was actually our seventh pregnancy. Jill suffered our first of four miscarriages in 1999 when she was a little more than three months along. This happened when we were in Seattle at a conference launching a journalism diversity recruiting firm at a national convention. The hemorrhaging began after the convention ended and we were in the hotel finally getting rest after staffing our booth fourteen hours a day.

We left the cleaning staff an apologetic note and a substantial tip for the mess on the bed. We both were devastated. We took a cab to the University of Washington hospital, where she received intravenous fluids and treatment. Believe it or not, we caught our red-eye flight home to Memphis.

So, twelve years after the vasectomy, I returned to my urologist because I have Peyronie's disease. It possibly sounds way worse than it really is, at least with the benefit of Internet diagnoses. I had all the classic symptoms. The men's restroom in the urologist's office had a poster on the inside of the door. Call it comic relief for the pitiful, middle-aged male. It showed fruits and veggies in various stages of Peyronie's: a red pepper shaped like a fishing hook, a banana with an exaggerated curve, a squash, a zucchini, a cucumber—some of them with turns that rival a Grand Prix course.

This condition happens to one in ten American men, usually in their fifties. It comes stealthily. And one day you wake up to a tallywacker "wackering" in a decidedly unnatural direction. I found it interesting that the condition is caused by a build-up of scar tissue as a result of years of "trauma." A surgical procedure is scheduled soon.

Men are notoriously wimps when it comes to things like this. I am no different, but I know that there is no comparison to what you guys have to endure on many levels (see breast examinations).

Nevertheless, I know if my brethren were to read this, there is a whole lot of wincing going on.

Love,

Byron

Older Bodies

Friday, June 26, 2020
Taos, New Mexico

Dear Byron,

Again, again, again.

Thanks for your candor. It is certainly therapeutic to talk through these family matters. I continue to try to not bring them up with Don. I am sure that I start to sound like a broken record.

I am sorry about Jill's miscarriages. I had one. One was enough. Brutal.

We were in the middle-of-nowhere Oregon at a family wedding. A "nature-y place." I called my doc in Cincinnati and explained what was going on. We ended up going to a small-town doctor (on a Saturday morning, and I still remember his name, Jess Hickerson) and I then had a dilation and curettage (better known as a D&C). I guess that is how some people have abortions. While I am firmly Choice, I cannot imagine deciding to terminate a pregnancy—that all made it real for me. So, I am the rare woman who may be pro choice, but not so keen on abortion.

Saturday morning, I lost a baby and went to a wedding on Saturday night, in a pink dress.

Your procedure and situation sounds well-in-hand, but also a bit nasty. Sending good juju your way. All of this stuff that deals with our reproductive systems has the yuck factor for sure and most of us never talk about them.

Speaking of, I had the total hysterectomy in January. So, first I found out that my uterus was the size of a twenty-six-week pregnancy and that it was time to get the plumbing removed. Turns out I ended up in surgery maybe at the last possible time one could viably do so before COVID.

The process itself was simple, but my incision was major so it took a while to heal. But I did heal and within a month was back to exercise. It is a strange feeling to have all of those organs removed. It feels like one goes from having babies to being neutered in a quick flash.

It is the most daunting way to see life pass.

Aging is real. I spend many hours engaged in healthy living. At the same time, as vain as I am, I have learned that I am pretty against plastic surgery. While we all like our younger faces best—there is something about living in one's real face, or the face that we have earned. I also believe that a doctor could actually make it worse—so there is that.

Don and I took to the trail today. We hiked about nine miles from 8.7K to about 11.6K. It was a stunning trail and we both needed time not tethered to the keyboard and phone. We may be living in beauty, but we will grind away daily with work. My body wasn't feeling it. Worried about Don's hernia and wondering if the constant steps were good for either of us. My heart was doing its racing thing (that is medicated) but I kept my mouth shut and plunged forward.

We made it. We said we were actually going to go about two miles extra and just stopped.

We talked later about giving up early. Don asked me if my heart had been bothering me. I said, "Yes, a little." I asked him about his hernia and he said, "I kept pushing it back in."

We move onward with life. Aging. Trying to minimize it.

Maybe not being as honest with ourselves and each other as we should.

Grateful to be in the mountains.

Pressing our luck.

You are in my thoughts,

Jennifer

Sorry About Your Goods, Hun

Saturday, June 27, 2020
Cincinnati, Ohio

Jen,

Today, I'm going to continue with a topic that we talk about a lot. Americans love to complain about it. It's our health. We've been going over our agreed-to allocated word limit, but to me it's OK. Short is better sometimes, but I have not been bored with any letter, regardless of its length.

I've told you about my up and down weight management issues. Up and down all my life. I became a pretty avid runner in my mid-20s and kept that up until three years ago, the first time I ever had a hospital stay, which led to my first leg procedure. So, I memorialized this visit a few months later. Sharing an edited version here as part of our "health" series of letters.

The second most embarrassing moment of my life happened on the first day of December in 2017.

I was on the 26th hour of lying flat on my back at Mercy West Hospital in Cincinnati after undergoing 10 hours of surgery over two days. The event that had brought me to this particular place, at this particular time was wholly unexpected. The day before, I was having coffee with a source. About a half-hour into the conversation my left leg felt like it wanted to explode.

It was as if someone had a blood pressure cuff around my calf and would not stop tightening the pressure gauge. Warm waves of pain came next, like a cramp but ramped up times five. If my source sensed something was happening, he did not let on because he kept talking and talking and talking. Finally, the meeting ended. I limped two blocks, essentially dragging the leg.

In July, I thought I had a torn meniscus, so I had an MRI, which revealed an intact meniscus but found something else.

"Looks like you have a couple of aneurysms behind both of your knees," said my orthopedic surgeon. "We will keep an eye on them."

"What?" I said.

"These are not the kind that you think about when there is bleeding in the brain and are fatal, but they are pretty common. I see a lot of these in folks your age. This is called a popliteal aneurysm. Essentially, arteries in both knees were being overworked. If the arteries clot, the danger is that you can lose your legs. Sometimes they can kill you if the clot spreads to your aortic valve."

The nurse practitioner in my primary care physician's office is Amanda.

Normally the bubbly sort, all the color went out of Amanda's face when she examined me. It was 5:15 p.m. She ordered a blood test, stat, and made some phone calls. She sent me home, told me to elevate my legs, and take baby aspirin. One of the calls she made was to Mercy's cardiovascular ultrasound unit, where I was to report at 8:30 a.m. the next day.

The ultrasound technician, Shannon, got right to it. She squirted warm ultrasound gel on my legs and scanned. She kept pausing minutes in the same spot. Her face looked like Amanda's.

"So, you see something? I asked.

"We'll see what your doctor thinks," she said.

"So, do you think I'm going home?"

"I'm not allowed to say, but we will have to see what your doctor says."

After about 30 minutes, she left the room. When she returned, she told me that—no—I wasn't going home. Instead, I headed straight to the OR. The race was to save my left leg.

Jill was told the surgery would take about 90 minutes. It was six hours before doctors told her about the complications. They could not finish. The clots were so extensive, they would need to administer anti-clotting medication intravenously overnight and go in again the next day. The technology is called an EOS machine. They did not tell me I would need morphine to handle the arterial pain in its aftermath.

After four more hours of surgery, things stabilized. But my journey had just begun. Finally, I got to eat after 48 hours. The lime Jell-O tasted great.

I had to remain flat on my back. At 1 a.m. Sunday, medical alarms started going off. A gaggle of nurses rushed into my room—five of them—all with a sense of urgency.

A racquetball-sized hematoma had formed. They removed covers and the thin hospital gown that gives strangers easy access to whatever they need easy access to. They took turns massaging and manipulating the lump, a result of new clots that could be deadly.

I had lost my modesty many hours ago, with the surgery, and the catheter, and not having been able to shower in way too long.

So, there I was, splayed out in a tortuous hospital bed, my meatless flaccidity in bas-relief, while The Five took turns battling the hematoma, which was right beside my manly parts.

One of the nurses, apparently attempting to add levity to the situation, went all #MeToo on me. "I'll bet you never thought you would have five women down there at the same time."

At about the same time, one of them said: "Sorry about your goods, hun." At that moment, I imagined myself as a Pangolin, all rolled up in a ball, hoping no one could see me anymore.

Sadly, that was just the beginning of my medical odyssey. But today I'm so much better.

Warmest regards,

I'm Just Not That into #MeToo

Sunday, June 28, 2020
Taos, New Mexico

Dear Byron,

Your letter made me wince and laugh. Five women and #Metoo. Me too; that was a moment that seems to have gone the way of the immigrants and the environment. The Svengali Trumpers have ensured that we look away.

Look away, look away. Then we stop watching the news—too painful. In the meantime, lots of what makes America "great" (like freedom and clean air) seems to be receding.

Re: your health, sending prayers that you stay healthy and that your upcoming procedure is minor. I too have had some challenges—some that are likely a result of aging, others that popped up, but I think my overall health is generally positive.

So, this aging thing. Yep, here we are. I will be fifty-seven in a few weeks. Not for the faint of heart, but, as they say, better than the alternative. On most days, I am glad to be here on this messed up, upside down planet. I have lost two friends to cancer in recent years. Don's brother left us when he was fifty-two and then my grandma lived to be 104.

None of us know how it all turns out.

Here we are.

I just had a long and positive facetime chat with my mother. We actually laughed lots; mainly about politics. I told her about a meme that showed Clinton, Bush, Shrub, Carter and Obama all running. Adjacent was big old red-faced Trump sitting on a chair in a golf shirt with folds of flab for the world to see. I don't think the dude even tries to be healthy. He has a belief that we each only have so much energy (across a lifetime) and that he should not waste his with exercise.

We also had a long talk about the removal of statues and her own history of growing up in Charleston, West Virginia and attending "Stonewall Jackson" segregated high school. She told me that one holiday her family drove to Washington, D.C. to see relatives. Gladys (who worked for her family) came with them to visit her own family in the area. Gladys was black and they, therefore, were not able to go into restaurants. Mom said they simply bought food and had a spread outside.

I am sure that you know many similar stories. Neither of us would have lived them—while we may be getting older—we were too young, except to hear stories from relatives.

Today was mostly a low-key day for us. Don did lots of outside work and I read and rested.

I am proud of you re: your steps on your overall health. It is important in these uncertain times that we minimally try to take care of ourselves and our families.

I'll be interested to see how things in Memphis go. I've never been there.

Love,

Jennifer

Room at the Table

Monday, June 29, 2020
Cincinnati, Ohio

Dear Jennifer,

How was your day today? I hope it was great. Summer returned here with a vengeance. It was ninety-nine degrees for a high today. And very, very sticky.

Today, I had my first in-person meeting with someone in the past three months. I'm going to be one of the virtual table leaders for the "Room at the Table" meetings, which were convened by the Cincinnati USA Regional Chamber and created by HR executive and counselor Whayne Herriford. I'm really looking forward to it. We will have five sessions lasting three hours before Christmas. The first will start July 15.

These are conversations about race and class, and they are needed right now.

Whayne came to Cincinnati after being recruited by KnowledgeWorks as HR director. He retired last year. Downtown remains about a quarter as busy as it was three months ago. There were very few cars on Interstate 71, and parking spaces were easy to find on Court Street, which is where Whayne's offices are located.

We talked for about ninety minutes, and I realized how much I needed to talk to someone like him. Like me, he is an African-American man from Louisiana. His family lives about one hour from my father's family and about three hours from where I grew up. So, at sixty-seven, he's old enough to have lived in the Jim Crow South and has also been able to live in progressive areas like Northern California. We are lucky to have him in the community. I hope you guys get to meet. With your psychology background, I think you will have a mind-meld. You are both wise.

Well, tonight's letter will be short and sweet. I have that meeting tomorrow at the hospital.

Wish me luck.

A final thought. As I was writing this, a newsflash came on CNN saying that the president was aware that Russia's Vladimir Putin placed a bounty on the heads of American soldiers in March 2019. Trump apparently lied and said no one ever told him. A lion with no heart.

Love,

Byron

Out of Options

Tuesday, June 30, 2020
Taos, New Mexico

My dear friend,

I am glad to hear that your interview went well this morning. Fingers crossed for you.

Like you, I would like to hear from someone who was an adult during the Jim Crow times.

I honestly don't think that I realized that it took over 100 years for black America to be treated even close to equally.

I am really tired of these "All Lives Matter" people. Too much.

I was in a women's leadership (national) program in 1998. One of my co-program friends raised that a man in her work organization asked if there was a similar program for men. Her response was "there is, it is called your life."

That is pretty much how I feel about "all lives matter."

We are headed over to Santa Fe for two days. I actually have a meeting with the CEO of a New Mexico agency about affiliating with them. Exciting. I am not sure how this will go, but as we get closer to being full-timers here, it is a working option. It is also uplifting to know that at this advancing age someone thinks my skills are worthwhile.

On the drive we heard Biden's speech about COVID. I agree with him. We are fighting for the soul of the nation and that current POTUS is a traitor. I spend so much time in total shock.

It is hard for me to believe that the dude is our leader and that so many people are OK with it.

Don and I have lost friends (by the week) in terms of TRUMP support. Between whether one thinks TRUMP is OK and the mask deal; it has become a time that we need more than a line in the sand. Yes, I have always been one who has friends with different opinions. However, the issues and people at stake are too big and too important to continue surface relationships with people who think that TRUMP and what he espouses is OK.

It is NOT OK.

This also goes for some liberal friends. Yep, we are sticking together. But we do not need to hear from the wealthiest among us that everyone should just stay home, period. Many don't have the option. Tone deaf. How does one think the supply chain works? What about the peach pickers, the grocery store workers, the hardware store clerks, law enforcement, fire fighters (many big fires now)? Do they stay home? Can they afford not to work? Those who "get" to work remotely (or not work at all) are privileged.

It would be a wonderful world if we could all stay home and be waited upon. But that is not the world in which we live.

I don't think the current state can even be called a battle between right and left—but it IS the battle for the soul of America. About who we are, about being tolerant and the right and the left can both be intolerant.

That's my own rant for the day.

On a more pleasant note, I am glad that our families are healthy (knock on wood), have food on the table and are relatively stable. I am glad to be on the planet, have another birthday and a big upcoming wedding anniversary. I am grateful for all of it.

Santa Fe has been interesting. I am taken by this smallish city. So old. While many people are brown, it is pretty gentrified as well.

If we are going to spend money (in these times) I CHOOSE the very local level. I purchased some more masks from a Native American (that his daughter made). A little while later, Don and I were on the old town square. We were approached by a reporter from *The Santa Fe New Mexican* doing a piece on the story behind people's masks. I had a good story and promoted the man and his daughter. Once a PR girl, always a PR girl.

And we plug on. Out of the house and in the community and wearing our masks.

Talk soon.

Love,

Jennifer

Santa Fe Doorway, June 2020

My Weight-Loss Journey

Wednesday, July 1, 2020
Cincinnati, Ohio

Dear Jen,

I just have to say how worthwhile this exercise has been. It has really become a therapeutic way to end the day.

I'm eager to see what the Santa Fe reporter creates with his mask story. You and Don had the coolest masks.

Interestingly, masks seem to have been the lead news story today. It seems that Republicans are breaking ranks with Trump and are calling for folks to wear masks. I have a prediction: Trump is creating a macho narrative to make it seem that he always was going to wear a mask. Watch him wear one in the coming weeks—personalized.

Did you see Ohio Democratic Chairman David Pepper's post about working on a project with Putin in St. Petersburg in the 1990s? Turns out, Putin was fluent in English but led everyone to assume he was not!

He wrote to make a point about President Trump being in way over his head with Putin. Frankly, this scares me to death. I fear Trump has made deals with the devil, and our country will pay the cost later. I can't believe this president would continue to undermine the intelligence community with impunity.

Finally, I want to share my adventure at UC Health's weight loss program today. The first session was today. I attended a ninety-minute orientation, paid $500 for the twelve-week program and purchased two weeks worth of nutritious products. Five meals a day with the fifth meal consisting of real food totaling 440 calories. The other four meals are meal replacements totaling 640 calories.

For me, this is life or death. I simply cannot allow myself to continue to live with the weight that is literally dragging me down. Since I have lived in Cincinnati, I have gained fifty pounds. That's about 2.5 pounds per year. Even though I had been successful in Weight Watchers (I lost seventy-four pounds once), things just have not progressed the way I need them to.

So, this medically guided program is the step I took before trying bariatric surgery. I just needed a little help and coaching. I've said this before, but I'm really thrilled that I took the plunge, no matter the cost.

Nothing is more important than health and life. I hope that I can celebrate my fifty-sixth birthday, July 2, 2021, 100 pounds lighter.

Thanks for being on this journey with me.

Love,

Byron

We Are Aging Well

Thursday, July 2, 2020
Taos, New Mexico

Dear Byron,

First, happy birthday and so glad that you are on this planet with me! Second, (and this is only what I know about weight management and I am NOT an expert) you are doing this the right way. I generally have been a thin person, but for about the last ten years (until September 2019) I did let myself go. While I was still very physically active, I was heavier than I should have been. Don's doctor said that he HAD to lose weight or would become a diabetic. So, I set out to develop a food plan for both of us.

For us, this has meant losing about thirty pounds each and drastically changing our habits. I can tell you this:

- It is a serious mind game, reminding yourself about the goal.
- I document what we eat.
- I pay attention to numbers.
- Carbs are somewhat evil.

Is it hard? In the beginning yes, but you know that. It is now a lifestyle. For us I would still like to lose another ten pounds, but my mom reminded me that my face has gotten very thin and now all of my wrinkles show, so there is that.

This entire country is being played. I am most concerned about the people who continue to rally behind Trump. And I am not at all sure that he will lose this election. We have a family connection to Biden, and I think that he is a great human, but well past his prime and I worry about his candidacy. I know that if he wins, he will have great people around him.

And I am not sure that he will win but lose as the election will be stolen.

Santa Fe was good. Such a magical place. Good meeting and it looks likely that I may do some work with the agency. My career has turned into a "show up at the same place for decades" to a cobbled together set of gigs. While the former way had the trappings, this method does make for a better life.

Most interesting. The woman with whom I met has parents who were Holocaust survivors. Her dad's family was good friends with Anne Frank's family, both when they lived in Germany and moved to Holland to flee. They were both kids together. Also, ultimately in the same concentration camp. Her dad's family was also one of the few in which every family member survived.

My contact made me laugh. She explained that people often asked her father, "What Anne was like?" and he said, "we knew one another when we were eleven." While Anne Frank was a mere one death, she most certainly has come to symbolize those wretched times.

NM is under very serious lock down now. People are now fined for breaking the rules. The numbers are in our favor in terms of COVID incidence. Important, since (in this county) there are only four ventilators. Many people (who live here part time) have arrived from HIGH COVID places and are ignoring the quarantine. I am not comfortable with this. Don and I are in high risk categories.

It seems like I am losing friends by the day—whether it is about Trump support, not taking BLM or COVID seriously. I have always been "live and let live" but it does seem like these are such important issues. More important than friendship—who is to say? And I don't want to be preachy. This one is tough.

We sit on top of a strange fourth for our country. I do love our country, but I stand behind almost nothing that is happening now. I feel most for our children.

Thinking of you on your weight loss journey.

Love,

Jennifer

A Road-Trip Surprise

Sunday, July 5, 2020
Memphis, Tennessee

Dear Jen,

So much to talk about in so little time and space.

Having taken some days away, I realize how much I have come to rely on writing these letters to keep me grounded and hopeful and up today with what's going on in the world.

Three things I have learned on this trip from Cincinnati to Memphis (there are others):

1. Be in charge of yourself and your immediate family (no one else).
2. Don't try to transport fresh fruit and vegetables in an unrefrigerated container.
3. Never surprise your seventy-four-year-old mother (mother-in-law).

We set off from Cincinnati Friday morning with a two-car caravan if you can call it that. Kevin and Loren drove their car, and Jill and the girls and I were in our car. We had six people and Ginger, Loren's dog. Age groups range from twelve to fifty-five, which requires all kinds of planning. I needed to take a potty break every fifty-five minutes. The girls needed potty breaks between my potty breaks, and we had to coordinate plans to eat. It's not super hard to coordinate vegan meals on the road, but you do have to think about where to eat.

Jill has the patience of Job. I am less patient, so I became frustrated with all the coordination. Jill wanted to bring fresh oranges and apples and celery and carrots to her mother, thinking that they would be OK with no ice.

Part of the reason for the trip is because we wanted to check on Mom to see how she was living from day-to-day. She was startled to see us. She lives alone and many of her friends have died. Few people seem to check in and she is slowing down. It was good we did this. We found things in need of immediate attention. Jen, old people are not meant to live alone. They need a tribe around them to help them through life the way they helped us through life. It was a wake-up call for all of us.

It's been a while since I've seen the whole city. It's much different than it was when I lived here twenty-five years ago. It's much less vibrant than Cincinnati. It's poorer. And the infrastructure is worse. The streets and sidewalks are dingy. And the chasm between the haves and the have-nots is stark. Over the past forty years, prosperous whites have moved out into Shelby County and created PGA-quality golf clubs, country clubs, gated subdivisions, and robust businesses.

The city of Memphis is now sixty-four percent African-American, many of them working multiple part-time jobs to make ends meet. It is a horrible indictment on the wealthiest country on Earth in the city where MLK's life ended.

We don't know if it's time to get closer to home yet.

Lots of decisions to make.

There were some bright spots. We got to spend time with my great-niece, Paisley Mae. She is the most alert three-month-old baby I have seen. I got to see my sister, Rolandria, whom I have not seen since Mom died. And I got to buy lunch for Kameron and Erika, Paisley's parents. They moved to Memphis one month ago.

Rolandria drove up from Louisiana with her boyfriend, Stephens. And the kids were able to connect.

Finally, I will never understand why people refuse to wear a mask. Two of my relatives were unmasked. Ohio and Tennessee are both red with COVID cases. We interacted with a lot of people this weekend, though we remained masked and all of us tested negative before we arrived.

Here's hoping we will remain healthy.

Love you, Jen. Love to Don.

Old Man Ernest

Monday, July 6, 2020
Taos, New Mexico

Dear Friend,

Your trip to Memphis is so interesting on many levels. First, in your usual style—it is humorous. I have an exact picture of your vehicles heading south and the rotting fruit.

Candidly, please let Jill know that traveling with the fruit without "refrigeration" would be something that I would do. It is a sign of caring and hope. Thinking of her mom and hoping that the fruit makes it.

I get it.

And Don would have gotten annoyed with me about it as well.

Second, that little girl is precious, and I love the name. Is it a "Prince" reference? So cute. Whenever I see babies (or young children now) like my step-grandchildren, I cannot help but wonder what this world will be like for them. It seems that we live in such a negative time and is there, in fact, hope?

But I guess people before us felt the same way. We have just been spared for many years. Yep, we have been fortunate.

Fourth of July weekend on the high desert—in the mountains at almost 8,000 feet—was a trifle different this year. In past years we have had a morning brunch and then the group heads to a protest parade. (One in which I once stood next to Donald Rumsfeld, Secretary of Defense Under Bush 44.) He lives in this liberal bastion and manages to fade into the background. Once though, he had Dick Cheney (former Vice President) in town as Cheney was thinking about buying property here—and within a day the protesters drove him away.

After the parade, we generally go to a pig roast and then go to bed early.

This year was unique. We had two couples over, had a distant barbecue in the yard and socialized briefly. Honestly, I am not feeling very patriotic or loving America much.

Back to the Taos liberals. So, by Taos standards, I am very much a moderate. I am finding that the people on the far left and the far right are equally judgmental, it just comes out in different platitudes.

This country is angry.

As POTUS would say "very very angry."

Ha.

I have been in close touch with my mom. I think you know that she retires in December. She seems to have adapted to being at home and not having such a tight schedule better than I would have expected, but it does raise the issue you said about Jill's mom.

While my mom is married, her husband is eighty-nine and she eventually will be alone and WILL stay at home. That is what she wants. I am wrestling with lots of guilt as my almost seventy-year-old husband and I are ready to move for good across the country. I love my mother deeply—and that remains static. I do however want the last phase of our lives to be far west.

So, we will head and return to Cincinnati often. I keep thinking of all of those people whether it was during the great migration, the wagon trains going west, those enslaved captured in Africa or the immigrants who got on the boats—all leaving their families which was likely forever.

And I sit here and seem to choose to do this voluntarily.

I do beat myself up about it some, but I think, deep down, we all need to be who we are inside.

I agree, old people are not meant to be alone.

And I am sure that you guys have some tough decisions to make.

The thing no one tells us (or maybe we are just not paying attention) is that we spend years getting our kids ready to launch and then (hopefully that goes well) it is time that our parents need us. And in these times of COVID, the timing is way off on everything.

I am trying my best to take pleasure in the outdoors, in the fact that (for now) we are healthy and, in the hope, that we elect a new president.

Or as Hemingway wrote in *The Old Man and the Sea*, "It is silly not to hope, and I believe it is a sin."

Safe travels,

Jennifer

Grandma Jean Loved Her Whiskey

Tuesday, July 7, 2020
Memphis, Tennessee

Dear Jen,

I'm still trying to process our Memphis trip. You and Don would enjoy it when the country opens up again. You can hear great blues, visit Sun Records and the Stax Museum of Rock and Soul. And, of course, barbeque!

I visited Jill in Memphis six weeks after we met at separate conferences in a hotel in Olive Branch, Mississippi. The second meeting was the week of November 20, 1994. Her mother came to the door, but I thought it was Jill. At forty-eight, she looked twenty-seven. Seeing her didn't hurt my decision to marry Jill. I thought *this how my wife will look at fifty*? She does.

Over the years, my mother-in-law, Evelyn, has helped us in many situations. She is reserved and is not one to show much affection, but she is generous. I think being reserved is a trait passed on to Jill. They have quiet strength and character.

Evelyn is four-foot-eleven and has been plucky since I met her. Like my mother, she became pregnant with Jill in college. Jill's bio father's name was Jan. He was from Dayton, ironically. We visited him thirteen years ago at his mother's house in North Dayton on Mother's Day. That day Loren, age nine, learned to prep Cornish hen, prodded by her grandmother. Thing is, I never saw her place it in the oven because she started drinking bourbon. And then she fell asleep on the porch. Grandma Jean loved her whiskey.

Jan was five-feet-two and a Vietnam veteran. The war damaged him. He once looked like George Michael, Jill said. At sixty, he looked like he had done hard drugs and was emotionally unavailable. He did love his pit bulls, though. I wasn't sure he was happy or indifferent that we made the effort to visit. That was the third time Jill saw him. On that day, Jill learned she had a sister who was two years older than Loren. She lives in Columbus. We don't even know her name. Jan died four years ago. I did an advanced search on him and saw that he was clearly a victim of racial profiling by Dayton police. I counted eighteen traffic stops for minor offenses or for nothing. This made me sad.

But he and Evelyn created Jill, my wife, the mother of my children, and an outstanding human being.

Evelyn's mom died when she was four years old, leaving her and her four sisters orphans to be raised by their grandfather. "Poppa" grew soybeans, corn and cotton—cash crops. Evelyn kept the books—even as a little girl. When the time came to integrate schools, organizers wanted kids from strong families. Evelyn was picked. She left Lincoln College in Nebraska to integrate Southwest Mississippi Community College in 1967.

Her grandfather had his house shot up by the KKK and a cross was burned in the yard. She and a few other kids who joined her in integrating Southwest rode a bus to the school. White students spat on them and pelted them with small rocks every day.

After a year, she enrolled at Memphis State University, where she eventually earned two degrees and became a public school teacher.

She raised Jill alone and sent her to The Taft School, a boarding school in Connecticut when Jill was fifteen. From there, brainy Jill got to go to Brown University. Evelyn set her daughter up for success.

I'm lucky to have her as my mother-in-law. And it makes me sad to see her age. We all will face it if we live long enough. She means so much to so many.

I have to stop now.

Love,

Byron

On Top of New Mexico

Wednesday, July 8, 2020
Taos, New Mexico

My Dear Friend,

I love the details on Memphis and your Memphis trip. So past wisdom has been never to make life-changing decisions during a crisis, but I suspect that this "crisis" is a new way of life. I feel like it is difficult to make decisions beyond the next day. I was raised to make plans, plans, plans.

This is not the time for much planning. It reminds me of when my grandfather was on his deathbed (in a hospital he founded in Charleston, W. VA). He first said, "I trained many of these people, they don't know what they are doing." And later I said, "I wish that you would get well." He said, "I am doing the best that I can."

This was a guy who usually answered with comments such as "I will." "Don't worry," etc.

Not the platitude that "I am doing the best that I can."

Which is maybe all that any of us can ever do.

We are all doing the best that we can.

Work has been on top of Don and me. Our clients are in crisis; COVID on site, people who don't want to go back to work, trying to generate revenue in a broken nation. And we are most grateful for clients. And we are living in one of the world's most beautiful spots. Yet, rarely a day goes by in which we are free to not engage with work product. This sounds like complaining (and maybe it is) but burnout is real.

I am grateful for the loyalty, the income, and the confidence. I am also very tired.

So, with this in mind, we decided to climb Wheeler Peak (roof on NM) which is also visible from our backyard. We ascend at least once a year. To me, there is nothing more therapeutic than a day on the trail. We succeeded with some effort and felt better on the steep up and the slippery down than we have in years. As I get closer to the next birthday, I remind myself that there is still a young person inside of me.

At the core of it, the only person to whom I want to prove something is myself. I have found physical challenges and accomplishments to mean more than any professional award or title. The physical makes me sleep well at night. The professional is vacuous. At least to me.

Generally, we meet interesting people on the trail. These are not times for making new friends. Most people are masked, and we all step aside (widely) when passing others.

I have given much thought to your stories about your family struggles. Being black in America is/has been tougher than I could have imagined. While I consider myself enlightened, educated, anti-racist and friend to many not like me, I never truly knew the daily struggles and the fear. I also know that, in today's America, there is not much room for anyone who is not your standard Anglo. I fear for this once great country.

I have always believed in the goodness of the human spirit. Evil is so prevalent now. Has it always been there? Is it just activated, again?

I have lived through the words of Holocaust survivor and psychiatrist Viktor Frankl (*Man's Search for Meaning*):

> We who lived in concentration camps can remember the men who walked through the huts comforting others, giving away their last piece of bread. They may have been few in number, but they offer sufficient proof that everything can be taken from a man but one thing the last of human freedoms—to choose one's attitude in any given set of circumstances—to choose one's own way. —Viktor Frankl

Through it all, it seems right that we can only control how we are impacted. To be sure; black American's have carried a burden almost too exponential to bear.

I have reconciled with my sister. We do argue some, but that is the life of many siblings. My reigning attitude is that for those with whom we share a modicum of alignment (on such critical matters) we need to rise above and "get along." This means putting past differences aside for the good of the whole. My mom keeps talking with me about the concept of existential aloneness. While she is onto something, I also cannot give in to the darkest thoughts.

It is simply too big to slay.

So instead, I go for a hike.

Not much of substance to report from here, except that I seem to be inside my own head.

Love,

Jennifer

Mr. Trump, Mr. Grinch

Thursday, July 9, 2020
Cincinnati, Ohio

Dear Jen,

Yesterday's letter was powerful and truthful in so many ways. It's hard to know where to start to respond. So I'm going to start with the prospect of another four years with Donald J. Trump as president.

Every time I see him saying or doing anything now on television, in my head I replace the audio with the singular voice of Thurl Ravenscroft and his Grinch. Just substitute "Mr. Trump." Amplify the bass clarinet.

You're a monster, Mr. Trump
Your heart's an empty hole
Your brain is full of spiders
You've got garlic in your soul
Mr. Tru-UMP!
I wouldn't touch you
With a thirty-nine-and-a-half foot pole

As you know, Jen, I once fashioned myself as a Republican. This was the party of my grandfather and the party of one of my mentors, Robert Brown, who worked in Nixon's White House as an adviser on civil rights.

When I arrived at Louisiana Tech University in 1983 to study journalism, I was Carlton Banks and Alex Keaton combined. I believed in self-reliance and free enterprise as the path to freedom. This was the philosophy of my grandmother, who never accepted welfare, though she probably needed it with eight children in the house. She was too proud to apply. We didn't need government handouts. Everybody who could work did work.

Only eighteen years earlier, Tech had admitted its first two black students, Bertha Bradford-Robinson and James Earl Potts—in 1965. I was proud to follow in their footsteps.

I was oblivious for so long. I thought I had risen above the effects of racism. Stuart, my white best friend from my hometown, and I were roommates (only later did I discover that this arrangement was juicy town talk). I was a proponent of a "colorblind" society because why dwell on the past you cannot change? We could only move forward together. Hard work, sacrifice, and a good education is your golden ticket.

Cue the scratched record.

Today, I feel ashamed because I bit deeply into the myth of the American Dream and opportunity for all. I feel betrayed and the same people I once chided for their non-belief, I now owe an apology. I have always spoken out against bigotry and racism. I have written from my own North Star guidance.

But, sadly, I do not believe in our country as I once did. I have suffered discrimination because of my race in the workforce for sure, but in many other ways that I will never be able to put my finger on. At fifty-five years old, when most folks grow more conservative, I feel like I'm having my own awakening. My optimism has waned as I see the scabs ripped off, exposing vile racism and bigotry EVERYWHERE! I wonder, like you, has it always been here simmering, or is this something else? I wonder how much social media has to do with it.

Trump was born out of the reduction of a sickly stew pot. We allowed him to happen. And now, like you, I fear there is no turning back. In my heart, I want Joe Biden to win. But in my head, I'm preparing myself for four more years of Trump. He is dangerous and his heart is an empty hole. I don't want my children to have to spend their formative years in his version of America.

Our democracy is at stake, and we will be the laughing stock of the entire world.

Love,

Byron

P.S. I want to talk about the Philadelphia Eagles wide receiver, DeSean Jackson, and his anti-Semitic posts and his praise of Louis Farrakhan. Just not today. His ignorance makes me sad and diminishes what we are trying to do.

Our Love Story

Friday, July 10, 2020
Taos, New Mexico

Dear Byron,

Happy Friday. For some reason (and I won't question it) I am feeling happy today. It may be because we talked to Nora (from Berlin) and she received the news that she officially finished her MSC in International Business, Economics and Finance from KULeuven.

I am so proud of her. She is the youngest of the four girls with three above her that have been remarkable. It is often not easy to stand out in this family. But she has chosen her own path of adventure. She also let us know that she and (boyfriend with whom she lives) Erwann will marry this summer. They are ready, and while it is not the time to have a wedding (nor does she want one), we are thrilled for the couple.

Her American mom will plan something (a party) once travel is permitted.

I feel such deep love for this girl; my youngest child. She is an exceptional human and has "seen" things on this planet that I could have never imagined. She also is so brave and world aware. She has been "anti" the way the USA lives before it was chic (NOW.)

So, a story for you and one that I don't think that I have shared.

My 30th birthday was 7/17/93. Don and I married on 7/17/93. Nora was born on 7/23/93. She did the math at some young age and figured out that she was not born to the natural order of life. Don and I wanted to marry well before. But we were both married to other people. We had lived together a few years by then and wanted another baby, so we proceeded. We thought that we would have another "out of wedlock."

However, he learned on July 15 that his divorce went through. Through Don's political connections he was able to get the Ohio five-day-marriage license-waiting period waived.

In all his years in politics; this was a favor that he so wanted. We went to the courthouse (me very pregnant) and processed our information and the bureaucrat did not even flinch as he typed in our license data.

Two days later we had a birthday party planned for my thirtieth. We called family and ensured that they would attend. And Judge Nadine Allen (an old friend) showed up and announced a surprise wedding. We have NO video tapes of our life. Weren't into that. Don's late brother had just received a camcorder for a gift and taped it all—it is very touching and very funny and good to hear his voice over—all of these years after he died.

So, Nora Esther was born days later. Our official love story.

At the time, this was a scandal. But also, it was one of the best days of our lives.

Marriage is never easy. This we know to be true.

But I love being married to Don Mooney. We have had our troubles (yes, we have) but I feel so fortunate to be where we are now.

The world is such a challenge. This president is frightening. The people who support him are worse. But in the middle of it all, I am thankful for the life that we have had.

This is for the four healthy and amazing girls and the whole of the family.

I'm ending today with another quote. This by another writer, F. Scott Fitzgerald from *Tender is the Night*.

"I don't ask you to love me always, like this, but I ask you to remember. Somewhere inside of me will always be the person, I am tonight."

Have a good weekend.

Love,

Jennifer

Black Compression Socks

Saturday, July 11, 2020
Cincinnati, Ohio

Dear Jen,

Hey there! How was your day? Mine was pretty good.

As an FYI, today is the 216th anniversary of the day that Vice President Aaron Burr killed his great political nemesis, Alexander Hamilton, in a duel in New Jersey. OK, I'm not that good or that smart. It came up on one of my "This Day in History" feeds today. Our family, like millions of other families, has its TV (or entertainment unit) tuned into Disney Plus, which is now streaming one of the original Broadway productions of *Hamilton*.

Two things I learned: 1) History was not taught well in the school I attended, and 2) History taught the right way can turn even a cynical preteen into a rabid history buff. That would be Laila, my twelve-year-old. She and her older sister, Simone, have memorized the entire soundtrack, which is to say every line of the play.

Hamilton was everything it was cracked up to be. Lin Manuel-Miranda has genius-level talent, that's for sure.

For me, today began with the best intentions. I was going to weed and mow the lawn. I put on my work clothes early and set the intention. My work clothes consist of cargo shorts, running shoes, black compression socks and a ratty white T-shirt with a picture of Simone on the front and her hand prints on the back. A caption back there reads: "Hugged by Mone. Father's Day, 2007." Oh yes, a cap. I look rather like an old man now who tells the kids to stay out of his yard.

I never made it outside to mow. Jill was gone all day. Simone needed help with something. Then there was lunch to make. And I needed to prep for a

Zoom lesson I'm teaching for church. And then it was time for dinner. And the day just got away.

I mentioned offline about the rough patch Jill and I are hitting right now. Our 25th anniversary is in November. Like all marriages, ours has been exhilarating and traumatic. We have been happy and devastatingly sad. And most of all we have been challenged to raise three incredibly smart girls with their own sets of complex issues. As great as we appear on the outside, I think it's important to admit that nothing is perfect, and everything that's good usually takes a lot of work and nurturing. We are always a work in progress, particularly now during the most stressful part of our life. We still have a deep and abiding love and like for each other.

There is a reason wedding vows make us promise to be there for each other "in sickness and in health, for richer or for poorer," because when those times come, and they will, they grab you by the throat and threaten to choke the life out of you. We need to remember who we are and how we can remember and rediscover the people we left behind.

Love,

Byron

A Mini Break

Sunday, July 12, 2020
Taos, New Mexico

Dear Byron,

Good weekend. We are heading to Colorado (about three hours away) for a few days to early celebrate my birthday and our anniversary. We will stay in a remote cabin, bringing food, and will minimize human interactions. Our plan is to climb Mt. Elbert; the highest Colorado peak. Colorado boasts fifty-eight peaks over 14,000 feet. They call them 14ers. The car is loaded with the cooler, all meals, our bikes, and hiking equipment.

We, too, are a Hamilton-obsessed family. My stepdaughter was the first obsessed. She lives in Union City, NJ—just blocks from the Hamilton-Burr (Weehawkan, NJ, 1804) duel. She saw the show on Broadway and waited outside the theatre (after) to say hello to "Lin." Apparently, he was quite friendly. Don saw the show in Chicago. (I had some other family plans that day.) So, my life (of late) has been to the soundtrack of the show with no reference. Sort of like football, I have been capable of totally ignoring it.

Yes, we watched the other evening, too. Lin is a serious genius and it was even more than I expected. So, I guess that I am a latecomer fan.

I have (like most) been recently ruminating on COVID and tracking where the incidence is high. Living in NM, it is always clear that this is a tribal place of many sovereign nations. These nations have "shut" their borders to outsiders (smart.) However, some of the tribes currently have significant rates of COVID. It has made me think about all of the terrible things that white man has inflicted on the Native Americans. We brought alcoholism, stole land, shattered families and now this.

I am sorry that things are tough between you and Jill. These times are trying everything. Don and I have been together since 1988, lived together since 1991 and married since 1993. While we have been happy; there were some brief challenges. For five years we had a commuter marriage. We came through it with a deeper commitment and deeper faith. There is so much that threatens marriage. I have realized that we can't ever take any of it for granted.

I have prioritized my own marriage over most else.

We had two couples (old, old friends) over for a distant outside dinner. One man was married to a woman who became one of my closest friends. She died three years ago. He has been in a relationship with a friend, from youth, with whom he reunited. They announced their engagement last night. He is close to seventy, she is in her mid-sixties. This later-in-life happiness for "older folk" is heartening. While all six of us share views on Trump, masks, life, etc it is clear that even among like-minded cohorts, opinions vary.

The group of us hails from Tulsa, Houston, Santa Fe and Cincinnati. One couple has a son-in-law who had COVID—and was hospitalized. The young man is a welder—and given very little time to get back to work. Part of me, while glad to be with friends, wondered whether we should even be within six feet of breathing distance from one another.

I talked with my mom yesterday. I know that she believes that you are VERY well positioned for the job for which you are interviewing. I realized I did know the man who retired from it; he was a good guy and had been there forever. She also believes that, over time, they WILL take care of the salary part. She reiterated that the "main" guys are very excited about your interest.

I just finished a book about women in the Hitler 1936 Olympics and the athlete's observations about Berlin. I started another book called *1939*. I have suspected and now believe that today is much like *1939* in that the world is on the brink of "something" big. In *1939* people knew that life was changing. We, too, are aware; and it seems that 2020 may be a watershed for much of what we have known.

We all seem to be on the edge of our seats, appreciating what we have and had.

And in the middle of it all the Disney Theme Parks open.
Really…
The World's Happiest Place on Earth.
If only for a few minutes.

Happy Sunday.

Love,

Jennifer

A Transcendent Moment

Monday, July 13, 2020
Cincinnati, Ohio

Dear Jennifer,

It's great how you and Don challenge yourselves to be great and do great physical things. Lots of people say they like to hike and climb mountains, but a lot of them aren't really climbing and hiking the way you climb and hike. I aspire to do this. I'm going to keep pushing myself to grow stronger and increase my stamina to one day get to the "roof of New Mexico" or, at the very least, a hill bigger than the short incline in my neighborhood.

The big news today (to sports fans like me at least) is that the Washington Redskins have decided to drop "Redskins" as the team's mascot. Owner Daniel Snyder had to be pulled kicking and screaming into the 21st century with the decision. I was happy to see that pressure from corporate partners, especially FedEx, began to work. Revered CEO Fred Smith, who has created a diverse middle class in Memphis, was the main catalyst. He has stadium naming rights and is a minority owner of the Washington team.

When I was younger, I did not give the name a second thought—just as I didn't give playing "Cowboys and Indians" a second thought. The Redskins was just part of the sports universe, and the Redskins were the rivals of my team, the Dallas Cowboys. So I hated them intuitively. But for the past few years, all the things that racist name represents I found abhorrent. I began calling the team the Washington football team. The use of Redskins represents the equivalent of a team being called the N-words or the K-words. Fans mindlessly perform a "Tomahawk Chop." They do the same thing at Braves games, Florida State games and Cleveland Indians games. I think those teams are next. And I'm even hearing the Texas Rangers may even have to consider a name change based on Rangers' savage history. ("Every Texas Ranger has Mexican blood. It's on his boots," goes an old saying.)

Back to the Redskins. No way this name and behavior would fly if this team was starting anew.

Because of the business you and I are in, we know the importance of brand equity. Imagine having to get rid of Charmin and all the years of work it took to make it a market leader? Only this is a bit different. The team's brand has been built on a slur that dehumanizes Native peoples.

You and Don are rare birds who live among the Native peoples and get a chance to embrace and honor the culture. How do they feel, I wonder?

You and I started writing partly because of what was happening in our country. We wanted to document history and our unique place within it. Indeed, this has been an extraordinary spring and summer, and it ain't over.

Institutions are rethinking their history and their deeds. (I saw where someone even pulled down the Conquistador statue in Albuquerque.) A team will spend millions to rebrand after resisting for years. The sitting president is reminded that "Black Lives Matter" on the street outside two of his homes—the temporary one in Washington, D.C., and the more established one in Manhattan. The movement has not waned yet.

The conservative part of me wants to make sure we do this the right way by organizing, setting goals and measuring progress. I want to have a multi-pronged strategy to get new civil rights laws enacted, and business investment and political power for the historically marginalized.

The heat will eventually die down, and I think that's when the real work starts. That said, this period feels transformational. Sorry to sound so philosophical today. Thanks for listening, Jen.

Love,

Byron

In Thin Air

Tuesday, July 14, 2020
Twin Lakes, Colorado

Dear Byron,

We continue to be in an undisclosed location (a remote cabin—Twin Lakes, an old west mining town) in Colorado. Our plan (in coming here) was to avoid the constant phone, email, texts and many client demands. While we are grateful, it has been way too long since we unplugged. However, as responsible grown-ups, we have continued to stay a bit plugged in.

I am thankful for the ability to find a slow connection.

Latest news, our Caroline, who lives on the South Carolina-Georgia line was just notified by her landlord. The couple living next to her (with whom she shares a driveway), both doctors, have COVID. Our otherwise healthy girl (as is her mama) is now worried. She is down there alone, which concerns me. Like, how will my baby be taken care of if she becomes ill? And she is living in a pretty opened-up part of the nation.

For the last three hours, I have not been manic. I don't do manic anymore. I am worried though. I am wondering who will take care of Caroline if she gets sick. Would I fly in and care for her? She gets sick, I get sick...

And I have gone from 0-60 in hours (minutes, really) but I am a mom and contingency planner.

What to do? Ugh. Nothing. That is the worst part of any of this. Families apart and nothing.

Nora got in touch today as well and has made the plans for her marriage to Erwann. Their date will be in Denmark in August. She has described Denmark as the Vegas of Europe. I am happy for them. Nora did not attend her high school graduation, her college graduation and there was not a grad school graduation—COVID. Nora determining to marry without a wedding or family—is very Nora.

And then there is COVID.

And we are thousands of miles away.

Our job (as parents) has become very much about answering the phone, being the coaches and reminding the grown "kids" that somehow this all works out. There seems to be little else we can do.

Yep, let's hope it all works out.

So, in the past two days, there has been some physical exertion. We (for the second time) climbed Mt. Elbert (highest in Colorado and second highest peak in the lower forty-eight). That mountain delivered a wallop. Weather: it rained, hailed, thunder stormed, bright sun and stiff and fast wind. We were (by at least twenty years) the elders on this peak. We both experienced health challenges that resulted in some stress and concern. By the time we returned to the cabin, we both wondered if "people our age" should undertake this sort of challenge.

On a side note, I have learned to NEVER trust the climbing guide-books. While we always research the trail, the following is almost always fact:

- The trail is likely longer than described.
- The trail is likely harder than described.
- The climb takes longer than described.

Sort of like life.

Maybe we are just old and slow, but yesterday was a prime example. Eleven miles, tough weather, aching joints and epic beauty. The good news is one becomes very focused during these expeditions with little time to worry about all else.

Today we put our bikes on the car and crossed Independence Pass (highest paved point in the USA and Continental Divide) and parked some distance from Aspen. We then rode in, strolled, were reminded that "touristy" small towns are still in operation, ate lunch and rode back.

Lots of people are vacationing in Colorado. They are wearing masks.

When I graduated from undergrad, my then future husband #1 and I moved to Vail, Colorado. Why? Why not? We didn't know how we would get jobs and were not ready yet. To this day, I am glad that I took out some time (when young), worked retail in a mountain town and had the experience. In those days, we often took side trips to Aspen. While always a "hot spot," in 1985 it still seemed like a cowboy town. Today, it is a very expensive and modern place.

You spoke of cowboys and Indians and the PC nature of it all. I think that we all likely (and by accident) said and did bigoted things. And I do feel for our Native American population. We are all intruders on this land. The white man owes much to the Native American.

When I sent you the photo (Sunday) of the Aspen trees (my favorite tree) you said, "You can hear the angels sing," and I have had the Youngblood's song stuck in my brain as follows:

Love is but a song to sing
Fear's the way we die
You can make the mountains ring
Or make the angels cry
Though the bird is on the wing
And you may not know why

I was also laughing to myself when you texted that both my mother and I have intimidating beauty.

My line on this (that I learned from her as a child):

Beauty is as beauty does.

Love,

Jennifer

A Beacon of Light

Wednesday, July 15, 2020
Cincinnati, Ohio

Dear Jennifer,

I've learned at fifty-five that my brain does not want to respond to the problems and stressors of a thirty-five-year-old. I get hot, break out into a sweat and become irritable if I feel overwhelmed. And lately, my days of feeling overwhelmed have arrived like multiple avalanches.

On my worst day working in the newspaper industry, I was associate editorial page editor working with a manager who was not the best planner or delegator. It was a fifteen-hour Friday that stretched into 3:30 a.m. Saturday. Jill would confess to me later that she wondered for a second if I was seeing someone. NO! She has never experienced this.

As a thirty-five-year-old I was able to handle it. This isn't so now. I promised myself that I would never place myself in a situation where that would happen again, but it has. I blame myself. I have volunteered to teach a weekly class at church on the biblical books of John 1, 2, and 3. I also agreed to be a table host for an initiative that brings strangers together to discuss deep issues of upbringing, our place in society, and the future. This, on top of what you know is happening for me on your birthday and my return to work after being out for a while.

Not doing this again.

On the bright side, this initiative, branded "Room at the Table," first was marketed by the Cincinnati Regional Chamber. The person who developed it is a Stanford-trained HR executive and mental health counselor. The Chamber is no longer housing it, so the creator has asked some of us who have gone through the exercises to lead.

We just finished our session, which was an unexpected gift.

Some takeaways:

- I remain startled at the depth of racism in America. Some of the participants discuss being spanked as early as age four for playing with a black child, which ignited a fear of black people well into adulthood.
- A person of color in the group with a white stepmom attended a local university known for Greek mischief. Her first exposure with overt racism was "Ghetto Week," where suburban kids found it funny to wear gold chains, afro wigs and boom boxes. This, at a "public Ivy."
- And a person raised in one of our suburbs never encountered a black person until she joined the workforce.

I could go on, but the good news is they all are in my group, voluntarily, because they want a future that is better than our past.

To which I say, "Amen."

I so cherish our relationship. I hope we can be a beacon of light in a world of too much darkness. In the end, what does it matter anyway? Why did we treat one another so unkindly? How can we not embrace one another as brother and sister and friends? Imagine the economic power that we have wasted because of the desire to oppress a group of "others."

Love to you,

Life of a Step-Mom

Thursday, July 16, 2020
Taos, New Mexico

Dear Byron,

We made it back from the very high country to the pretty high country. With the number fifty-seven coming tomorrow for me, I am glad to have accomplished some fitness.

If anything, the "climb" requires such focus, that it leaves little time to worry about Caroline with the COVID positive neighbors and Nora getting married in Denmark. I am happy for the latter, yet it just shows me how far apart we are. The world seems suddenly big. We have extensive technology but remain outside of hugging distance.

Weird times.

My late best friend and I used to have these youth conversations (called predictions) in which we would predict what would happen to us as adults. We never considered that she would be dead by thirty-two and that within a few years, the world we knew would cease to exist. While I have always been a planner, I never realized how futile an exercise planning is. I keep thinking about the blasted corporate "five-year plans" I used to have to develop. Really, five years; give me five hours.

I keep thinking about this huge part of America, those who are truly down on their luck. I was reminded (by my mom) as I gave her a version of the work that you and I are doing together, that we (you/I) are both privileged. We have our families, work, health and the things that matter.

So many folks are alone and frightened.

These times are frightening even for the best and most ardent of us.

Family has been top-of-mind lately. We are empty nesters, with the kids and other relatives far away. These times make for much reflection about our years together (mine and Don's). We moved in with each other when his children were eleven and six, and soon after I had Caroline and Nora.

I have been a stepmother for decades. I have a stepfather and had a stepmother. The "step" lifestyle is an integral part of our lives. My stepdaughters have been good to me—they place value on someone to take care of their dad. I have never tried to be their mother. They have one. And we all sometimes only get one and maybe a "bonus" step. I know my place.

In our early days together I was blamed by (people outside of the family) as the instigator in what happened when I was in my twenties. I was young, impressionable and in love. Do I regret any of this? No. Definitely not. Yet it does fall in the camp of "blaming the woman." We have been together happily since we met in 1988—many lifetime's ago. So, it seems that the love, drama and all that followed was more than an accident.

We were and are a love story.

After all of the decades, Don is the family patriarch and I, his wife.

On the eve of my birthday and our anniversary, there are two titles that matter most to me, mother and wife.

I know that you are worked-slammed. Talk soon.

Love,

Jennifer

Is This the Job for Me?

Friday, July 17, 2020
Cincinnati, Ohio

Dear Jen,

Do you know what today is?

It's your birthday and your anniversary. Who gets lucky enough to celebrate the two most important days in life on the same day?!

I hope you guys had a great day filled with fun and thankfulness.

Today ended a busy week, for which I am thankful. I've been talking to Julie lately. One of the things I said to her is how blessed we are to be able to choose whether we lie on our navels, unlike some of our intubated and ventilated comrades. I'm trying to be mindful of how blessed we are, as Judy said. We are!

I want to give you a quick update about my chat today. The whole crew seemed happy and seemed to appreciate what I have to bring to the table. Hard to read through a screen though. They asked great questions, too, not "gotcha" questions, but legitimate scenarios that are meaningful to the work. Funny how I can draw a blank in these circumstances sometimes.

I don't remember stumbling, but I should have asked them to talk about challenges and whether they feel like they have the time and resources to do the work. Also, I find myself second-guessing or hoping my confidence was not interpreted at something else.

Alas, it will be what it will be. You asked me about next steps. I have more information about that. If it is decided that I am to move forward, I would meet with the director and the VP. And then, presumably, they would make an offer!

Fingers crossed.

On a different note, have you been paying attention to what's going on in Portland? Federal troops are detaining protesters without identifying themselves as law enforcement! Remember the Clinton Administration and the term "jackbooted thugs" coined by Republicans in response to Janet Reno's department of justice?

Look at what we've become under this very small, insecure Republican president. Jen, if he could he would not leave office. I also believe he would round up America's undesirables and establish a gulag if he could get away with it.

This is ending darkly, but I fear for my country and our democracy. He has to go. Our country has become a laughingstock.

What do our ex-pats Nora or Stephanie say?

Bye for now,

Byron

¾'s Past Middle-Age

Saturday, July 18, 2020
Taos, New Mexico

Dear Byron,

Lots to say today. Turning fifty-seven and twenty-seven years of marriage in the books. We had a nice out-to-dinner, outside dinner last evening. We are blessed. Blessed to be on the planet, healthy, here and together.

To quote Hemingway again, "Now is no time to think of what you do not have. Think of what you can do with what there is."

I have little patience for the privileged with a constant litany of complaints. Do something—march, write, take action, pray, love. Do it. We are here because our ancestors pressed on and prevailed.

Speaking of. Got in the car after dinner and learned that John Lewis had died and MARCHED until the end. His passing is a loss. His voice is needed.

Recently you wrote about not having the patience, motivation and perhaps the energy to deal with the "avalanche of stressors." I get it. I began to feel the same way in my earlier fifties. There is something that happens to us—it all becomes too exhausting. I still have the physical energy for fitness and the mental discipline to read and to write. But I hit a wall with too many appointments, too much negative brain work, etc. I am not sure if it is age or just being fed up. I wonder how/why my mother (at eighty-one) still does it.

There is much to be concerned about—but (maybe it is just me) I have to keep smiling. I can't do this thing called life with a frown. As long as I can remember, I have always sought the silver lining. Many believe that we are constantly steps away from the entire bottom falling out. They are likely correct, but I can't do my own life that way.

I sometimes note my daughter's correcting me. They sometimes even say, "Mom, this is bad," and I keep pressing forward with the bravado. Maybe Trump and I have something in common. Frightening thought.

With regard to your team interview…

In the Jennifer wild sense of optimism, I cannot imagine that there is a more qualified candidate for the position. I am so glad that it went well. My only concern is that you are far above the other people in the room—and people have to be secure to accept that concept. They have to truly want what is best for the organization, not just their own tiny role. My husband used to say (when I sat at the corporate table) that what drove people nuts about me was that I often knew people's next steps before they did. You are the same way. I learned the hard way to not unwittingly point out this fact.

My fingers are crossed. They need you.

It was great to hear from so many folks via social media yesterday and via text and phone. I received very COVID times gifts; anti-aging home beauty products, couture masks, designer cookies, flowers and books. We had pre-dinner drinks with our LatinX (now I think that is the term versus Hispanic) neighbors. I mention their ethnicity because living beside them has given us a front row seat to the fabric of a large LatinX family. Their families are part of the pre-statehood NM history. They are smart, interesting and full of love. They have taken us in.

They own restaurants in Belen, NM and I have not heard one word of complaint about life today. They innovate, create and move forward. This couple (now late sixties) has been together since their late teens.

I was especially pleased to hear from all four girls today. Their greetings seem to matter most.

On an inspirational note, there was an interesting FB Anniversary post from an old friend.

He said:

"You two are truly an inspirational couple. You took risks and it paid off." There is much for which to be grateful. We are the fortunate few.

Talk soon.

Love,

Jennifer

Dad Has Covid

Sunday, July 19, 2020
Cincinnati, Ohio

Dear Jen,

I just got off the phone with my dad. Moments before, I was having email dialogue with a reader who seemed to take offense to today's column about "freeing" Dr. Amy Acton, our former director of the department of health. The reader doubted the legitimacy of COVID-19. He presented as evidence four people at his workplace having contracted COVID and all returning to work healthy.

He even offered that NPR (that bastion of liberalism) is signaling a new-found skepticism but without supporting facts.

So, I turn to my dad, now facing the November and December of his life without Etta, his wife of fifty years, one of Louisiana's earliest victims of COVID (the editor of the *Lake Charles American-Press* printed my column on the oped page about losing her). I have mentioned before that he tested positive for COVID as well, and today he told me how much it messes with his mind. How can it not?!

Lake Charles is between New Orleans and Houston, two of the hottest places in America in the summertime. He is always hot in the summer, but he told me this kind of "hot" feels different, so he checks his temperature many times a day. And he wonders if pain or a cough that would have been dismissed ten years ago are the lingering effects of COVID. I imagine it must feel like post-traumatic stress disorder.

I imagine his pain everyday. I'm not sure how long he wants to hang around. And I feel such a profound loss that I didn't really get to know him during the prime years. Because I know him and what he has gone through, I have a very short fuse with some asshat who comes at me with "COVID is not real."

Maybe it's the Cancer in us, but I am following your good habit of being optimistic. So I also had the most animated conversation with him that I have ever had. It was about guns. He's a huge gun advocate (who knew?)!

Changing lanes, a final thought on that new job that I'm seeking. If I do get this job, I know I will miss the ability to share my thoughts in the public space, but I think it's for the best. I believe this staff to be solid, and I do believe they embrace the big picture.

And the reality is that I'm so tired of hiding my light under a bushel. So I just won't do it ever again. I will just be the only me I know how to be, which is collaborative and seeking to exceed expectations.

Love,

Byron

Dying Without Funerals

Monday, July 20, 2020
Taos, New Mexico

Dear Byron,

I am so sorry to hear about your dad. His graphic description of COVID is unnerving. Have you thought about going to see him or is it just too challenging with all else? I am not the best source on fathers and how to interact. Mine died and we were estranged. For many years I was at peace about it. Things happened in a certain succession. I was cognizant of why and the ramifications. It was and is painful.

I do know that I feel terrible for him, even with his own mental illness, and what it meant to go through a large part of his life without having a relationship with his children. Just keep talking to your dad. It matters.

I have lost patience for Trump supporters and COVID deniers as well. Sadly, I seem to know more than I expected. Mostly people with whom I grew up. The same group "posts" comments that border on bigotry. I just don't understand.

I just finished Mary Trump's (POTUS's niece) book, *Too Much and Never Enough*. POTUS's father (Fred) was one horrible dude. His mother (Mary) sat back and did nothing. Yes, family dysfunction and psychological damage that could have been treated. These are people who are not self-aware and simply do not care who is hurt.

Most disturbing is that this is known to the public and a huge slice of America is OK with it.

Life is currently a combination of beautiful, disturbing, dark and sometimes uplifting. Yes, it's hard to be an optimist now. But it is also hard to even know what reality looks like. We are living in the middle of what will (decades from now) be called a significant time in world history. Like people before, we are caught in the day-to-day without the ability to observe the 30,000-foot view.

I am afraid that, if we had this vision, we might not get out of bed.

My own husband's family is BIG. All former wives and relatives ever related to the Mooney clan are still involved. My late brother-in-law's first wife, the mother of a Mooney, is one of us. Her mom died of COVID over the weekend. Older woman, but tragic. A scene with her four children talking to her and saying goodbye through a window.

Daily, I hear so many of these stories. Like your stepmother, dying without funerals.

We look back at historical times, follow the thread, and it usually makes some kind of sense.

Not sure this time.

Not sure at all.

Have a good evening.

Love,

Jennifer

Life is Rough

Tuesday, July 21, 2020
Cincinnati, Ohio

Dear Jennifer,

I reached something of a breaking point today.

I have a counselor, but she didn't work out. I'm seeking another one.

I hate to be gloomy. But today the world was too much.

So I cried for a while. I broke down talking to a coworker. Work seems so secondary. I want to talk about it to you in this letter. It feels too personal for some reason, though we have been forthright.

Truth is, journalism is making me ill and tired, physically. The time has come to leave. To do something else. The thing that made me rage this morning was a little thing but a big thing. A person at work whom I don't respect was asked by another editor to look at my column before publishing. She changed my lead, edited in an error and published it. For forty minutes this morning, I looked like an idiot to anyone who read it.

Thankfully, another co-worker pointed it out and I was able to change it. I called her out on it and copied the editor who asked her to read it. Crickets from both of them. Of course, there is a racial component to this. She is from the Deep South and her personality reminds me of the horrible folks back home who would get you killed (think Emmit Till). She did not acknowledge her error, nor did she apologize to me for committing it. And so it goes. This is how you lose good people and when you are gone people wonder why. Quietly, an error and, in my opinion, unseemly collaboration of editors, were just swept under the rug.

And I'm not going to let it rest. Jen, they operate from a position of privilege (and maybe they are jerks) and I feel it everyday. And I'm tired.

This, on top of marriage, and kids and worry over my dad's wellbeing. And I found myself silently raging. I need to find a place of peace in order to be useful and loving to others.

But right now, I'm not finding it anywhere.

Sorry about this mood. Tomorrow will be better.

Byron

On Any Given Day

Wednesday, July 22, 2020
Taos, New Mexico

Dear Byron,

On any given day, this is how it goes:

- Nora is driving across Germany and I worry about fast German drivers, the Autobahn and accidents.
- Caroline writes that she just stepped off of a body fat monitoring scale (in Georgia at Orangetheory) and her body fat is just over 24%. She is fit, beautiful and healthy.
- My sister Leigh (living on the Gold Coast in Chicago) is nervous as Trump says that he will send in his "troops."
- Don's hernia continues to act up. I am ready for it to be fixed. I worry. And his job stress is nuts…as you can imagine. As the lawyer for the teachers union he is dealing with frantic teachers, the school board/administration, and parents. Not fun.
- I am dealing with work-clients and pretending that life is normal.

On any given day in the United States, this is what privilege looks like. The life of currently healthy people still dealing with the ins and outs of daily living.

I wonder, during the wars and at times when life was at a fever pitch, how people functioned? Did they concern themselves with the details of daily life and shun away the macro? Psychologically, it may be the only way that we can get through.

Such as my rumination with masks. Do I have enough of a variety to match my outfits? Seriously, I concern myself with this.

On any given day. Regardless of the fact that I rarely dress in anything meaningful, I rarely put on make-up and wash my hair only occasionally. My only attempt at beauty is exercise, doing my own nails, and coloring my own hair.

And for what? So that I can look in the mirror and feel that it is OK.

This is any given day and yes, every day.

We see old friends (from a distance) in backyards and on porches. We talk about our fears. We are happy for two friends who found each other late in life. I was good friends with the now-deceased first wife, Karen. I have grown to love the new mate—I know that Karen would have liked her, too. I wear Karen's jewelry on many days. Being around people who found one another (after so much heartbreak) gives me hope.

Hope for the human spirit. I can find that optimist in there somewhere.

In July of 2020, I think we are in times similar to a blend of Europe 1939-1945 and USA 1968. Our ancestors were here before. Many of them still remember.

I hear you loudly about work and feeling negative. Journalism is tough now. Nowhere to hide. Even tougher when one feels that the people with whom they work are competitive rather than collaborative. I had a call this morning with a co-PR professional (we are working on a client together). She asked for some advice re: a client who had truly disrespected her. She asked, "Has that ever happened to you?"

I laughed. Yes. More than you think—on any given day. We are the consultants, the scapegoats. We are a place to affix blame. For "good" clients, we are on their team. One of them. In it together.

Like you, I rage, more than I would like. Riding my bike helps me evacuate bad energy. I am finding that I continue to have these deep COVID dreams and wake up troubled and tired. There is no escape. There are people who "bring the bad stuff" to the surface.

You may remember that my M.A. is in workplace psychology. Workplaces are especially tough. More often than not people pretend to have your back but are truly only looking out for their own interests. It is often a phony environment.

I also focused on positive psychology. There is a man named Martin Seligman (leader of this movement). I have found him to be inspirational.

"The optimists and the pessimists: I have been studying them for the past twenty-five years. The defining characteristic of pessimists is that they tend to believe bad events will last a long time, will undermine everything they do, and are their own fault. The optimists, who are confronted with the same hard knocks of this world, think about misfortune in the opposite way. They tend to believe defeat is just a temporary setback, that its causes are confined to this one case. The optimists believe defeat is not their fault: Circumstances, bad luck, or other people brought it about. Such people are unfazed by defeat. Confronted by a bad situation, they perceive it as a challenge and try harder."

We can only try to do our best and be our best.

On any given day.

Some days are far more difficult than others.

You are truly an optimist my friend.

Love,

Jennifer

American Gothic meets Covid times. Don and Jennifer Mooney, June 2020.

¿Qué Pasa?

Thursday, July 23, 2020
Cincinnati, Ohio

Dear Jen,

Fifteen is the birthday that holds the most significance in my memory. 1980.

We are July babies, so at the very least our birthday memories are possibly tinged with vacation. When I was fifteen, I went to Dallas to visit my aunt, who just one year earlier had moved there to work for one of the Bells—Southwestern Bell Telephone—now AT&T.

She warned me: There won't be anything for you to do. I work long hours. You'll be home alone. But I needed the break because months earlier Buddy had the catastrophic stroke that blinded and paralyzed him. I did not have to feed cattle in the summer and mom was depressed and stressed.

So I took my week away. The solitude in the big city was liberating. I watched FIVE channels, including a Spanish-language channel with this one show in which they repeated "¿Qué pasa? What's happening?" over and over again. The song still gives me an ear worm. I walked three blocks down to Jack in the Box everyday and bought a burger and fries.

My Aunt Debra was dating Joey at the time. He was a nerd and was working in advertising. He LOVED to watch commercials and he marveled at their intent. He laughed like nobody was watching. I grew to love Joey because he always seemed positive and encouraging—at least to us kids. Debra and Joey eventually married. Joey was the only man in my immediate family who had gone to college, and I hung on his every word. Even then, I placed education on a pedestal, good or bad. After all for any Black man in the South to have a job with clean hands was exceptional.

On the Saturday night that ended my week away, I went to a party with them where lots of dope was being smoked and there were a lot of Africans with braids, short afroes and beautiful teeth. I was completely out of place and a little bit terrified when I lost Debra and Joey.

I was a (too-young) country mouse among these "city slickers."

Today was my daughter's fifteenth birthday. She is growing into an accomplished and beautiful young lady. She has blue hair. She is a theater nerd and she loves cooking shows, adventure cartoons and food. She is an excellent dessert maker; her younger sister is the chef. I can see their carry-out store front now: "L&S Hearty Bites and Desserts."

Simone is finding her way. I do not see myself in her at all. I'm proud to be her dad. I thought I had pressure at that age. It does not compare to what our kids are experiencing now. I wonder if Simone wants a week away? Where would she go? The world is moving too fast. (Your July 22 letter was evidence of that.) I wish I could slow it down for them and for us.

Love,

Byron

Keeping Hope Alive

Friday, July 24, 2020
Taos, New Mexico

Dear Byron,

Decent week. Like Simone, Nora's birthday was yesterday. She turned twenty-seven. I continue to struggle with how we will see one another with the travel restrictions in place. At the same time, I am glad that she is in a safer place than the USA. It is hard to believe that the health of Americans is getting worse by the day. Now, the troops are sent into our cities to "attack" our own citizens, for protests.

I agree with what you say about the summer birthday. Nora, Simone, you, me. I have always loved summer most. The days are longer, and the attitude is tamer. Summer 2020 is a major exception. However, I anticipate a tougher time dealing with COVID in winter. People will be truly housebound.

On Thursday we took our (what has become once per week) day away from the world. We went to Los Alamos which may be diving deep into the most frightening version of our planet. I hadn't been there before. It is about ninety minutes from home. We hiked in the hills and visited the historic Atomic Bomb areas. My grandfather was in England during the war. He was assigned to study the impact on chemical warfare on humans. Can you imagine? A doctor.

Los Alamos is truly "in the middle of nowhere." At least it would have been in the forties. It is still a national laboratory, and likely still involved with top secret invention. Apparently, Oppenheimer (who managed the construction of the Los Alamos laboratory, where he gathered the best minds in physics to work on the problem of creating an atomic bomb) went crazy once he understood the real impact of what they created.

It is hard to get one's head around.

Have you read *Man's Search for Meaning* written by Viktor Frankl, Austrian psychiatrist and Holocaust survivor? Both inspirational and depressing all at once. He ends the book with: "For the world is in a bad state, but everything will become worse unless each of us does his best. So, let us be alert-alert in a twofold sense: Since Auschwitz we know what man is capable of. And since Hiroshima we know what is at stake."

If you haven't read it, take a read. It is worth it.

I keep repeating myself, but I can't shake the notion that "we," like others before us continue to go about our day-to-day lives. We get up, dress, exercise, work, go to the market, reach out to loved ones and do our best to get ourselves together. We continue to repeat the ritual hoping that better days are ahead.

And then more news, more disruption.

You asked whether it is easier to be an optimist in our current mountain life? I think that it is. Natural beauty makes a difference, at least to me.

We return to the city in the middle of next month. To more COVID, more people and the crowded apartment building. While we have enjoyed our life there, it now seems like a potential germ trap. Don is scheduled for surgery. We will see family, friends and deal with business matters.

It all seems so much different this time. So tentative.

We have never known where we are headed. We thought that we did. We had that great American sense of optimism. Fleeting. So strange.

In the beginning days of the pandemic, I witnessed humans behaving kindlier. I witnessed some hope and that typical human concept that "this was temporary" and we would get through. People are now seeming haggard, despondent, angry and hopeless. Not all, but many.

There are some people missing from the national conversation. I have noted Jesse Jackson. I am thinking that he is just not well. Stuck in my mind though is Jesse shouting "Keep Hope Alive." I saw him live several times, once on Fountain Square. His energy and passion were all consuming.

For today, I am keeping hope alive.

Love,

Jennifer

I Lost My America

Saturday, July 25, 2020
Cincinnati, Ohio

Dear Jen,

I'm starting this note by repeating something in your letter that I found utterly profound.

"We had that great American sense of optimism. Fleeting. So strange."

A few hours ago, I was talking to Jill about why I think I am feeling the way I feel. The answer is this: the America that I thought I knew was never really there. And I mourned and wept, as I might if I lost a close friend or relative. And, the tears well up even as I write this. (This is super weird.)

Finally, I get it. I'm mourning the loss of my country.

A few days ago, Jill told me that she feels I have accumulated so many hurts that I find it difficult to be optimistic, even about a possible pending good fortune. (You know the thing to which she refers.) I harbor so much anger and bitterness today that is so foreign from what I used to be. Jennifer, as I have mentioned earlier in our writings, I was the most optimistic, almost Polly-Anna-ish person you might have met. My world-view was colored by what I experienced in my little town—raising food and livestock and defying vile stereotypes and knowing hundreds of others doing the same.

Being blissfully ignorant of the sacrifices made on my behalf.

After college, I mentored kids, became a Big Brother, joined the board of Boys and Girls Clubs in two cities, and had at least a half-dozen major speaking engagements a year. I was the one who always sought to be a part of a diverse group of friends in my New America, my New South.

I (thought I) had transcended the racism I saw and preached colorblindness and inclusion. And I benefited, too, from a journalism standpoint, especially when I moved to Alabama, where my publisher was a Clinton-hater. And I had known his editor since I was in high school. I love him to this day. He was a Marine (a Vietnam vet, a former D-Senate candidate and a fellow Louisiana Tech graduate). He hired me to join their editorial board after I had become the first African-American editorial page editor in Mississippi.

Jill and I went into our young marriage with a new suburban house, with an American flag, a pool, two red sports cars and in short order, Loren, a fluffy new baby. (We even briefly attended Jeff Sessions' United Methodist Church!)

In the 1990s, people probably thought Ken Blackwell, J.C. Watts, Colin Powell and Condoleeza Rice were paying me, because of my deference and praise in my writing. Here were examples of Black people who validated my vision of the world as I knew it. Work with the system. Lead. Inspire your brothers and sisters to do the right things, i.e. get an education, avoid the crooked road, use the king's English, etc. (We are not monolithic!)

Somewhere along the way, somebody ran the needle over my thirty-three rpm vinyl record. Someone lifted the film from over my eyes. I took a "promotion" to Cincinnati because of the perception of a better opportunity. In retrospect it was a trick bag. My reputation within Gannett did not matter. These individuals didn't know me from Adam. And it showed. (Note: Cincinnati transplant Peter Bhatia, a five-time Pulitzer winner who served as editor for two years before moving to Detroit, made me a columnist, for which I'm eternally grateful.)

Meanwhile, my America (our America) has changed. I changed. And I am truly ashamed for what I was and believed. I always felt that I lifted up my own people but there was a time when I might have done more harm than good. Never again.

Jen, our generation was supposed to make the world better. How is it that we elected Barack Obama twice AND Trump?!

You mentioned Jesse Jackson has been absent from the current discourse. I think it's because he is ill. He has Parkinson's, and he is beginning to sound like Muhammad Ali sounded at the end. I grew up in a household that revered Jackson. I have interviewed him no fewer than six times in my career, including three editorial board appearances. (He worked with Jill's uncle during the Civil Rights Movement.) I covered his 1988 presidential campaign. Somewhere in Arkansas there is a posed picture of him and me shooting "thumbs up" signs. During that 1988 bid after covering a speech he made in Pine Bluff, Ark., I returned to the newsroom to file my story. My editor first asked me something to the effect of: "What kind of trouble is Jesse stirring up now?"

Great. And he has to edit my story.

Last year, Jackson visited the editorial board to protest Kroger's "abandonment" of poor communities. I wrote this column, "Dear Rev. Jackson, boycotting Kroger is a mighty big ask," essentially telling him he was wrong. But in retrospect, he is right and I was wrong. We still need his voice, even though there is truth in his extortionist methods.

This is the quandary I find myself in now. The whole: "Are you Black or are you a journalist first?"

Along the lines of having the shades lifted, during my interview I realized something that stopped me in my tracks: Here I was again, in my fifth decade, sitting before the same potential supervisor that I have sat before asking to be hired all my life, almost every time. What is wrong with the picture? And how do we get better by doing the same thing over and over again?

The only time I have been interviewed and hired by a person of color in thirty-five years of employment is when I was hired by a historically Black college. What does this say about our America? 1) I should be grateful to be considered for employment? 2) How in the world have we allowed the gatekeepers of employment and upward mobility to essentially remain the same? This may lie at the root of Jill's observations about my current state of mind.

And I can't help but wonder that in the September of my work life how things could have turned out differently. These are a lot of words, but good Lord I felt like I would explode if I didn't get them out at this point in time.

Thanks for listening, Jen.

Byron

P.S. I'm going to read Viktor Frankl. Sounds like I need him more than I realize.

Byron McCauley and Ljillauna Watson were married in 1995 in Memphis, Tennessee, thirteen months after they met in Olive Branch, Mississippi.

Growing Up

Sunday, July 26, 2020
Taos, New Mexico

Dear Byron,

So, there you are/were in front of the same guy whom you have always sat. Different name, different title. Telling the same story. He is half-listening. He doesn't get it. And you are the guy who has edited big papers, a columnist, on TV and the radio and interviewed one of our true treasures (Jesse Jackson) six times.

How does it come to this?

I think that we were raised by people who told us that if we studied, followed the rules, presented ourselves well and told the truth, we would succeed. My mom said my first long word was "responsibility" and little Jennifer pronounced it "responsibillowe." At a young age, the mantra was drilled into me.

I think that you had the same experience.

So here we are; often passed over for the job, the title, the money or even the opinion. I have not voiced it often as I am too proud, but I achieved early success and was ultimately relegated to a back seat. The center did not hold. There was one "boss" who took a chance on me, a White man from El Paso who also was raised to respect and value others. He positioned me well, but once I became the province of future bosses—things changed.

Why do I consult and not work "in house?" Because consulting is what was left for me. I wasn't anyone's type and I was no longer willing to play the game. I reached high heights and it was over. My consulting has been a reprieve and fortunately I have a husband with a stable income as there are ups and downs.

You, Byron, can get into any door to which you set your mind. You have the brains, presence, success and appearance. You succeed at the drill. I suspect that the "man" on the other side of the table is thinking, "Wow, he is smarter and better than I am. He may not play the game the way I need him. Should I hire someone this talented?"

It takes someone with self-confidence and goodness to hire you. Trust that it will happen for you, but it takes sublimation—that with age is tough to muster.

The American Dream was a fallacy. We believed it. Shoot, I believed it until very recently. At times it seems that I constantly espouse these "great American novelists" (read: old White guys) and their wisdom. It seems that writer F. Scott Fitzgerald felt human flaws viscerally. And yes, it seems that many of these deep thoughts have come through the mouths of these White men. I am hopeful that (the ones whom I select) are more wise than most. The truth is many of my selections checked out early—the world simply destroyed them.

So there is that.

Fitzgerald wrote in *The Great Gatsby*, "Gatsby believed in the green light, the orgastic future that year by year recedes before us. It eluded us then, but that's no matter—tomorrow we will run faster, stretch out our arms farther… And one fine morning— So we beat on, boats against the current, borne back ceaselessly into the past."

I, too, mourn for our country. For what I thought it was, but what it really is. Deep down, I think that it has always been this way—but we were busy, working, raising kids, living and bit by bit we noticed—and all at once, here we are.

Personally, I am too numb to be frightened about what another four years of Trump looks like. Where do we go? What do we do? So somehow, I stay optimistic about the parts that I can manage—checking in with family and friends, baking, exercising and valuing our lives.

I will be back to the Midwest soon and look forward to seeing you "in real life."

Try to be hopeful and remember who you are.

Love,

Jennifer

Men Can Be Jerks

Monday, July 27, 2020
Cincinnati, Ohio

Dear Jen,

Thank you for the affirmation. Wind in my sails. Warm wind.

Yes, and so we are here. Consulting and yet seeking one more staff role to eek out a roller-coaster career. If I'm honest, I'm apprehensive about the hospital possibility. I have been so blessed in my life. Truly, I should be thankful.

As I have been displaced or downsized, I pouted for a while. I then asked God "why not me?" The period of general unpleasantness can be translated as LIFE. Everyone has problems. Everyone. Dwelling in the valley has lasted much longer than I anticipated. But when things were better, I wonder if I was more Henry Potter than George Bailey. I should have done better.

Jen, is this what a midlife crisis is? What do you think?

In my twenties and thirties I was shining and soaring. Recently, I thought about the "older" men and women of forty-five, fifty, and fifty-five in my first workplace, a big newspaper in the South. Some were revered. Some were hidden do-nothings making good money and meting out a few more years. Some were mid-managers with titles and the cachet of being someone at the paper—gatekeepers. Once upon a time, all of them were "somebodies." And then who was this new kid?

Mike Tyson said he is making a boxing comeback at fifty-four "because you can do it if you feel as beautiful as I do," he told an interviewer. But

119

America Lost and Found in Letters

George Foreman, who won the heavyweight boxing championship at forty-four, said this is foolish. The body and the brain do strange things at that age. It doesn't respond properly anymore. Know when to step away.

I don't want to stay too long and not realize what the others around me are thinking, feeling and perhaps not saying. I want to know when to step away.

Meanwhile, I agreed to disagree with a good friend today in order to keep the friendship strong. I cherish our relationship. I don't like how the disagreeing feels, but I'm thankful for the emotional maturity it takes to choose a third way and not obstinance.

Again, what you wrote in yesterday's letter was profound, particularly the sexual harassment part. My friend is exceptional and pretty. "You are the best-looking piece of cake I have ever seen and it's a shame I don't have a fork to eat you with." That came from her most recent boss, who fired her six weeks after saying that to her.

I was incensed. I don't think about sexual harassment that much. I assume that it is a relic and too much of a career-threatening #metoo liability. Yet, her situation happened within the past year. And when you wrote, you casually passed over it, ("Who wasn't?"). Gosh, the perpetrators repulse me, but when and how do you decide to go to HR on these vulgar fools when perhaps you need to pay your mortgage or feed your kids?

Seldom, it seems. Instead, you leave your workplace or you just tolerate the horribleness of it.

Just as I didn't think about harassment that much, my friend (maybe rightly in her mind) minimized what I was trying to explain in regards to ethnic workplace discrimination and racist hiring and promotion practices. She saw the two as the same. She was punished because of her "boobies and—." The kick in the head is that she ends up with the guy with the power and influence and capital with the benefits. And so many guys (for whom the system does not bend) do the best they can to support their families. And, again, I'm blessed.

She thinks I have the skills and the know-how and the appearance to succeed but that I haven't tried hard enough or tried for the wrong jobs. Is this the truth? Should I listen harder and receive that critique?

One other thing.

This friend believes in the current president. I love her and I will grow to love her because I'm a loyal friend.

However, if I have lost my friend a little bit today—and I think I have—it breaks my heart. I have to figure out how to navigate this new chapter, considering how difficult it is to justify the behavior of our sitting president and to be friends with someone who supports him. Looking inwardly, Jill and I have sometimes nullified each other's votes (it's not about party for us) over the years (rarely now). Our love and respect remains constant. Mary Matalin and James Carville seem happy, though they are polar opposites, politically. A perfect example of this is Kelly and George Conway.

It's just that the president is so polarizing. And I feel his rhetoric endangers my life.

And now it all feels weird.

Love,

Byron

P.S. "Responsibillowe" at three years old is gangster-level genius.

P.P.S. The cookies are to die for. When I take a break off my plan, I want the recipe.

Yes, I Bake Cookies

Tuesday, July 28, 2020
Taos, New Mexico

Dear Byron,

I am trying to be hopeful and optimistic, but negativity is coming at me sideways. I am finding myself being "angry" with people, being "petty" and just not demonstrating high-road behavior. It is tough to shake. I also think that I am a bit freaked about returning to Cincinnati—to life in the high rise where people are blowing off rules.

On that topic, I have tried to adapt the "live and let live" attitude. However, the pandemic demonstrates that when individuals do not abide and wear masks, it threatens us all. I see many good friends on Facebook in large groups and not social distancing. Friends have told me that they are going to parties and have essentially returned to normal. I am starting to believe that people in "certain" social classes think that none of what is happening applies to them.

I am becoming quite judgmental of people. The other evening, another couple told us that their young adult is following white supremacy groups. I adore this couple, they are friends. WTF? True or darker natures are taking hold, including my own.

Today I actually Googled "What does it mean if I think negative thoughts about people?" Nope, not a quick answer. I am well-educated (and in psychology) and I am searching for this answer.

The more I dive into deep *1939* reading (have been obsessed with this time period for decades), I believe that we are crossing the Rubicon into dark, dark times. I believe that frightened is the wrong descriptor, but more a state of shock.

Everyone always said that the *1939* sort of evil could not proliferate in the USA.

Yet, here we are.

And now the "boys of summer" are widely infected and it looks like our first foray into live sports may fail to continue. I am not a sports fan, but I do recognize the entertainment value that it delivers—and that it gives people something else to ponder besides the myriad of issues at stake.

In the meantime, I am baking cakes, making cookies, preparing large "meal" salads, doing laundry, spending time with my sweet cat, reading, exercising, working and sleeping. In other words—constant distractions.

We have done our share of COVID cocktails and distant meals. We both are tired of people. Tired of the discussions about today. It has gotten hard to have conversations. Because anything other than the issues at hand seems off base.

BTW, I love that you called three-year old Jennifer "gangster-level genius."

Like you, I cannot abide friends who think that TRUMP is ok. And sadly, I am learning that I have too many of them in my history. I just don't get it. This economy has strengthened their wealth position which has hardened their stance.

With regard to your friend implying that you haven't tried hard enough, I think she isn't listening. I am not sure that she is a friend. People hear what they want to hear (and "disregard the rest"). Most humans don't listen well.

I have non-politically correct thoughts about sexual harassment. Honestly, I endured it, did not report it and marched forward in my career. It is certainly NOT on the same level as racism in the workplace. I was lukewarm on the #MeToo movement. I felt for the female factory workers, but not the film stars. Is it acceptable? No.

Don has significant expertise in the area and obviously believes that workplaces need to be well aware and guard against an environment that proliferates sexual harassment. Yet, (my point-of-view) in the broad scheme of discrimination, is that it is lesser than other ills. I will be chastised for making this claim.

I don't think that the dilemma that you describe re: your own career is a midlife crisis. I do think that when one has been "at it" a long while, we become more jaded. It becomes more difficult to drink the Kool-Aid and to believe the brass. We recognize limitations of both ourselves and others. Re: ourselves, I think we "self-limit" as we determine what and whom we will tolerate.

Like Tyson says and does, I continue to push my physical limits. When we are young, we even become lazy, like we will always have a certain prowess. It becomes more of a challenge as we age and pushing ourselves (to me) delivers greater gratification.

I think what you describe is the real recognition that life is truly random and unfair. That the good guys often don't win, that the winners are often dishonest and great humans leave us all too soon.

And, in the meantime, I will continue to bake and send you the cookie recipe when you say the word.

Love,

Jennifer

A Democracy If You Can Keep It

Wednesday, July 29, 2020
Cincinnati, Ohio

Dear Jen,

It seems amazing that we are nearing Day 60 of our letters. We started writing because the world went mad and we wanted someone to digest things with.

But it has morphed into something that I couldn't have predicted. I'm better for it.

You mention *1939* and what was going on. This terrifies me, but it also confirms and illuminates how Hitler comes to power. He who consolidates and has the gumption to wield power is the person who has power. And we are left to soldier as best we can.

Was it Ben Franklin who said, "A democracy, if you can keep it?"

I feel like we are all just watching and wondering when someone in charge will "do something" about the attacks on our democracy by all corners of this administration. I'm repulsed by Barr, who used to be someone, right? And I'm repulsed that the president is so mentally ill that everything is a popularity contest. While lives are at stake, he is picking a petty fight with the only person of reason who seems not to be afraid of him—Dr. Anthony Fauci. How can the leader of the free world and the most desired republic seem to have such little regard for the welfare of the American people?

I'm eager to hear you talk about feeling traumatized. I completely understand why. I fear we are entering into a period of reckoning, and I don't believe it will end well. This I know for sure: We all need to be prepared for anything, including government intrusion into our homes and property.

Trump's ads seek to scare suburban women with the ominous dark man breaking into a home. It will drum up irrational fear. But he's playing smoke and mirrors to keep us from noticing he's committing rape against our democratic republic.

Yours,

Byron

Drift Away

Thursday, July 30, 2020
Taos, New Mexico

Dear Byron,

You asked about my being traumatized. I think that it is more that I am numb. And maybe a mild case of shock. I am beyond worry. Because what is one exactly supposed to worry about?

There is so much and then what will really happen. The energy that comes with worrying is not in me. Many people talk about having trouble sleeping. I am finding that I sleep deeply, long and dream heavily.

This is not keeping me up at night—it is taking my mind to other places.

Last night we went out to hear music. There is music at one place in town that is still open. A friend of ours plays. We sit over twelve feet from him, very distanced from other tables and all is very remote. This is a place (about half a mile away) that we love. It is also generally a very socially engaged place. Now, it is a mere glimmer of itself. We continue to patronize—to help everyone out and get out of the house.

Last night he (Jimmy) was playing the song Mentor Williams wrote called *Drift Away*. Mentor's most famous tune. Mentor lived here with his wife, Lynn Anderson, as in "I never promised you a rose garden." We used to see them around. They both died here.

The song goes like this:

Day after day I'm more confused
Yet I look for the light in the pouring rain
You know that's a game that I hate to lose

I'm feelin' the strain, ain't it a shame
Oh, give me the beat boys, and free my soul
I want to get lost in your rock and roll and drift away
Oh, give me the beat boys, and free my soul
I want to get lost in your rock and roll and drift away
Beginning to think that I'm wastin' time
I don't understand the things I do
The world outside looks so unkind
So I'm countin' on you to carry me through
Oh, give me the beat boys, and free my soul
I want to get lost in your rock and roll and drift away
Give me the beat boys, and free my soul
I want to get lost in your rock and roll and drift away
And when my mind is free
You know a melody can move me
And...

I realized that this is exactly how I feel.

More confused.

No wonder this was a Grammy winner.

In other words, I don't think we are special in our disillusion.

I was also thinking about past times in life and how I got through. You may remember that Don and I had a commuter marriage for five years. I was in Florida; he was in Cincinnati and he flew to Florida to be with the kids and me every Thursday until Monday. It is often painful to think of those times as the ultimate reason that I walked out on my gig: for the family to be in one place. Yes, it hurt my marriage. Yes, we recovered. Yes, it took a long time. All these years later (twelve years) I finally feel that the scars have faded.

The time in Florida did have some good parts. Florida, in all of its weirdness is a truly interesting place with a bizarre and painful history. It is also intensely diverse. Ultimately, I believe that it was good for the girls. We met lifelong friends.

While in Florida, I spent a load of time in Tallahassee. I made the mistake of asking questions about times like the "civil war" in which I was told it was "the war of Northern aggression." Florida is very southern, as most northerners don't know and I realized that I was a true woman of the North.

We lived one town over from where Zora Neale Hurston was raised. We dove deeply into Floridian Black culture.

I also learned what crooked politics really looked like. And loving politics, I met many whose names I had only heard on the news. In Florida, one gets to go to political events held at a mobster's home for the future governor. I hired this terrific lobbyist named Bill Rubin. A truly honest man and one of the most competent.

One night (near the end of my time there) we were sitting at The Governor's Club in Tallahassee, a stately southern place that I am guessing didn't admit anyone not White, not Christian and not male until sometime in the last two decades. I told Bill that I was probably leaving and that I was quite depressed, that my family might be falling apart.

He looked at me and said, "Jennifer, this is not the last chapter."

That's how I feel about now Byron.

This is NOT the last chapter.

There will be some tough ones ahead, but we will wake up to some clarity, clear skies and find a way to have lives.

The John Lewis funeral today told me that. We can't give up.

We can't give in.

As he said, "If you see something, you must say something."

It's up to all of us to be the voice for which he calls.

Love,

Jennifer

Front Porch Sitting

Friday, July 31, 2020
Cincinnati, Ohio

Dear Jen,

Hey. So, I had an interesting visitor on the front porch yesterday. I was socially distancing with one of my Leadership Cincinnati friends, Sharon, a former Unitarian Universalist Church minister. And a silver-haired lady sees us and comes over, still social distancing. Sharon and I wore masks. The lady did not. She was warm. She had a nice smile. She appeared wise.

Turns out, she lives on the next street over, and had been walking by for a year. We had a Mount Notre Dame High School sign in the yard for a while, signifying Simone's enrollment. She had a Chinese exchange student who attended MND who is now in North Carolina. Apparently, she is in the system to board Chinese students who come to good American high schools—part of their journey to get into American Ivys or other good schools.

I invited her up and poured her a bourbon with "one cube of ice." Hmm. Insightful.

Her name is Pat. She is seventy-nine. She worked for our first female mayor and was a community organizer in Chicago in the 1970s. She is a mediator, now retired. Her party had five delegates on Mayor Richard Daley's Council. And, to the delight of Sharon, she had worshiped at the Unitarian Church, so they shared a few common acquaintances. We talked for an hour and a half on the front porch, our lives intersecting through former bosses, current friends (Bea Larsen, Chad Wick and many more).

We delved deeper. Her granddaughter is a rising 8th grader at the School of the Creative and Performing Arts. Our Laila is entering 7th grade there.

Then she talked about how her three grandchildren, who are biracial, began to express their identity after the George Floyd killing. And then she went to her home and returned with a BLACK LIVES MATTER banner with a beautifully drawn sketch of a doe-eyed child wearing a mask with the words "I CAN'T BREATHE."

The artist is the granddaughter! Sharon, a social bee who is charged by meeting new people, is holding in tears of joy, and I am feeling renewed at the wonderful randomness of it all. So, now, we have a new friend. And we hope Laila and Ella, Pat's granddaughter, will meet.

Sharon marked the moment. "You never know who your neighbors are."

It also reminded me of the times pre-COVID, and even before I allowed the world to bludgeon me a little bit. Early in our marriage, Jill and I invited strangers to our house for a meal and discussion. I did this through my column, writing in Alabama. Can you believe it? I would not do the same now. What changed? That's a good question.

The next day, Pat walked over with another banner, this one with grommets to make it easier to hang on our porch.

Goodness happened the other day. I appreciated it, even as COVID rages. It was a reminder that we must carry on during this time and we can never, ever lose our connection with others.

Long live the front porch.
Love,

Byron

My Adult Girls

Saturday, August 1, 2020
Taos, New Mexico

Dear Byron,

So glad that you had a surprise good day. Those are the best. It is hard to find much to complain about at all in my life—yet I do know that around the corner there is some evil. It ranges from a close friend getting sick, to the continued troubling scene in the USA. It is just this low-level anxiety thing.

I think I have told you, but we are going to move to Taos (full time) sooner rather than later. I am ready, but I get sick to my stomach at the thought of letting my mother know. She knows that it is coming, but maybe not so soon. I am hopeful that she will spend a decent amount of time here.

At some point one needs to live their own life. I am fifty-seven and have been a doting daughter. I certainly will miss her.

There is no easy choice.

I have been back and forth often with our mutual friend Stephanie (now in Amsterdam). She moved in January for a terrific job and never guessed that she would go so long without seeing her grown kids. It has been almost a year since we saw Nora. It has been since March for Caroline. I am a daughter and a mother. We were not raised, nor did I raise my own kids to stay in one place. While I am proud of their independence, living it can be tough.

My favorite line from Jackie Kennedy is, "If you bungle raising your children, I don't think whatever else you do well matters very much."

To some extent, both Stephanie and I did what we were supposed to do. This still doesn't make it easy, just like my not being around as much is certainly tough on my own mother at age eighty-one.

Hope, Interrupted

The front porch life is an interesting one. To some extent, we have gotten to know people better (during these times). When we do get together (on the porch) the conversations are deep, long and real. No one is wasting their time. We seem to have a sense that the future is not certain. It is interesting that now, today, we connect with those who have been in our backyard for a long while. Hence, your neighbors.

Ironically, we spent last evening with our own neighbors (Tenci and Pete). They are warm, gracious and interesting. Their own son (who is forty-eight and in Chicago, a father of two daughters) has tough cancer. They can't go see him now. They are doing anything but feeling sorry for themselves. They are demonstrating optimism and hope. They raised three terrific children (now in all in their forties) who display such commitment to their parents.

We ran into Tenci and Pete at the farmer's market this morning. All nearly seventy years of Pete were there in shorts and cowboy boots. Married since their late teens. Love these folks.

We return to the Queen City shortly. While things could change, it is likely to be our last stint there for a good long while. My heart has been in New Mexico for decades. While I am certainly ready for the next phase of life, there are things that I will miss: namely family and good friends (you) and also that the city holds memories for me around every corner. So much of my life has been spent in Hamilton County, and this is bittersweet.

The truth is that I have tried to "live West" since I was a teenager. While there were a few years in Colorado in the 80s—the balance has been in the Midwest. It is a time of transition—some on purpose and some dumb luck.

It is also clear that, for all of my life's moves, this is the last stop. So strange to be of this age and at this time.

Have a great rest of your weekend.

Love,

Jennifer

Me, The Astronomer

Sunday, August 2, 2020
Cincinnati, Ohio

Dear Jen,

I wanted to be an astronomer. So much so that my poor mother had to buy me collectors' books that held stamps of every known galaxy in the universe. I had dozens of these books. I would study the night sky with my binoculars. I would always know about comets and meteor showers. I even wrote a paper once about the "Night of the Leonids."

And then I discovered writing and left science behind. In a way, I regret that because they say the thing you loved as a child never really leaves you. It's true, but it also seemed impractical for a little Black boy from a tiny, Southern town to be an astronomer. About as impractical as Neil DeGrasse Tyson becoming one, or me becoming a newspaper reporter.

I say this against the backdrop of today's splash landing of the SpaceX capsule carrying astronauts Doug Hurley and Bob Behnkin, childhood friends no less. They left Earth in their cool, new Tesla-designed spacesuits two months ago and returned to old school, in a capsule.

I felt a little nostalgic. While I was ten years old the last time a space capsule touched down in the water, I remember the wonder of it. Seeing SpaceX with four deployed parachutes slowing it down safely was history making. Some might say the pursuit of space discoveries is a waste of money, considering all our issues on land. I disagree. The applied science that powers space travel transforms technology and gives us a bit of hope.

I remember when the *Challenger* exploded. That was the same day that the *Los Angeles Times* offered me a summer internship. Both events will never leave my memory, an extreme low and an extreme high, both life-changing.

Space travel is certainly anxiety-inducing, considering past catastrophes, but it remains inspirational and exciting. Even Laila, my resident curmudgeon youngest daughter, watched. She also liked "Hidden Figures," so there is that.

I hope this generation of kids is inspired to pursue science and space exploration. So much to learn and so much we can never know. But ah, the wonder!

Love,

Byron

Byron McCauley takes a selfie with television journalist and producer, Soledad O'Brien, host of "Matter of Fact With Soledad O'Brien."

Remembering Gordon

Monday, August 3, 2020
Taos, New Mexico

Dear Byron,

I found it interesting that you were taken with astronomy. I get it. More than you know. It is the wonder of what else is out there. Many people out here believe in UFOs. Many. I do not. I have routinely made the mistake of making snarky comments about them only to learn that others in the conversation have "seen them." However, the sky is HUGE out here.

Maybe beings from another universe actually care what is happening on planet Earth.

Maybe.

In fact, artist Georgia O'Keefe said that she loved it out here because of the "big sky." The night sky is something to behold. Seeing planets with the naked eye. The Milky Way…all within view. You guys need to visit.

The western sky is magic. I have seen the southern hemisphere sky a few times. It is strange to see a different sky above—the southern cross.

I too loved the sciences. I double majored in journalism and geology. I did field work in Wisconsin (Baraboo Quartzite), New Hampshire (rotated garnets and the Connecticut River Valley), Black Hills and Wind River Range (general mapping). I loved it. I was with a bunch of super smart people who were thrilled to be in the middle of nowhere with few people. At that age, I needed people more and I am not sure I was smart enough to move forward.

Well now, I am fine with a few people and I could be a park ranger as a second career. Oh well, missed opportunity.

I love that (when we were young) we had that wonder. We felt that the world was opened to us. We had dreams. We felt that anything was possible. We believed. I am pretty sure this does not exist for young people today. They just want "A Job." Any job. They don't feel heard and they are feeling powerless.

That hope is what kept me going—through lackluster jobs, through bad bosses, through the general BS that happens to an individual.

And we still have that hope. We were raised on it.

I was thinking the other day about our chat re: Gordon Parks. (The famous first black fashion photographer for *LIFE* magazine, artist and musician 1912-2006.) He was one of the most amazing humans with whom I interacted. The height of my own corporate career. Not only was he humble, talented and authentic—but he had a great sense of humor and style. At one point I moderated a discussion with him and others. Someone raised their hand and asked whether (in his own family) they talked about things like race at the dinner table. He chuckled and said, "we usually talked about fashion or what dress my daughter liked at Saks."

While Gordon certainly soared with the greats—Ali, Gloria Vanderbilt, Bergman and others—he never lost sight of the regular folks. I never felt like he fought to make a point; he just lived.

The recent years—and during these times of COVID—have offered so much time for reflection; I have remembered my own life. What I know to be true is that I am just an ordinary woman who was raised in the Midwest. I have done nothing extraordinary, but I have certainly had a solid and good life.

I raised two daughters and was a step-mom to two step-daughters. I married twice. I paid my bills. I served my community. I have kept myself in shape. I have traveled. I have been fortunate. And that is all for which any of us can ask.

What I know is this. To me, it is the most important to make a difference to the people in our own circles. The people who matter to us. To live well and honestly.

And on that note, I have noticed that my grey hair is starting to pop back up. Time to color it again … maybe I am not so honest after all. It's also about waking up each day and doing our best. My best happens when I don't look exactly my age.

Love,

Jennifer

Ranchos Church, painted in 1930, Ranchos de Taos, New Mexico.

UFOs

Tuesday, August 4, 2020
Cincinnati, Ohio

Dear Jennifer,

The sky where I come from was very dark and the stars were bright. I loved it. I sometimes reclined on blankets in the side yard and gazed for hours. Some of my best nights were spent outside in Plain Dealing, Louisiana. Lord knows there was not much else to do there, but it did allow room for a kid with a big imagination to let it run wild.

Funny you should talk about extraterrestrials. I do believe we are not alone in this vast universe. But I find it perplexing that if there are other beings, especially more intelligent beings, where are they? And what are they waiting for? The movies assume they want to seek to destroy us, but perhaps they want to share. One reason I do believe there is something out there is because two credible people I know have witnessed what they believe to be space vehicles and the Navy's recent admission that they were essentially buzzed by a UFO.

Back in the early 1980s, Jill's dad observed what he thought to be one flying over Memphis. Others noticed it, too. But again, where are they and why haven't they come?

After such a busy and long day yesterday, I rested much of the day. I cleared emails, researched ideas for two more columns, and watched too much CNN. The news is quite depressing. And CNN is more star-driven, just like the others. The Axios reporter who interviewed Trump did a good job, I thought, and journalists who ought to own Trump with the power of CNN instead are interviewing the Axios journalist.

So, Jen, get this. Phil Heimlich, Michael Anne Johnson and others have formed a group called Operation Grant for Ohio: Republican Voters Against Trump. I was thinking about writing about it at the end of the week. In truth, I hate to continue to give Trump publicity. But if I can illuminate the fact that some Republicans are coming together as anti-Trumpers, maybe it can change the minds of others.

"In Trump's Republican cult, there is no discussion, no dissent, no vetting of policy and that's what you get when you let hate-filled populists take over the party. In my view, populism is nothing more than a perennial search for a villain to slay with no plan as to what to do with the body," said Christoper Gibbs, former Republican Party and Shelby County Board of Elections Chair.

Phil said if we allow Trump to be re-elected, our country will soon "resemble Putin's Russia more than Lincoln's America."

Whenever I write about Trump, even a minor inference, I get four or five trolls who leave messages or write to me in a huff. It's good to know some of them are waking up and are trying to rustle others.

Love,

Byron

No Roads Lead Here

Wednesday, August 5, 2020
Taos, New Mexico

Dear Byron,

We will be back in Cincinnati around August 19. It seems that it is time. Time for Don to prep for surgery and time to finish our final pack up and wrap some things up as well. While I am excited, it is also (as I have written) strange.

Strange to be at this point in life. Past middle age. Kids launched. Life. It goes fast. Unbelievable.

We climbed a weird peak yesterday. We have found that we need to take one day weekly to unplug. Working virtually is great, but it never stops. Starts early, ends late. Don is in the middle of dealing with the teachers— many are fearful about returning to the classroom. Lots of manic behavior.

Who is blaming anyone?

We are all in a tailspin.

And then there are the parents who rely on the schools for childcare. I get it re: the single parents without options. I DO NOT get it from the wealthier folks—what are they thinking? People's true selves are showing for sure.

The peak (Ute Mountain) is only 10K. No roads lead there. No trails on her. We drove across vast fields and found a start point. The rest was about bushwhacking. The view from the top included miles of sand desert, the Rio Grande river valley and distant mountains. It was worth it. I have bloody legs and scratches. I don't trust people without scars—one needs to put herself out there. I only feel whole when I am in contact with Mother Nature.

My scars on my legs and lines on my face tell the story of my life.

Perfection is not important to me.

It is about the experience.

I can point to any scar and tell a story.

I started Isabel Wilkerson's new book *Caste*. She may be, truly, our best writer. This tome is prescient. I am certain that it took her years to write. The research is deep. It is very much indicative of why life now is as such. It is generally about the caste system in the USA. You and I both live that.

She may be my new hero.

"The price of privilege is the moral duty to act when one sees another person treated unfairly. And the least that a person in the dominant caste can do is not make the pain any worse." —Isabel Wilkerson, *Caste: The Origins of Our Discontents*

I truly can only read nonfiction (at the moment).

We also watched a movie called *The Eichmann Show*. It's about how permission was granted to tape the Eichmann (SS Officer who often is credited with The Final Solution) Israel hearings and then show them around the world. Yes, heartbreaking, but apparently most people (even Israeli's) did not truly believe what happened during the Holocaust. It reminded me and harkens to Hannah Arendt's *The Banality of Evil*. (There is another good movie about that.)

None of us can believe the inhumanity of which humans are capable. The director of the filming (Leo Hurwitz) is fixated on provoking emotion-reaction out of Eichmann. It becomes clear that Eichmann believes that "he" was only a cog in a big machine and doing his job.

How many people truly justify behavior through the "making a living" fabrication? Shoot, I did. While I was only a minor player in the cable TV business, I was part of the world that gave birth to channels such as FOX news. I am part of our world problem. I am not proud.

We delivered valuable content as well. But does one justify the other?

Most disturbingly, both Wilkerson and Arendt head in a dystopian direction. We humans have not changed much. We may look at Maslow's Hierarchy of Needs and say to ourselves "food, shelter, protecting our kin" and extrapolate that that means that as long as our bad behavior provides for our offspring—well, then it is OK.

To end.

And here we are today.

"The point is that both Hitler and Stalin held out promises of stability in order to hide their intention of creating a state of permanent instability."

—Hannah Arendt, *The Origins of Totalitarianism*

I like bushwhacking better.

Love,

Jennifer

Joe Biden, Interrupted

Thursday, August 6, 2020
Cincinnati, Ohio

Dear Jennifer,

What a treat to FaceTime with you and Don today! You guys are setting an example of how to work hard and play hard—simply. (Also, I want that watermelon-feta-smoked trout salad!)

By now, you know. Gov. Mike DeWine tested positive for COVID-19. And then he didn't. And I'm confused. My column posted for about three hours then I took it down. I have re-written it saying that we do need to double-down on testing and be diligent with all the rest of the safety precautions, but you know what's gonna happen, right? The president is going to manipulate the facts, muddy the waters and continue to dispute science.

It may be the worst thing that can happen. You have to wonder how other nations have managed to reduce their incidences of COVID and start to return to normal. It just doesn't disappear. They did things to usher it out, which is what we are not doing in America.

Meanwhile at the NABJ-NAHJ (the Black journalists and Hispanic journalism organizations) Joe Biden apparently inserted foot in mouth today. Some of my colleagues are mad, including my best friend Vasin, a former journalist, now an artist, sculptor and car enthusiast. He posted on Facebook: "Vote for the one who is less racist." This makes me sad.

At issue is Biden seemed to infer that Blacks in America are monolithic, where Hispanics are not. Here is an excerpt:

"We can build a new administration that reflects the full diversity of our nation. The full diversity of the Latino communities. Now when I mean full diversity, unlike the African-American community, many other communities, you're from everywhere. From Europe. From the tip of South America, all the way to our border and Mexico and in the Caribbean. And different backgrounds, different ethnicities, but all Latinos."

I get what he was saying, or at least trying to say, but he is only part-right. Hispanic history in America is much different than African history in America. Hispanics are much more disparate, and it's true that they are not monolithic in their political preferences. However, Blacks or Africans in America are very diverse, too.

I just hate that we don't pause and take a breather before belching out premature anger.

I'm going to start taking my own advice. Because I was desperate for a column today, I immediately jumped on DeWine's "positive" test and used it to criticize Trump. The whole argument was blown up when DeWine tested negative. And so now I look like a Trump-basher again. I am sometimes that, to be sure, but when I bash I can't afford to be wrong because the trolls are always ready to pounce.

Love,

Byron

Feet First

Friday, August 7, 2020
Taos, New Mexico

Dear Byron,

Another interesting day. Yep, we hiked again. Twice on weekdays—indulgent. But the phone just keeps ringing and ZOOM started at 5:30 a.m. MT. While I know that this is 7:30 am on the east coast, who is really that important? Yuck. And I was asked to facilitate the call so had to be perky and on.

After the call we heard from our peripatetic Nora. Nice chat. She is busy making her plans to go to Denmark for her marriage to Erwann. While we only talk with Nora about once a week—these are usually long and deep calls. Lately—mostly about the USA. We discussed racism, bigotry and *Caste*. I am truly taken with this tome—and candidly pretty shocked. When you follow Wilkerson's logic, one realizes just the depth of the cracks in our nation. Sort of like mask wearing, we will not be FIXED until we (as a people agree) to be part of a solution. Too much denial. Lots of pain.

Nora texted me after the call and said:

"I am proud that you are learning more about racial injustice in the U.S. Most people from your generation seem so clueless."

Right on. Hence, I am losing friends as I have been strident on the subject.

I have had titles, compensation, awards. Nothing means more to me than hearing praise from my children. They are the ultimate critics. They have seen us for who we are. As I have aged, I have learned that I care little what most people think of me, of professional honors, of job titles. I do, however, care deeply about what those in my innermost circle think. My adult children thinking well of me matters most.

I also want to be thought of as a good human.

We have been financially generous with our offspring. While we are not wealthy people, we worked hard and long (still do) and our greatest pleasure is in knowing that (through our assistance) our kids don't have to panic if something goes awry. There are many different philosophies about this sort of "help." Mine is: "The world is tough enough—if we can make the landing softer, we should." Or why else am I here?

A long-time acquaintance of mine (who is also a multi-multi-millionaire) once explained to me how they were teaching their children the value of money. This included not letting the offspring get their millions until a certain age. They then lectured me about the "fact" that I "let" my youngest move abroad. Eye roll here. Needless to say—our kids learn by how we behave, not what we dictate. I am pretty sure that their kids did not learn meaningful lessons.

She is a pretty lonely person.

When we talked with Nora, we further discussed racism—part of the chat was about Wyoming High School—where both the kids and I graduated. Yes, it was all about the quality of the school—high ratings and safe neighborhood. I only recently learned (as I think I wrote) that it was the last school district in Ohio to integrate. This breaks my heart and makes me sick.

I have been in touch with several classmates about this revelation.

My mom and I discussed this, and she said, "Did you have Black friends, Jennifer?" I reminded her that I did. I thought about my friend, Brian. My first husband's best buddy who was in our wedding. I loved his parents. Brian also dated my friend, Katie. Katie's parents were not pleased. There was much sneaking around. Her father was especially awful. I recall a scene in which he literally chased Brian out of their yard. This was in the early 80s—and it sickens me. Did then, does now. Katie's adult life turned out fraught with challenges—including (as I learned last summer) some near homelessness.

Did her parent's control and behavior lead her to this life?

Our behavior (as parents) does predict our children's lives.

Yep, it is often the fault of the grownups.

We set the tenor, model the behavior and are looked upon as examples.

All this thought on parenting, our country—the past, present and the future and what is in both our personal and collective DNA. We are responsible for all of it. For who we are and what we do. Our children heard us.

We truly reap what we sow.

Love,

Jennifer

The Warmth of Other Suns

Saturday, August 8, 2020
Cincinnati, Ohio

Dear Jen,

What a day!

You know a book is good when you fall asleep with it and you can't wait to wake up to pick it up again. This is what happened with the book I completed this morning by Mira T. Lee titled, *Everything Here is Beautiful*. It's going to make an excellent Netflix movie.

It is an epic story of the love of two sisters, one of them mentally ill and brilliant, the other not mentally ill and brilliant. The story takes place in Connecticut, New York, Israel, Switzerland, Ecuador and Minnesota. I think you will like it. When I read her piece in the *NYT* that I asked you to read, I bought the book. I hope you get to read it. Tonight I'm diving into *Warmth*.

Now then, let me tell you about the woodchuck. At 11 a.m., I was ready to tackle the yard. But first I made myself an omelet from my Southwest egg powder and one egg (Nom Nom! Thanks, UC Health). I looked outside the kitchen window and there, standing upright and munching on grass was a puppy-sized rodent. Google, help. It was a woodchuck and it had burrowed under my garage door.

Ruined my plans. It stayed in my yard all day, fearful of nothing. So I faced my fear. Not of the animal, per se, but of its unpredictability. I can't get rabies right now, nor do I need it to bite and bleed me out. So I rushed out with a broom. It scampered into the hole. I retrieved my tools and went to work. I left the garage door up. One hour later, all done, I gathered some lavender out of the urn on the front porch, layered it under the garage door and walked away.

Not ten seconds later as I climbed the back steps, I heard loud squeals and banging on the garage door. Not one, but two woodchucks squeeze under the door like little bats out of hell! I kid you not. Google said they hate lavender. Apparently, they do.

What's chilling to me is that they were not burrowed in a hole. They were actually in a corner of the garage behind boxes. Eek!

This is my fourth animal adventure. I think it might be time to sell. Blackbirds are inside the pitch above the third floor. A family of squirrels are above the third floor. Nancy the chicken stayed with us a few days, sunning herself on top of the garbage cans. Nuclear Rat squeezed into sewer pipes in the basement and made its way upstairs. Oh, and how can I forget? MOLES!!!

I'm done here. It's time.

Love,

Byron

Me Worry?

Sunday, August 9, 2020
Taos, New Mexico

Dear Byron,

Truth be told, I am smiling widely about the family animal situation. There has to be a column on this one. I am pretty convinced that the animal kingdom is as confused as we are. They sense that the planet is tilted sideways. Your "rodents" are merely frightened.

I have noted (and confirmed this with others) that the birds are in a strange pattern. I have never seen so many hawks flying low and observing— it has given one the chance to see their strange and kind of freaky bodies. We also have loads of magpies and hummingbirds in the yard.

There is some confusion for sure.

Today was a quiet one. We did see some folks over the weekend. On Friday, we went to a home for distant listening to live bluegrass music (yep, all the way out here and listening to that Kentucky stuff). The home was on lots of land. The couple has been here over forty years and they are serious off-the-grid hippies. It was a mix between mini-Woodstock and being on a commune.

I left a little in awe and frightened. I am good with stepping into another universe for a few moments but am fearful of becoming quite that laid back.

But I do like the thought of it.

Last night we had a few people over for an outside dinner. We laughed lots. It felt good. We even saw a meteor shower—nothing like looking at the full western sky. We told the story of the possibility that Ohio Governor Mike Dewine "faked" COVID seemingly to avoid Trump's Ohio visit.

Well done sir. Well done.

I realized that I have written lots about Nora, but not so much about Caroline. The reality is that Caroline is a low maintenance and independent girl. She went to Miami University—studied nutrition and dietetics and married her college boyfriend. They moved to Georgia (for his job). They were a young, in love and beautiful couple.

They had a spectacular wedding and sadly their marriage failed. As my first did—as Don's, as yours.

It happens.

A few things about the wedding. I am glad that we were able to get together family and friends—for what might be the final time. I am truly impressed at how she has managed her own life. Do she and I talk enough? Not for my taste, but we send each other Snapchat photos of food, our cats, life. I am proud of the young woman that she has become. Somehow both of my daughters have learned to take care of themselves.

No one gives food advice like Caroline. She's my coach and role model.

I packed up some things to send to Nora. She warned me, not much of value as they have to pay duty. As I folded up table linens, something that invoked normalcy and family history (these are linens on which she has had meals). I knew that I was attempting to place some order on our lives, with love thrown in. I loved Caroline's wedding for what the time together meant for the family and I love Nora's "elopement" for what it says about Nora. My girls are so different from each other, but I see us in both of them.

Do I worry? Of course. Of the strange occurrences and evil out there. Of the germs (much smaller than a grain of salt, I hear) and of all that could go wrong. Do I wish that I could still peek into their rooms and check on them?

Every day.

This is why our cat (formerly Nora's cat) Lolli gets way too much attention.

I visited Caroline in March and we went to the coast. Since she has been South, I suddenly have spent lots of time in a part of the country that I felt forbidden. Like us, she is progressive and bothered by much of the rhetoric. Yet, she has built a life.

My mom asked me today (on FaceTime) what I am most concerned about.

I quickly said, "Everything and nothing."

I also added that we can worry, worry, worry—but what will go wrong will come at us sideways and is something that we never considered. Either our heads are in the sand or we are just not that creative. I added though that I worry about my children.

I asked her the same question and she said, "Trump getting re-elected." Yep, true enough. The proverbial elephant in the room. I am immersed in *Caste* and *1939* and am firmly convinced that these days have been in the plan for decades. We didn't behave properly, we became fat and happy, we believed in our exceptionalism, we lost our way.

Joe Biden is correct. This is a fight for the soul of the nation.

It is my hope that we find our way.

Love,

Jennifer

Out to Pasture

Monday, August 10, 2020
Cincinnati, Ohio

Dear Jen,

Thanks for spearheading our picture-taking next month. I think it's good to be thinking like that. Plus, our PR/Marketing skills can be put to good use.

Today was a fairly good day, uneventful, which is sometimes the best kind of day. Kevin is out this week, so I'm assuming some of his duties. My manager is out, too.

I've been thinking about the hospital opportunity lately. Judging by the way that whole process was handled, I'm inclined to think they were never really serious. I really appreciate Judy's help. I have not told her yet. Do you think I should? I don't want her to do anything, of course, but I feel like I just need to thank her again.

I did not watch much news today, which was also a good thing. Usually, my TV watching goes something like this: *The Today Show* for thirty minutes, then CNN until it becomes white noise in the background. This six-month routine has made me realize that I'm not so sure I like CNN any longer. In fact, I can't say that I like any of the cable news programs. Or the content of the news, in general. Lester Holt is pleasant. Rachel Maddow is smart. Maybe I should just wait and watch Judy Woodruff at the end of the day on PBS. It takes a lot to remain relevant all day, every hour on the hour.

The hospital experience, the school district experience, the Port experience and the Strive experience (and that's just this year) have shown me that perhaps it's time to push pause on the job search. It doesn't matter how smart or qualified you are, at our age I feel like they want to put you out to pasture and I think they secretly wonder why you are still hanging on. They erroneously imagine all the money you're making and they imagine you not pulling your weight.

"Print" journalism (air quotes because it doesn't really exist anymore) has gotten very weird. We, too, act a lot like TV news. Our two lead horses are good at this kind of gossipy news. I'm not very good at it. I could be hard and seek to make a ruckus with my column, but it's not my style. Someone needs to make readers laugh, make them smile, make them happy and sometimes even sad. Someone has to illuminate the realities of the "least of these." If not me, there is no one left who will do this.

Each Friday, the editor sends out an internal memo, noting good work. He is informed by his managers, who convey the good things their teams accomplished through the week. Do you know what the metrics are? Page views and subscriptions. Sometimes good writing is mentioned (usually from Miss Texas), but the notes are driven by the number of page views and subscriptions.

Consequently, my manager very rarely pushes my work, internally. I find it deflating. I sound like a broken record, and I don't mean to. But my time here is done. I just need to exit properly. When one overextends the time or the welcome, it helps no one. I remember poor George, a reporter in his sixties, and feeling pressure from all sides. One day, his face beet red, he lost it and walked out of the newsroom.

I feel that way often.

I will say that when George Floyd was killed, and I wrote the series of meaningful columns about our inhuman condition, there was appreciation. But it's like all that never happened in our newsroom. You and I have talked about why it seems that the same guys are always in charge. I wish I had the answers.

OK. Enough of that.

I did write the column about the woodchucks/groundhogs. I named them Phil and Phyliss. I talked about Louisiana and Pennsylvania and Ohio. I even included Zoo Director Thane Maynard, who was kind enough to answer an early-morning email about the nature of woodchucks. THEY ARE

ACTUALLY THE LARGEST SQUIRRELS ON EARTH AND THEY CAN CLIMB TREES, TOO!

Horrifying, simply horrifying.

Love,

Byron

Midwest Bland

Tuesday, August 11, 2020
Taos, New Mexico

Dear Byron,

As always, good to hear from you. Again, the day is dominated with Zoom calls. I believe that people schedule these things to prove that they are actually working. I have taken to ensuring that my "background" looks good, but I generally am dressed plainly. No makeup, little jewelry, etc. I am well beyond trying to impress or prove much.

I too have given thought to your "job" dilemma. You are most talented, an extraordinary human, super smart and easy to work with. You are the "perfect" employee. But you are so much more than an employee. There is a saying, "You will be too much for some people—those are not your people." You and I live in this camp.

Once I abruptly left the corporate world, this became all too clear. I went through many interviews and was often the second choice. I understood that folks knew that I was a skilled leader, but I had come from a "big" position, would be taking a pay cut and was not a controllable entity. I always knew that I would do OK with the movement "down," but I started to comprehend that my own experience was threatening.

Yes, this sounds like ego talking. They might have known something that I didn't. I would ultimately not have been thrilled with the situation. Yet, we all need to be able to support our families and pay our bills.

You have such personality and presence and (at the risk of sounding "bitchy") you are being viewed by those who are Midwest bland. You operate on a different plane. You likely will play by the rules, but not love it.

America Lost and Found in Letters

You know more than those for whom you would work. This is a blessing in disguise.

You are anything but Midwest bland.

For the past decade-plus, I have had to be scrappy and creative. Luckily people like us come to those attributes naturally. This means using your own ingenuity and peripheral vision. Opportunities will appear, but maybe not in the form anticipated. You will meet people who will change your life—like I met you.

And being free of the judgments of those to whom we are too much is liberating.

Interestingly, the COVID dreams are often about my old work life. And they aren't pleasant. People are often undercutting one another. I sense my own insecurity. I wake up tired—as if I just sat through long power point meetings with self-important people.

The latter part of my corporate life was working for (at the time) the world's most prosperous privately-owned media company. At first blush, I liked the folks—we were all Jews. I felt that we would connect. Until I learned that I was owned. With the exception of the "religious" element, we had nothing in common. I was one of their servants deemed to make their own family even wealthier.

Ultimately, the family that I truly cared about was MINE. Not theirs.

And they cared less about mine.

After decades of success, I have watched their business decline. They have sold many assets. They didn't pivot fast enough. They relied upon their own name and what they knew. They didn't listen. Are they still one of the wealthiest families in the world?

Yes, but there isn't much of a life there.

I have a complicated view of money. I was raised amongst some people who had "too much." Many were not happy. Because for those who care about money, there is never enough. Of course, we all like to have "things." That's America. But things do not bring joy.

I have thought lots recently about raising my girls. They were with us for about eighteen years and then off to their grown-up lives. My own life will be spent without them more than with them. I spent many of those years working, stressing, rushing, not being present.

What a waste. Yet that is what we did to send them to college, to pay for our family experiences, to be part of the community. At the time, I knew that it would go fast and that I should not miss a moment. I remember trying to sear these times into my memories.

I think that I was a halfway decent mother. The girls turned out to be good people—caring about others, not materialistic, concerned about the state of the planet, independent and respectful of others.

They are no longer in my orbit, but they are making a difference and learning daily.

It is strange how this happens. We do everything at once for those early years and when they end, we have time and they are miles and head time away.

You still have two in the house. To the extent that you are able, treat this time as your most valuable. Know that your own flexibility and attitude are what will carry both you and your family. I so wish that someone had told me this sentiment.

Somehow it all works out.

Love,

Jennifer

People in Your Life

Wednesday, August 12, 2020
Cincinnati, Ohio

Dear Jen,

Thank you for your kind words. It was important for me to be reminded that life-changing people will enter your life—and that I am one of yours! Thank you. You are one of mine for sure.

I always love to hear about how you and Don raised your girls because, of course, of my own three. They seem to be pulling away from me the more I try to hang on, so I just try to let them be and be there for them when they need me.

This is hard. It is especially hard for me because of the way Laila, my youngest, transformed. While no child is an accident, we did not expect to have her. But what a delight that she arrived as the third and final daughter. She was always curious, always a cut-up and clearly the baby of the family. She always went from zero to fifty in seconds, and always came to a screeching halt once the thing that upset her passed on.

Simone was not kind to Laila. (This is her own admission.) And when Laila became old enough to hold her own, she was not having any of it. She changed from the little one who was there to give love to everything and everyone into a mostly brooding, quiet, self-contained preteen.

Stop touching me. What are you doing? *Breathing.* This has been the case for four years now. She has always made As and tests two grade levels above her normal class. We have chosen not to elevate her to a higher grade; instead, we just give her more work and try to enrich her learning ourselves.

Loren and Simone have remained themselves, for the most part. I remember watching Richard Williams, the Shreveport, Louisiana-born dad of the tennis superstars talk about how Serena would be a greater champion than Venus. She was still a little girl and had never won a tournament when he said this. Now she is the greatest tennis champion of all time. Parents know their children, just as you know yours. At first, I did not follow Mr. Williams. Now I do.

Loren is a free-spirit, a roller-coaster, where Simone is a solid, black Model T. Steady, steady, steady. The fewer changes, the better. Loren will be seeking and searching and creating. Simone will get a job and try to keep it for as long as possible and hope it will not require her to move around. Laila will invent things and her mailbox money will likely support the three of them. That's OK. I just hope things work out in the end, as you say.

On another note, the house two doors down contains a lot of people— men, women and children of many ages. Perhaps six or seven at any given time. We accepted extra fruits and vegetables from the school, given to all CPS students. We had an abundance, and wanted to give away the excess. Jill was hesitant to give them to anyone, for fear that we would violate Midwestern sensibilities. *We don't need your charity?* Yet, I ambled down there with a box of apples, oranges, celery, potatoes and beans.

A boy who looked to be fourteen, and a man who is always on the porch were there. The boy's eyes lit up. He was so excited to get the food because he said he didn't have anything to eat. Incredible! I was so happy that I went down there. I took a chance. I went back to the house and got more oranges and more canned goods. Poverty and hunger looks like normal life happening right beside you.

The second thing I did was to $CashApp just a little spending money (maybe for gas or dinner or a pedicure) to my Aunt Debra in Dallas. She has written two books, owned several sandwich shop franchises, and has given so much to the family, especially to my mother over the years. They sold the stores and she now consults. She is handling the estate of my Aunt Lucy, an accountant.

Maybe my little offering helped, maybe it did not, but the givers need to be given to sometimes, even if the amount is symbolic. This is the same aunt who forty years ago let me spend the week on her couch and who took me to the party where the smiling Africans with beautiful teeth were.

Mom did not share her funeral plans with me; she shared them with her sisters. She shared everything with Debra because that's who took care of her most often, financially and emotionally. Mom kept her affairs close to the vest. Each time I went home, I asked about plans. Her doctor called me just past 10:30 p.m., Nov. 17, telling me she was gone. It was too late.

But Debra and Doris and Lucy took care of everything. Mostly Lucy. I signed over Mom's life insurance to handle partial costs of the funeral, which was double the insurance proceeds. It was a spectacle, with dancing pall-bearers and a Bentley of a casket, glistening black and silver. The pallbearers danced down the aisle with her casket. This is what she wanted, I was told.

It was beautiful.

But, Jen, we don't do a great job with estate planning. I have seen this re-peated over generations, and it complicates things. Hiring legal and financial help becomes a luxury most people can't (or won't) place in their budgets. But it makes for quite a calamity in the end.

I did not know Mom took out a second mortgage on our tiny, 80-year-old farm house to make repairs. And Debra had been making the payments. Debra told me that Mom told her to make sure "they don't lose the house."

I'm thankful for this. But, as you can imagine, I also feel a tinge of guilt.

While I have tried to hold things together for my little family all this time, I'm sure I have conveyed one too many times how busy I was or how things were "tight" this month or that month.

She didn't want to burden me, clearly. Things feel incomplete still.

Love,

Byron

Simone and Laila McCauley are not so sure about Santa.

The America That I Love

Thursday, August 13, 2020
Taos, New Mexico

Dear Byron,

So much to think about now. Mostly good. Like you, I believe that Kamala Harris on the Biden ticket will make all the difference. She is America. She is the American Dream. It does feel like Obama 2008. I am weary of the Bernie supporters making snide comments. Do they want Trump again?

One, a "friend" and former candidate for mayor of Cincinnati, is a good woman. We know her well. She "married" Caroline—quite graciously. She runs an organization that Bernie started. (I voted for Bernie in the 2016 primary—so I have liked Bernie.) The words coming out of this woman's mouth on national television that sound like a "wait and see" about Kamala…WTF? Really. We all need to line up behind Biden–Harris and put pettiness aside.

Too, too much.

I keep thinking of this poem by Langston Hughes. One of my best educational lessons was from my fifth-grade social studies teacher (Isabel Stamler) in Wyoming, Ohio. We memorized important historic poems. This was one of them:

Well, son, I'll tell you:
Life for me ain't been no crystal stair.
It's had tacks in it,
And splinters,
And boards torn up,
And places with no carpet on the floor—

Bare.
But all the time
I'se been a-climbin' on,
And reachin' landin's,
And turnin' corners,
And sometimes goin' in the dark
Where there ain't been no light.
So boy, don't you turn back.
Don't you set down on the steps
'Cause you finds it's kinder hard.
Don't you fall now—
For I'se still goin', honey,
I'se still climbin',
And life for me ain't been no crystal stair.

To me, it seems so much about what life has been like for many Americans. And Kamala Harris comes out of the story—and still climbing.

Ms. Stamler also taught me my most important lesson about plagiarizing—which shaped me. I turned in a paper about "India being a melting pot." She asked me what melting pot meant. As a fifth grader, I had no idea. She then explained to me that copying others' work was not OK.

Good to learn this one early.

I get choked up reading about your neighbors and their troubles. So tough for so many people these days. We don't have to venture far to politely help those who need it most.

The climb (and often falling) is real. Many have fallen far in recent times.

I have been thinking about our stories, about our own families. Many families keep secrets from one another until the end—just like your mother did. I am confused (always have been) by how we often don't discuss the most important matters with those who are supposedly the closest to us. It starts to feel too difficult. And I wonder—as the years move forward what it is that I will learn? And then, scratch my head, and wonder why it was never discussed?

I am certain that there will be information that comes forward. People learn about their parents, their spouse, their friends—once people are gone.

I have been obsessed with reading stories about people who others felt that they "knew." Yep, we think we know a person, right?

Parental relationships are challenging.

Like Langston Hughes writes, life sometimes is just about getting by. And I think this is true for all of us. Nature and the natural world (to me) feels like a soft and understandable cushion—that no matter what else is happening can be relied upon. It is the most real.

I love humans, but darn, people exhaust me.

For the first time since 2016 though I feel true hope. A reason to believe. That maybe we are turning the corner.

That maybe, finally, good will outweigh evil.

See you in real life soon.

Love,

Jennifer

Sweet Home, Ohio

Friday, August 14, 2020
Cincinnati, Ohio

Dear Jen,

Growing up, I never, ever thought I would end up in Southwest Ohio. I wanted to live in New York, Los Angeles, or perhaps Atlanta. My unlikely arrival came in 2002 when I was transferred from my hometown newspaper in Shreveport, Louisiana, where I was editorial page editor. "We need some new muscle on our editorial board. I think you would do well here," an *Enquirer* editor told me as we both attended a meeting at Columbia University.

Seven months later (it took that long), and I was here. Nearly twenty years later, I'm still here. And as this week concludes, I find myself firmly in a love-not-like relationship with this region. Earlier today, I had daydreams of leaving. Here's the thing: the deep South has no attraction for me anymore. And if I'm true to myself, I long for a place where there are mountains and water nearby (South Carolina?), but with family and friends close enough to visit within a few hours drive. I also want a place where I could feel free to be me fully, without worry.

This place may not exist.

What got me to thinking about this was e-mail and telephone calls in response to things I wrote in Cincinnati.com this week. No fewer than 15 people thanked me profusely for writing about groundhogs. And when I wrote about Kamala Harris, the responses were either tepid, neutral, or angry.

When I came to Cincinnati, I expected to find a more progressive North. And for a while, it felt so much better than Northwest Louisiana, where I knew what to expect. The area has a lot to offer, but as our favorite author mentions—the state is steeped in a caste system, and it is brutally stifling. Cincinnati is better than it was when I arrived on the heels of the "riots."

The editors in Cincinnati apparently saw in me an ability to be a community bridge-builder. I performed my duties well. Between then and now, I have grown weary, Jen. Few in our young newsroom know how much of my blood I have given to the cause. It is a different time now. Everything has changed. I have to find a way to thrive as things around me seem more chaotic. You play a huge role in helping me to focus and stay grounded. Thank you for that.

The Democratic ticket of Joe Biden and Kamala Harris gives me hope. It makes me believe in the America that I love. It's so hard to believe that the same America that elected Barack Obama also elected Donald Trump. Finally, after nearly four years of tornadic insanity, we may be on the cusp of positive change.

I'm praying for their victory.

Love,

Byron

Packing It In

Saturday, August 15, 2020
Taos, New Mexico

Dear Byron,

I know what you mean about Cincinnati. I was born in Canton, Ohio, and we moved to Cincinnati when I was three months old. I have lived in Michigan, Florida, Colorado, and now New Mexico. My "roots" have always been in Cincinnati, and life there comprised most of my life. I, too, have a love-hate relationship with the place.

To be sure, it is a beautiful city. There are enough arts and culture to keep one engaged. Being "raised" in Cincinnati gives one some entrees. However, when one is a first-generation Cincinnatian, and from a non-classic sort of White class, one is merely given crumbs. Enough to be part of the region, but not a player.

Some folks (like me) confuse themselves. They believe that they are part of the "power" group, but they are merely deluded. The decision makers are the same individuals from the same families since the early Cincinnati days. And they are not Jewish, Black or Asian. They are a bit homogeneous. Decent folks, but quite similar. These key folks have been decent to me, but I most certainly know my place.

Yes, it is a good place to raise children. No, they are not open-minded. It is considered the most Northern city in the South or the most Southern city in the North and a point of historical freedom. Some days I get choked up when I know that we will soon pull out for the final time. I also know, having left there before that, it is heartening to live in new places. This time though, I won't come back to live in the future.

Once one is fifty-seven, there are likely not that many years left.

So, my friend, I understand your conflicting views about the place that we have each called home.

I, too, am inspired by Kamala Harris. I am sickened by the birthers, and then the people who believe that she is not Black enough, or not Indian enough, or too female or too much of a ball-breaker. She is America, a blend of many attributes. She is terrific.

I only have one (and I am not petty) small suspicion about her. Like me, she is a stepmother. She has been one for five years. I moved in with Don when his children were five and eleven. We quickly added two more daughters to the family. Being a stepmom has been part of my life for over half of it.

I wish that my stepdaughters had developed a cute name for me like "Momela." I would have liked to help decorate their dorm rooms. I recognize that Kamala is attempting to show the world that she understands motherhood. I get it.

However, I also know that (except in rare instances), the stepmother is a title with no authority with a tentative seat at the table. Early on, I learned my place. Don's late father and brother went far to include me. We have been together decades, and I accepted the status (or lack thereof) long ago. We are happy. We raised two great girls and I was part of the lives of his older two.

No one actively dissed me—no real complaints. But I find it suspect that Kamala is as involved as she claims. Nope, this is not a reason to criticize her role. I do question (privately) whether she is merely creating a part.

When grandson Abel was born (the first) he started to call me "Nif" when he was about two. All of these years later, I am Nif to five grandchildren. I'll take it.

From the mouths of babes.

I am thrilled that she will be our next vice president. If I ever had the chance to see her privately, I am pretty confident that she would admit that being a stepmother can be a lonely experience. She would be in the support group that I joked about creating.

It's been a busy last few days. We had dinner at our neighbors for Pete's (Pedro's) seventy-first birthday. Out of eight of us, we were part of three "gringos." I find this refreshing. I love the lyrical nature of the voices, the rolled "r's, the family New Mexico history and the sense of total inclusion of us. I like that we are a minority here. These are solid people. Their home is filled with love.

We have had great neighbors only twice, once in Florida, and now in New Mexico. It is truly beautiful to have friends who happen to live next door.

We went to the farmer's market today and then came home and went for a bike ride. We ran into (not literally) Dave, who guided us on Kilimanjaro and is one of the planet's foremost climbers. (More summits on Everest than any non-Nepalese) Kili, for him, is a fun walk—for us, well a life accomplishment. We have seen him some this summer. He usually is on the "really tall ones" this time of year, but, like many, COVID has changed his life.

When in town, he lives up the street. He is a truly decent human and concerned about the state of the nation. We chatted about what would become of ski season this year (the ski valley does employ over 900 people), and he quipped, "What will happen to any of this?"

Sometimes it's easier to worry about the simple things. Do we have enough eggs for breakfast tomorrow? Am I exercising enough? Are my clients happy? Because concern about the big bad bumps in the night becomes too much.

We get on the road in two days—to cross the nation for the fourth time since March. Once there, we have things to manage—not the least of which is getting into the dreaded storage unit and determining the future of "stuff" and packing up our apartment.

The day comes soon when we leave Cincinnati to a place with tall mountains, good neighbors, and open minds. I will miss my roots and likely get teary when I think about life without them. But it's time to land on our final location—where we are Don and Jennifer, not the premarital history, and where we carve out our own life—while we still have the energy.

Love,

Jennifer

Eighteen People Shot in One Day

Sunday, August 16, 2020
Cincinnati, Ohio

Dear Jennifer,

I'm simultaneously crestfallen and hopeful.

Crestfallen because early this morning in our city, before sunrise, eighteen people were shot, seventeen of them within ninety minutes. So far, four have died. Shortly before noon today, one of our reporters was on the scene at Grant Park. Officials were cleaning away blood from sidewalks and basketball courts. So far, we have had sixty-six homicides, sixty involving gunfire. We have logged 300 shootings.

This is madness! When we began writing to each other, we wanted to record history and reflect our feelings about what was going on around us. We were responding to the brutal killing of George Floyd and the nationwide aftermath. We also wanted to celebrate life and all of its ups and downs. I did not expect that two months later in our town to bear witness to Cincinnati making national news for a weekend of mass murder. The problem is so complicated. It is rooted in poverty, boredom, anger, lack of opportunity. And, let's be truthful, the shooters either have no moral compass or have lost it somewhere along the way.

Either way, this is not the kind of city in which I choose to live. I don't know what to do right now, or how to address it, but I will.

Hopeful because we are on the verge of political change. If we elect Donald Trump to a second term, Russia will have its way with our country, and Trump will dismantle our democratic republic. Most of our cabinet and undersecretaries hold "acting" titles. And to see a political appointee who has donated millions to Trump's campaign become Postmaster General sickens me.

On the heels of the Democratic National Convention, I am hopeful that Kamala Harris and Joe Biden will restore America to greatness. When I lived in North Carolina in 1990, Charlotte Mayor Harvey Gantt, an African American, ran for the Senate as a Democrat against Jesse Helms, the notorious bigot known as "Senator No." So many of us thought Gantt would win. And then Helms' campaign produced the "hands" ad. It showed a picture of white hands, with a voiceover, "You wanted this job, but because of a law, they had to give it to a minority." Gantt ended up losing by five percentage points.

The Gantt-Helms race was the first political race that broke my heart into pieces. The second was the 2016 presidential election. I want to believe Joe and Kamala can win. I want to let go and feel with all my heart.

I'm hopeful, yes, but I'm also cloaking my heart just a little bit—to protect it.

It's going to be a wonderful week for national restoration. I cannot wait!

Love,

Byron

From Atlanta to Denver

Monday, August 17, 2020
The Red States

Dear Byron,

I have been thinking—head spinning. So much.

The eighteen shootings in Cincinnati are surreal. Cincinnati is a lot of things. Namely a middle-of-the-road city. Horrible and great things rarely happen. The economy rarely surges or dives. It is predictable and safe.

Like the person one might want to marry, but soon becomes boring.

And then eighteen people are shot in the part of town that has been gentrified.

I have long thought that this neighborhood (OTR) was at risk. When Caroline was in college, she was assigned to write a paper about her city. She wrote and questioned what would happen to all of the people who had lived in this now Disney-like place and been priced out. At the time, she and I drove through. I pointed out the swank new restaurants and shops. She said;

"Mom, what about the people?"

My kids (somehow, someway have the right values). Nora told me today that I needed to stop quoting Winston Churchill—that he was in fact a racist. He likely was—and I rarely let one off the hook. But I credit the guy for beating Hitler.

I am not sure that she buys my rationale.

And today you interviewed some of the people impacted by the shootings.

The sad folks who lived in the middle of now a war zone. The place in which so many have been disenfranchised. And now with COVID and a fraught economy, have given up. Others in big cities have said "make the killing stop—or make 'them' stop." And when I hear "them" I hear a dog whistle.

We both know what is being said.

Nope, no one should brandish a weapon and shoot, but I actually get it. And then the innocents, the people who have lived in the neighborhood for decades and are merely frightened.

Truly heartbreaking as we make our way back from Taos to Cincinnati, to the place that I continue to refer to as home. It will always be home.

Today we should have been en route to the Democratic National Convention in Milwaukee, with Don as a delegate. He has attended almost every convention since 1968 and was a delegate at many starting with Ted Kennedy.

Did I ever tell you that we named Caroline—after *that* Caroline? Caroline Kennedy. We have both been Kennedy-obsessed for decades. Don said that he would only marry someone born while JFK was still alive. He died three months after my birth. My mom said that I cried so much that she couldn't focus on the news coverage.

However, I didn't care for the "old man" much. Jack, Bobby, and Teddy—amazing visionaries and humans. And there is that time that Teddy "flirted" with me (1991, New York City). And yep, Bill Clinton too (in 1988) but those are stories from a different time.

Instead, we get into the Subaru tomorrow (with our furry cat girl Lolli), crossing the first of many red states, and will land in Cincinnati in two days.

We have come to the ground in Garden City, Kansas. And because I can find a literary connection to any place in the world—this is the place in which the famous "Clutter Family" "In Cold Blood" trial (1959) took place.

On other trips, I have required a stop at the Clutter family home. We stopped at the end of the driveway. We saw the snaking trees and felt 108 degree air (seemingly coming from the gates of hell) and imagined the horror.

Capote portrayed the vibe perfectly.

So, it is here in the Comfort Inn, with our cat running around the room, that we watch the virtual convention.

Yesterday, I was not feeling well. I said, "Certainly it is not COVID." And then look up the symptoms—well I can still taste and smell, so there is that.

I baked healthy cookies for the road and sampled. Not taking any chances. They taste great.

Today, I am a bit better. Fingers crossed.

I have only been to two conventions.

First in 1988 (Atlanta) and that is where Don and I connected.

And then in 2008 (Denver). Don was a delegate and I attended with CSPAN … sat in their box, got all of the speeches in advance. It was magic. So much hope.

That got me thinking. Don and I had some troubles in 2008 (I was working in Florida, he in Cincinnati) when we were commuting. In the middle of it all, I wrote this poem. As a young dreamer, I wrote poetry—as an old cynic, it never happens anymore.

Take a read. We will continue to be tuned in to the news on the radio and crossing America. See you soon.

20 years later…. Atlanta to Denver by Jennifer P. Mooney

My younger self remembers,
The white negligee,
That you
Gave me in Atlanta for my 25th birthday,
And, how, we
Never slept and sweated, because almost no place, is,
As hot in Atlanta in July.

We thought that we were different, and could breathe,
Rarified air.
Only today, 20 years later, do we know,
That we too…
Are a statistic.

We were hopeful, we had a candidate,
Albeit,
A weak one, but he,
Was ours.
To me, the political scene was purposeful,
And, full with desire, promise and life.

We knew, that the bonding of our flesh,
Was different, maybe transformational.
We knew, even then, that the price to be,
Permanent,
Was high,

And that,
We would pay,
A sum total,
Impossible to calculate.

In those days, I could survive,
On three cups of coffee and too little sleep.
Each day, I awoke, ready, to
Begin it all again.
My muscle memory, long and of heartbreak,
Short. For who,
Would ever break my heart?

I was young, so young... and never envisioned, things
Like, the towers coming down,
Your younger brother,
Dying,
Two teenage daughters, who are
So like me...
The matters of love and loss, who knows?
Who really knows?

From May 12, 1988, I adored you,
Your mind, your vocabulary and the use of the word,
Bizarre.
Your body and seemingly, unwavering,
Affection,
Just for me. I thought...no, I knew
That we,
You and me,
We're something special.
Something better.
Something real.
Something forever.

As I sit still today,
What I know to be true.
We are here,
With the best presidential candidate,
Perhaps,
In a lifetime.
We are married,
With four daughters,
And a grandson.

We are moved,
By the promise,
Of Hope,
That the storms won't rack our old cities,
That,
Honest words and the right intentions,
Are enough,
To believe again.

We basked,
In the clear sun,
In the mile high, city,
With the belief,
That we can be young, free
And new again.
This time,
We know, that,
In so many ways,
We are one, of many.
Not unique, not special,
But,
Not alone either.

20 years later,
We have,
The trappings of "happy people."
Three homes,
Endless books and lingerie,
Good jobs
And,
Can pay our bills.
We have faith,
And a dream.

We are forever, but a bit wounded.
My heart is broken and,
My body, oh, so tired.
It doesn't bounce back,
Like it once did, and it
Is the only thing, that,
Can help to heal my heart.
The pleasure it seeks, perhaps
Can sew the fissure,
Right down the middle.

We face the future,

America Lost and Found in Letters

Together,
With any luck, and a prayer,
A new president,
A new chance,
A future and,
A dream that breathes, in
The light of day.

It is, yes, it is
20 years later. But 20 years was really,
Just moments ago.
At that time, who would have known,
So much pleasure,
So much beauty,
So much change,
So much pain.

Who would know?
What we can endure...but,
What choice is there?
The heart is not rational,
Nor is the body...
20 years later,
We press on, and, as idealists know,

That,
The sun will rise,
The sky will be blue again,
All of the children grow up and
the girls will leave our home.
What I know for sure, is
That the heart muscle has no mind,
Only its own direction...
Only its own path and that,
I have fallen in, deep, and that
I can't help myself,
But to love you forever,
And to join you,
In reconfiguring,
Our own version of the dream.
20 years later.

And that was twelve years ago, wow.

Love,

Jennifer

Hope, Interrupted

Brutal Aftermath

Tuesday, August 18, 2020
Cincinnati, Ohio

Dear Jennifer,

Happy travels. Safe travels.

It's fun keeping up with your cross-country trip back to the Queen City.

Your last letter moved me, particularly Caroline's insight about where will the people of Over-the-Rhine go when the price of living there becomes unattainable. A powder keg of frustration explodes, and then one day, you get a mass shooting in a children's park.

It's not that simple, of course. There is an element of moral bankruptcy. There is also an element of economics, surely drug-turf battles. And there is no excuse for what we saw there this past weekend. But fifteen years after the "OTR Renaissance," the chickens are coming home to roost.

This evening at the park, they set up tents. I heard that even Chief Isaac came. TV reporters were there to talk, and camera operators framed the park to record the moment. A soulful singer sang a hopeful tune. Life wants to get back to normal. But killers still walk the streets and residents hunker as if they are in Aleppo. And blocks away sits "Disneyland" with its cute shops and haughty drinking places.

We will write about how cool they are. Where to get the best pizza that you "never knew you needed" and fawn over the struggling business that's making it despite COVID—and we should! Because, you know, small business.

But I keep learning new things every day about my adopted city. I'm still an infant. My sponge-brain consumes just enough to realize how little I know and how much I need to learn. When readers come at me and dismiss the powerless, the destitute, and challenge my solutions to "Black-on-Black" crime, it is sickening.

But we must—I must—continue to fight for the people in my little corner, doing whatever I can do, offering whatever I can offer.

Love,

Byron

Looking For America

Wednesday, August 19, 2020
The Red States

Dear Byron,

I, too, am troubled about OTR (Cincinnati neighborhood). I feel like some White people (generally in our age range) bought places cheap there, renovated, joined the community council, acted like they would blend in and help the community, and really just drove people out.

They complain lots, but mostly just about things that impact their precious lives—not the people who were born and raised their families there.

Like you, I am not surprised that the chickens have come home to roost. I have spent a share of time here—but tired of the scene and the obvious gentrification. It is a community with a deep history. I am kind of a "senior" citizen in Cincinnati, but still don't understand it all.

Don and I were on a Zoom call (while driving) with the Ohio Democratic Caucus today. Cincinnati Mayor Cranley was today's big speaker—as he is obviously trying for statewide office. He (and don't fall off of your chair) espoused that Cincinnati has turned the corner (under his reign) and mentioned positive things about the police.

Wow. I guess he isn't paying attention or is trying to change the narrative.

Day three of the virtual convention and day three of the drive across America. Whenever we do the drive I think of the Simon and Garfunkel song "America."

And walked off to look for America
Kathy, I said as we boarded a Greyhound in Pittsburgh

Michigan seems like a dream to me now
It took me four days to hitchhike from Saginaw
I've gone to look for America.

It feels like the consummate "immigrant tune." For the past years things have not been hopeful. Whenever we are on the road, I, too, look for America. This week feels different.

There was something about the roll call last night to put Joe Biden's name forward as our candidate that gave me the chills (in a good way). We watched from our bed at The Iron Horse Inn in Blackwater, Montana. We have crossed the country four times since March. This Inn has become our place:

1. It is lovely.
2. We are basically the ONLY guests.
3. It is well-priced.
4. They accept cats.
5. Blackwater is an historic town.

Blackwater was founded in 1887. It now is pretty empty and looks like a movie set for an "old" middle-of-nowhere town. We also always eat breakfast at Kimberley's. To be sure, we were likely the ONLY people watching the DNC last night. This is a Trump town with giant Trump banners. In 2016 I was spending time in rural Ohio. All of my liberal friends felt that Hillary had bagged the election.

I witnessed mass Trump signs everywhere. I repeatedly told Don that (to me) it was clear that she was at high risk of losing. It was not just the signs, but the attitudes. While this week feels hopeful, middle America is a different animal.

Kimberley's displayed a Trump calendar. The older farmers were friendly to us as we listened in on their chat. These are roughhewn men who have struggled. They are NOT Biden supporters. They noted (off the bat) that we were out-of-towners.

Yesterday we ate lunch at another regular stop. This one is called Boss Hogg's and is in Abilene.

Our first time in Abilene was by chance. We drove into Ike's hometown and must have been speeding (going 30 in a 25). The lights flashed behind us and we were pulled over. Don apologized and said that we were visiting and looking for dinner. The officer smiled and said, "Let me take you to a local spot." So, we had a police escort. We have stopped ever since.

However, this was Trumpland. President Eisenhower might be surprised how far away the nation is from America that he knew. There is much Ike memorabilia on display. They also have a basket of paddles. Signed paddles are on the walls. When it is one's birthday their waitress paddles them, and the injured party signs the paddle, and it is hanged. Marlin Fitzwater (former Whitehouse Press Secretary) was spanked. His paddle tells the tale. It's pretty funny.

Yes, I am a solid Democrat who has voted (and raised money) for many Republicans over the years. But Trumpsters are a different style of Republican. Folks like Sen. John McCain and House Speaker John Boehner were of a different ilk.

We live in a contradictory time and I am living in a contradictory week. As we watch the faces that make up this diverse nation, I feel proud of my own ethnicity. I am grateful to be part of the diversity in the USA. Yet, step away from the news coverage and we are immediately "outsiders" and likely considered part of the group that has made life "harder" for the standard White folks (or so they think).

This is an existential crisis and while I am hopeful that we end up supporting our huddled masses—I am never certain that we will get there.

Day three mask update:

Colorado: wearing masks
Kansas: mostly wearing masks
Missouri: not wearing masks
Illinois: not wearing masks.

Will update on Indiana. Into Cincinnati in about four hours!

Love,

Jennifer

Bated Breath

Thursday, August 20, 2020
Cincinnati, Ohio

Dear Jen,

I'm going to keep it short today. I stayed up, against my better judgment, to watch Vice President Biden's acceptance speech.

I thought he knocked it out of the park. What I heard from him was everything that Donald Trump is not. And thirteen-year-old Braden Harrington, who stuttered, was the star of the whole night. I'm proud of the Democrats. And it makes me proud to cast my vote for hope, not bitterness.

In contrast, media reports have said Sandmann, the Northern Kentucky kid who stood before the Native American elder in front of the Washington monument, will speak at next week's GOP convention. Also, the gun couple from St. Louis will speak, as well.

At a basic level, this is the difference between a Biden-led country and a Trump presidency.

Now, we need to go to work, protect voter rights and be watchdogs. Finally, in a few hours, I go under with anesthesia for the fifth time in three years after having never spent a night in a hospital. Fun times.

Love,

Byron

Breathing Thick Air

Weekend, August 21–23, 2020
Cincinnati, Ohio

Dear Byron,

My head is so heavy this morning. I think it is a combination of being back in thick air, COVID dreams, some super intense emotional challenges and the constant pelting news. I have not been around this many humans in months—it is an adjustment.

On top of the heavy head though is the sincerest HOPE that I have felt in months as well: Biden-Harris is for real. And they must win. We are going to be poll workers and do all that we can to be part of a fair election. No complaining, time for action.

So glad that you are through your surgery. I know that it was rough. You will be OK.

We are here in the high rise. Living among many of the non-mask wearers and COVID deniers. I have already had arguments with some people in the building. It is stunning to me. My remedy is to wear my Obama t-shirts (I need to obtain Biden-Harris) around the building with a smile and a mask. This is my attempt to "go high."

We are walking lots. Hiking in the urban basin. Of note, not many masks. We have been out to have "outside drinks." Because if one is going to do the walk, one deserves a reward. BTW, as long as I live, I will be enamored with the beauty of the riverfront and living on the river. I could stare for hours at the river traffic and activity. I am grateful that I have had the opportunity to swim across (and back) the Mighty Ohio many times.

This is something that I will miss.

So, the drinks. As you know, the building across from us (the former Anna Louise Inn) was initially a structure that housed women with life struggles. The organization started in the 1800s to provide shelter for women who lived down river and sought employment in Cincinnati in order to send money back to their families. For well over a century it continued to serve as a safe place for young women.

Until it was determined that it would be acquired and turned into a hotel.

On Friday night we found ourselves on its roof top drinking libations.

Yes, it is a beautiful place. Yes, it's difficult to get one's head around the structure's past and now future. Lytle Park and its environs are a beautiful spot. It is also whitewashed. It is groomed, pristine and forgetful from whence it came. Not even a historic plaque. There is one brick (in the stone) that claims its provenance.

People were socially distanced. The air was fresh. The staff worked hard. Yet it feels phony. It is a bunch of White people from the suburbs in clothing that is too tight, lots of blonde hair and not a care in the world. After being in a brown city for months, it is strange to observe this much homogeny. Don and I observed (from our perches at the bar). Yes, I am being judgmental, but this falls into the category of people likely not knowing history.

Sort of like the current political columnist at your paper. Do some homework, do some research. Pay reverence. Know from where you and "it" came. Maybe we are just getting old.

Yes, definitely getting old(er).

On Saturday we took a bike ride into Kentucky. A different vibe than riding in the mountains, but interesting as well. I truly love this region and that we can merely cross one of five bridges and be in a different state. And back from South to North and a point of freedom on the Underground Railroad. This reality has always given me the chills.

I met my mom for lunch (outside) in her town and the town of my childhood—Wyoming, Ohio. It has occurred to me that she has given me something that I have failed to give my own daughters—a constant home since I was three—to which I can return and remember. While it is said that one "can never go home again," this place has remained a constant across my own life.

We ate outside at a place to which we often return. The proprietor (Dino) is a robust Italian man who has always been grateful to his patrons. He also catered Caroline's rehearsal dinner.

Over our salads I let her know that Nora is getting married on Thursday in Denmark and that we are officially packing up our Cincinnati apartment to move after Thanksgiving. On Nora, she is happy for her as are we. It is hard for me to truly think through this without being bittersweet. My youngest girl, married, across an ocean and here I sit.

COVID has wracked all of us.

And then the subject of our move. Well, we both cried. This is the right thing for Don and me—emotionally and financially. My husband will be seventy in November. It is time to move to the place in which we will live out our days. On a side note, the wildfires (in the west) are burning like mad (not far from us) which is a worry.

Life today is truly biblical.

I went through the usual list of reasons for the move. My mom lifted her hand. (Every time I see her hands, I think that she has beautiful hands.) I did not inherit those hands. She said, "Stop, no reasons. The point is that you are going." It was a difficult conversation.

At about the same time, a friend (from across the street) waved to us. This friend, a community leader, was the first black President of the Wyoming Board of Education (Debbie). She came and sat with us. I probed her about the history of Wyoming and school integration. Yes, as a young girl, I was on the front end of integration. Throughout the summer I have learned of stories from my Black classmates—of their parents and relatives who went to a different school during the Jim Crow times.

And embarrassingly, this is something that I did not know.

To be sure, I noted Black Lives Matter signs throughout the community. I also know that this is no longer a staunch Republican enclave. The community is changing. It is time.

Debbie then looked at my mom and said, "How are you doing?" My mom is retiring soon, and they recently named her replacement. While my mom is eighty-one, she founded the organization. It is tough for her to leave it behind.

And here I am, the daughter that is leaving.

We left lunch, I came home and went straight to sleep. That heavy head.

We woke and "hiked" deep into OTR. It was a combination of screaming drinkers on that weird peddle vehicle that yuppies ride while drinking, to people giving us the thumbs up sign as Don was wearing a Biden-Harris American Federation of Teachers shirt. We put about five miles on across the city. Throughout the central business district, it is a ghost town.

It feels dystopian. My mom did phone me later. She did let me know that it is time to do what I need to do. She did let me know that she just wants me to be happy. She said the right things.

So, we move forward. One step at a time.

And we are going to her home for dinner tonight.

In Wyoming, Ohio—a place of contradictions.

That holds so many of my own memories.

Just some miles North from the first point of freedom.

A place in which there are many "tunnels" beneath the old homes leading to a better life.

As our next President Biden would say, "hope, not fear."

Love,

Jennifer

Judy VanGinkel, Jennifer's mom and frequent lunch partner.

I Migrated Too

Monday, August 24, 2020
Cincinnati, Ohio

Dear Jennifer,

I am about 190 pages into *The Warmth of Other Suns*. It is breaking my heart so far. Isabel Wilkerson is indeed one of the finest writers the world has to offer, and she won a Pulitzer Prize for reporting in 1994 while at the *Chicago Tribune*. I find that fascinating, but not surprising, having read how meticulous she is with research and writing.

The day the Space Shuttle *Challenger* exploded, nineteen-year-old me received a call from Larry Lane, a recruiter from the *Los Angeles Times*. I'd met Larry in Dallas three months earlier at a jobs fair with ten clips to sell myself. Larry gave me a crisp $20 bill and dispatched me to the hotel copy machine to make more clips after our interview. I had run out of clips and money.

My clips were solid. I returned with fresh copies and about $15 of change.

"Byron, how would you like to come to L.A. this summer and work for the *Los Angeles Times*?"

I was speechless for a moment. "Of course," I said. "Thank you so much, Mr. Lane. And thank you for believing in me." At that moment, this kid from Plain Dealing, Louisiana, a sophomore at Louisiana Tech University, which only fifteen years earlier had admitted its first Black student, had scored the most significant internship in the history of the journalism school.

Reading the journey of Pershing from Monroe, Louisiana, in *Warmth*, I'm remembering my journey from Plain Dealing, Louisiana, to Los Angeles in June 1986, in a blue Chevrolet Chevette with my mother and my nine-year-old sister.

We stopped in Dallas to see my aunt. And we spent the night in the West Texas town of Odessa, where we had an amazing diner meal of chicken fried steak, mashed potatoes and green beans. We rested at a hotel. The next day, we drove to El Paso. We had no problems with lodging. And on the next day, we reached Phoenix. No problems. We arrived in L.A. during rush hour, having struggled over those mountains that drove Pershing insane.

I can't imagine having to drive nearly the whole way, alone without the luxury of lodging, a bath, or the assurance that I would eat. And so many of my people, some relatives, had made that tenuous journey before me. I was going with the assurances of a job and a place to stay.

I remember as if it was yesterday when the family who lived two houses down from my grandmother piled into a Ford station wagon with faux wood panels made the journey themselves, the car loaded down from roof to trunk. The dad's name was John L. Bryant. He had one arm. I never knew why. He pressed the horn and held it for a long time as they passed my grandmother's house. We stood on the porch and bid them adieu. This was in 1973–74.

All of them gave up everything to get away from hell. Ironically, his son, Erving, now sixty-one, reached out to me on Facebook two months ago, asking if I remembered him. Of course, I said, and I told him about my memory of their passing the house. It was like they were going to dreamland.

I feel thankful that we have come such a long way. And even though it seems our nation is coming apart, we are so much better off than we once were.

And with God's help, the Biden-Harris election will bring us all back together again and restore America's promise anew.

Love,

Byron

They Said "I Do"

Tuesday, August 25, 2020
Cincinnati, Ohio

My Dear Friend Byron,

I am glad that you feel well enough to write. My head is again full and heavy. I am experiencing sensory overload due to being back in the city, the Republican Convention and, most importantly, that my daughter is marrying this Thursday in Copenhagen.

That is foremost to me.

I think the following says it best. There were letters between Nora's new mother-in-law and myself. I have included mine, but not Bieke's to protect her privacy.

These strange times.

Here goes:

Dear Bieke,

Nice to meet you via letter. These are such challenging times and I wish that our meeting was in person.

We are very happy that Nora and Erwann will wed this week! We are especially glad that Erwann was able to come to the states (one year ago) and spend lots of time with our family. He is loved by all. You have raised a brilliant, caring, funny, independent and superb young man. We are fortunate that he and Nora found one another.

Nora (our youngest of four) has always been highly independent and a person of the wider world. When she left for Europe in high school, it became clear that she would eventually call it home. While she lives far from us, we are glad that she has found happiness. As her mother, I miss her daily. Yes, this is difficult but that is surpassed by how proud we are of Nora and impressed by her compassion, accomplishments, integrity, spirit and zest for life. I feel certain that Nora and Erwann will have an interesting life together.

I have asked that they please send a few photos of their ceremony. As soon as Americans are permitted to enter the EU, we will come over. We very much want to meet you and your family and see Nora-Erwann. Sadly, it may be a long while until we are permitted. I also would like (once travel is ok in the future) to offer to host you at our home in New Mexico. I know that you are an archeologist and NM offers much to see. It is my hope, as time passes, that I am able to come to Europe with some regularity. We just have to keep our fingers crossed for good health.

Thank you for being so good to our daughter. As parents we worry. It is heartening to know that she has a family close by.

Please stay in touch and I so look forward to meeting you.

Love,
Jennifer

Bieke wrote back quickly. We had both asked our children for the other mother's contact. She explained that she had recently been with Nora and Erwann and expressed their happiness. She also let me know how impressed she was with Nora's passion, stability and smarts. I can tell that I would connect with Bieke, and only hope that comes soon.

Dear Bieke,

You have reflected my feelings exactly. I have found myself crying, though I don't let Nora know. It is sad that she marries and that we cannot be there. Erwann is your first and oldest, Nora is my last and youngest. It is all difficult.

I am glad that they have you nearby (nearer than we are) and I know that she has another mom to look out for her.

I do believe that they are truly happy together. I was glad to see that close up last summer.

I look forward to the day that we meet and hope that it is soon.

Love,
Jennifer

The Day I Got Religion

Wednesday, August 26, 2020
Cincinnati, Ohio

Dear Friend,

Today, I'm prayerful.

Neither of us has spoken much of our faith in these many days of letters. I have written about my faith in columns, not as a bludgeon, but simply to note that I am a person of faith.

I was baptized in 1972 in a tributary of the Red River, which ran alongside and about 100 yards from the church that was founded by my grandfather and a dozen or so other men. A handful of kids were with me in white robes. This is the same river that we are hearing about today as Hurricane Laura lashes my home state of Louisiana. We caught catfish and fatty, bloody buffalo fish there. Animals drank there and did their business there. And every year, at least a few scared new Christians were indoctrinated into God's kingdom there.

When I think about it, Pilgrim's Rest Baptist Church, founded in the 1940s, was really built on the edge of a cotton plantation owned by Mr. Charlie (C.A.) Rogers. My grandparents were sharecroppers on this land. And not far from the church was my grandmother's house, which is where my mother lived after I was born in Confederate Memorial Hospital.

The names on a masonry stone mounted on the front of the church shape my history and my earliest memories: Deacon Clarence Graham, Deacon Walter Bryant, Deacon Bennie Williams, Versia McCauley. Clarence was the unquestioned leader and one of the founders. Walter wore thick, tinted glasses, was prematurely gray, and had two gold teeth. He sang like Sam Cooke. Bennie was my grandfather, who perspired from his forehead and temples when he prayed. Versia was my mother, my love. (After Walter's wife died, Mom told me he tried to date her and had always "been sweet" on her.)

What I learned about religion and prayer, I learned from them all, first in the little church on the edge of the plantation. And when I was twelve, a new church was built further into "town," about 200 yards from the six-room house my mother built on cinder blocks atop red clay for the family.

Bible reading and prayer were as routine as dinner in our family and that unshakeable faith has sustained me all these years.

And so today I am prayerful. Prayerful for the family of Jacob Blake and George Floyd and Breonna Taylor and the others. Prayerful for the shooters' families and the victims families everywhere. Prayerful for those in the path of the storm and those who have lost their livelihood.

Jen, when we started this journey after the horrible, public death of George Floyd, I would have never imagined that our efforts would be bookended by another Black man being shot in the back seven times in front of his children. I would have never imagined that we would still be losing our neighbors and friends to COVID-19 and that I would be sending one of my kids to a school building and one spends the day in front of a district-issue-computer.

Both scenarios are not optimal.

How is this different from the public lynchings that we know happened but we can only access through literature and photos today? It's hard to watch the RNC participants not acknowledge any of the cop shootings but seek to repress the visceral responses. They are tone deaf. And they are pouring salt in the wounds of those who feel as if they have no one to help and feel unheard.

I am happy to see the sports world take action. Rich athletes are the only ones in the world it seems with autonomous power. They make a lot of money and they make their bosses even more money. They are not beholden to a board or a well-connected boss who is afraid of losing his stature in the community. Leading that charge is a young man from Akron who was blessed with the gift of basketball and brains.

Jen, we have so much to be thankful for. I know this. Some days I think I'm in the wrong field because I must address the things that are wrong in the world. I do try to provide enlightenment. It's a struggle. I'm up for it still. Thank you for your inspiration.

Love,

Byron

Six Time Zones Away

Thursday, August 27, 2020
Cincinnati, Ohio

Dear Byron,

My daughter married her love Erwann today, at 5 a.m. EST, 11:00 a.m. in Copenhagen—with neither of their families present. I wish them a lifetime of happiness. Nora has always been avant guard and not followed social convention.

I am so proud of her independence. My stepdaughter Maureen asked each family member to make a video to congratulate the couple. It made me happy and sad. It was heartening to see our family on film from across the nation. I am touched to see the outpour of love for Nora. I am sad for any moment in which I doubted anyone in our clan. These are good people.

Strange things happen in families.

Life continues on the banks of the Mighty Ohio. I was reminded (when talking on the phone with an old high school friend this morning) that we were taught that Cincinnati was the first point of freedom on the Underground Railroad. But there is so much more than that, right?

This is a city with its own conflicts. We are Cincinnati polite—we tend to skate on the surface and "get along." Recent months have borne out that it is time to dig, learn and connect. Our fractured nation depends upon it.

As I look out to the river, I see hope. The barge traffic seems low (commerce is down) yet some chug along. It is hard not to think of the history of this town. And I wonder, fifty years from now, what will be said about the time of COVID and the possible dismantling of what we call America.

The city is both full of tributes to Black Lives Matter, adjacent to COVID deniers without masks and young wealthy White people drinking "their lives away." Street by street, it is a confluence of events. When one has lived in a place for most of her fifty-seven years, each sign, building, crosswalk and road is a part of my own history. We look out through wrinkled faces with the same set of eyes with which we were born.

Maybe we are wiser. Maybe a little sad. But glad to be here.

On Sunday, we walked along the river. We ran into the city's last female mayor. I first met her in the 1980s at an event with the then-Attorney General. I was new to the political scene. I was young, brash, full of hope—and (as is often said) with my whole life ahead of me. She was an unknown and a house-painter. A lobbyist said, "Lookout for her, she is going places."

I hung on her every word and believed it all. Yes, she became mayor. And was one of the few politicians who did what she said that she would. Like many, I watched her transformation from no makeup and earthy to fully glammed and married leader. But through it all, yes, she remained authentic. We chatted from a distance as she walked her dog. Like us, she is far from the center of influence now—and is as real and grounded as one who is an elder stateswoman.

This gives me hope.

We have not watched the Republican Convention. Don says that his blood pressure can't take it. We have watched the clips. Of course, we believe it to be vastly misleading and dishonest. I sit back and think of like-minded friends with whom I have had disagreements.

Enough. It is time to stick together. We are up against corruption and the minor issue-related details are dim minus when parsed. The sake of our democracy is at risk.

I was reminded today, that NO we are not as bad off as in 1968. The racism and divisions were deeper then. I believe we are more aligned today.

The days click by.

Our lives are lived.

We do the best that we can.

To support one another.

As a great sage once said: "Yes we can."

Love,

Jennifer

Bad News in Her Voice

Saturday, August 29, 2020
Cincinnati, Ohio

Dear Jen,

You can always tell when someone you know and love is calling to share bad news. They try not to sound too sad or too happy, so the pitch becomes awkward and predictable. My sister was on the other end of the phone today as I drove.

"Have you heard from the aunts in Dallas?"

"Lanny, what happened."

"Bennie Junior just passed."

That would be Bennie Williams, Jr., the fifth of eight children born to my grandmother and grandfather, his namesake.

The story is often told that I lived because of his earnest teenage prayer. "Junior," as all family members called him, was thirteen when I was born. I was the ninth sibling. I was born at 4 lbs., 6 oz.—a baby in the segregated South to a single, twenty-one-year-old mother who had no prenatal care. I was a prime candidate to die as an infant. Mom concealed her pregnancy through the seventh month with a rubber girdle. Apparently, things seemed tenuous. They had never seen a child so small.

Junior slipped out of the house and onto the front steps, where he prayed. He returned and announced that the baby's going to be alright, "because I prayed for him."

Junior had a big heart and was full of compassion. He was also wild. He was so good at playing the trumpet in high school that he earned a band scholarship to Wiley College (home of "The Great Debaters"). He attended for two weeks and returned home. He wanted to make money now, and college would not be for him. So he went to work for the notorious Anthony pulpwood mill north of town. The work was dangerous and hot, but it paid well. I once saw his check stub for $378 in the 1970s.

At least once, a worker fell into a tank filled with hot water used to process the pulp. They recovered his bones.

Bennie always smelled like sweat and pine.

No one in the immediate Williams family touched alcohol except Bennie. He liked Schlitz Malt Liquor. And when he got paid on Friday that money was gone Monday morning, spent on partying, spirits and illegal gambling in one of six cinder-blocked juke joints/pool halls just outside the city limits (just a half-block over) of Plain Dealing. When Louisiana Downs opened in 1974, it was the worst thing that could happen. His gambling addiction intensified, and he was always broke.

My grandmother (or someone) bailed him out of jail countless times. He shot two men six years apart, both during illegal gambling parties. One man took a slug in the ribs. The other in the temple. Miraculously, both men lived and they all ended up friends. He never seemed to miss work and kept his job until a stroke ended his career and he became disabled.

The last I had heard was that he was in and out of a local hospital and had beaten COVID. My sister told me that he had been in a rehab center that has become notorious for losing patients. When Bennie died, hospital officials could not reach his wife, so my sister got word from the Dallas aunts to drive to the wife's house. Sister found the wife sitting outside smoking under a tree.

She called the hospital with my sister present and activated the speaker function. The voice on the phone told them that Bennie expired in the ambulance that was taking him to the nearest trauma center. He had suffered a blood clot in his lungs. He was sixty-eight.

The aunt who was born after Bennie is profoundly saddened, having lost three siblings in five years. "We are down to four," she said.

Love,

Byron

Broken Whole

Tuesday, September 1, 2020
Cincinnati, Ohio

Dear Byron,

It has been a few days since I have written. It has been great to catch up on the phone. I am still getting accustomed to city life and the thick air. And it is still bittersweet. While I am ready to depart this place, it has been home for most of my life. I am in the midst of wrapping "things" up while plowing forward on others.

At the same time, I am in a state of shock. I know that Biden is ahead in the polls, but my gut says that a larger swath of our nation supports Trump. My biggest concern is that we live among bigots. There are too many folks (whom I have known for years) coming out of the woodwork who are OK with a Trump America. I have always had friends with different views—the new definition of "different" is an ilk whom I don't condone.

I have also learned that it is NOT the time to split hairs and seek perfection on the issues. Nope, Biden is not the perfect man and many have concerns about where he might stand on certain causes. No, I might not agree with each and every of my "like-minded" friends. It is the time to "love them anyway."

To me, this is truly a choice between good and evil.

In the last ten days I have seen many family members and a few friends (from a safe distance). I have made the rounds to doctors and dentists. I am going through the motions and tying up loose ends. My dentist seemed seriously choked up that I was in his chair for the last time. He said, "I have taken care of you and the girls for over twenty years—such a good family." In all fairness, being a dentist is so high risk now, that he might be on an emotional ledge.

We spent some time at my stepdaughter's house (Ryan). They live on eleven acres in a hard-core city neighborhood. Yet they have goats, ducks, chickens, roosters, bees, dogs and a cat. Ryan, her husband and four children have managed to make COVID life idyllic. They have dug a pond and their yard is strewn with play areas. The kids were clearly happy to have visitors (and their Grampy Don on site) and no one complained about the sort of summer endured.

I stopped by my friend Sara's home and sat on her back porch. She gave me a wedding gift to send to Nora. Sara and I have been friends since we were three—and walked to and from school together for twelve years. Her husband is from South Africa and left due to apartheid. Enter USA 2020. We spoke of our joint worry.

There is too much rumbling about people "not being permitted to vote." We visited with our neighbor who is running for the county Sheriff seat. She is a married lesbian and liberal. Her win would be history making for this area. We talked about racism and the changes that law enforcement must make. She explained (and she has spent her career working in law enforcement) that the entire pipeline is filled with White men with attitudes. Hence, the challenge and not a quick fix.

My personal favorite (sarcasm here) comment from the right is, "Obama had eight years; why didn't he fix racism?"

Really? Wow!

Don has his surgery on Thursday and had his COVID test today.

These times feel like so much happens in a day, even as we sit still.

Leaving you with some words that mean something to me:

"Do not be daunted by the enormity of the world's grief.
Do justly, now.
Love mercy, now.
Walk humbly, now.
You are not obligated to complete the work,
But neither are you free to abandon it."—The Talmud

No, I am not a religious woman. Yes, I am culturally Jewish. Yes, I believe in something bigger than, we, humans. I seem to practice on my own terms. When one comes from a people who has been put to death due to their "religion," one often keeps it to themselves. The life of one who grew up post-Holocaust.

Love,

Jennifer

Love Unconditionally

Wednesday, September 2, 2020
Cincinnati, Ohio

Dear Jen,

You had to be in the familiar position that Jill has experienced way too often within the past four years—waiting on your husband to wake up from surgery and hoping everything is OK. I'm with you in thoughts and prayers.

There's a lady in Kings Mills named Dana Gendreau who makes the world a better place every day. She and her partner have a bevy of kids, and she rallied the community (known as the Helping Huddle) to adopt the Kings High School football team. She provided extra food and sports drinks and, most of all, support. She's doing it to this day. One kid grew three inches and gained thirty-five needed pounds. For the first time in school history, Hughes High School made the playoffs last year. The Hughes team returned the love to their PeeWee football teams. The Kings boys wear Hughes jerseys to school.

Dana did another grand gesture very recently. She helped a young lady from Avondale study to earn her driver's license and paid for everything. That seems small. But the young lady is a twin whose beautiful mother was looking out of her living room window on Sept. 10, 2019, in Avondale when a stray bullet took her life, and her twin daughters stood as witnesses. She had five children, three of whom went to relatives. The twins, eighteen, are freshmen at the University of Cincinnati and living in the Scholars House. One wants to be a doctor; the other a social worker.

The Helping Huddle wrapped around these girls, providing Christmas presents, helping them with financial aid and college applications, and also with testing.

Having transportation and the ability to drive provides the twins with freedom and opportunity to move about the city easily. Dana also babysits for one of her Hughes students and has supported her as she improves her life. I asked Dana why she does these things.

"We should take care of each other. That's what we were put on this Earth to do. It takes only one person to help make a change for another. We should all be doing this with each other," Dana told me. "And personally, my goal is to support anyone who needs an ally to walk with them in this racially divided world. Let's keep breaking down barriers with these kids together."

Dana is a beautiful human being. She read in the *Enquirer* the desperation of coaches who told us kids come to practice fueled on potato chips, having not eaten since lunch. She did something about it. She showed me a side of Kings that I needed to see amid the horrible racist basketball team scandal, where kids wore racist names on their jerseys and parents, coaches and referees were complicit. Dana has compassion because she became homeless as a child.

"Good Morning America" surprised her at Hughes, paid for a day off for her, and treated her to a day spa. So deserving. She exemplifies Margaret Meade's most quoted declaration:

> *Never doubt that a small group of thoughtful, committed, citizens can change the world. Indeed, it is the only thing that ever has.*

Love,

Byron

Waiting

Thursday, September 3, 2020
Cincinnati, Ohio

Dear Byron,

We have been at University Hospital most of the day. They took Don back into surgery at around 10:30 am. We are part of the wave that is now letting family (one member) into the waiting area. So, here I sit, with my pager and Don's code number #598363, waiting (with the other masked family members) for news.

This is straightforward. His hernia has popped out again. The surgeon fixed it three years ago and apparently that didn't hold. I packed my breakfast-lunch-snack, three flavored waters, two Atkins bars, some blackberries, mixed nuts and cheese. As I type, I have eaten all but one fluid and the blackberries. The hospital has the good sense to not have any political cable news on. They are running a benign local news channel and the governor is giving his daily news conference on COVID.

I sneezed once and quickly looked around the room. A woman said, "Bless you." I announced, "It's just allergies" and she smiled (I could tell) and said again, "Bless you." She meant it. I announced that I believed us all to be COVID-free as we knew that our households had been tested forty-eight hours ago.

This is the teaching hospital. Many residents and learners came in to check on Don and to explain his hernia situation to one another. I am always mesmerized by these young people and how "on it" they all appear to be.

The OR called me moments ago; said this is taking longer than expected. So, I wait.

In the hospital that was once called "General" and in which the late Charles Manson was born. Like the rest of us, he was once a child for whom someone cared.

Like you, I have been in review of our letters and smile, laugh and 'well up' at the past months in our lives. We are and continue to experience, moments of heartache and heartbreak. And I still come back to the original fear—that we have left our children a "hell of a world."

Byron, I know that you place value on religion and faith. I, too, have faith, but not in an organized fashion. Being a reform Jew means enabling great freedom. Freedom to worship on our own terms. Cincinnati is the home of Reform Judaism as it was born here. Mainly, so that families like mine, could assimilate and not be scary to non-Jews. I have learned to keep my views private, to not take off the Jewish high holidays from work (as that places a mark on my back) and to blend.

Nora, our world traveler, will do anything for a free trip. This included going on the Jewish Birthright experience. This program says that any young Jew can go to Israel "free" before they are twenty-five if they have one Jewish parent. She (and her college friend Chloe) qualified. Both have a Jewish mom and Catholic dad. I will never forget the call that I received from Kennedy airport prior to departure. Nora said, "Mom, all of these kids had bar and bat mitzvahs. We know nothing about being Jewish. This is awkward."

I took my girls to temple several times for the high holidays and we celebrated Hanukkah. We belonged to a congregation once, while living in Florida. I figured that knowing a group of Jews may feel like kin. The rabbi sang his own home-written rock songs each Friday night and the temple was an over-the-top structure that Jim and Tammy Fay Baker would have liked. The fees were crazy, and the congregants seemed to place more emphasis on their wardrobes than their prayers.

Once we left Florida, our days as members were over. In the way that only can be so in Florida, the temple ended up selling their structure to a right-wing Christian Faith group.

Once in a while, I still attend the evening before Yom Kippur service (Kol Nidre) with my friend Sara. This service is solemn and pays tribute to our dead.

I have witnessed (for the past two Sundays) one of our region's largest multi-denominational Christian Churches' meetings on the riverfront. Lots of loud music and prayer and thousands of people sitting in the bright sunlight. This gathering certainly brings them solace. I believe that it may also spread COVID.

I continue to wait. To believe that my husband will be well tonight and that God looked out for a lapsed Catholic (he was an altar boy and considered becoming a priest) and lapsed Jew.

Hope your day is well.

Love,

Jennifer

Don't Fret

Friday, September 4, 2020
Cincinnati, Ohio

Dear Jennifer,

They buried Uncle Bennie today without a funeral—just a graveside service. The closest I was able to get was a photo sent to me by my sister, who was among our extended family in attendance.

Something similar happened when Etta, my dad's wife, died. The mortician took Etta home for him to say goodbye to her after fifty years of marriage.

This is another new normal in the time of COVID. We are going to have to take care of one another better, or this pandemic will forever undermine our country. I was talking to a physician friend today who said every pandemic throughout history has been somewhat of a leavening or even a disrupter. Certain classes have been eliminated and others have taken their place on the hierarchy of life.

Earlier today, I saw a new number: 410,000 COVID deaths by January if we keep up this pace. I don't disagree. What I can't understand is why Americans cannot seem to do the work to make things better. Do we crave "freedom" that much, to endanger the health of our fellow citizens?

We have 6% of the world's population and 25% of the world's cases and 10% of the world's deaths from COVID. Countries will not allow American citizens to travel. Jen, what does Nora say about this? What are her perceptions and the perceptions of others about our plight?

Trump and his apologists are to blame for our predicament. He was the one who called this a Democratic hoax. He has defied wearing a mask in public. And his lemmings follow suit. This is so hard for me to swallow.

Remember when bed bugs were a thing? Remember President Obama's beer with Henry Louis Gates and the police officer who accosted him in his own home? Remember when they talked about Obama's beige suit? Good times.

Meanwhile, I talked to my aunt who is the person with the biggest heart in the family. She was among about ten members of our immediate family at the graveside service. The two remaining sisters were offered no part in the planning of the funeral. Seems there was a disagreement years ago with Bennie's only child; thus, they were shut out. My aunt was disappointed with the errors in the funeral program and lamented the fact that Bennie's name was spelled incorrectly.

The emotions of death and the activity of laying a loved one to rest can bring out the worst in people. My advice to my aunt was not to fret, because in the long run none of this matters anyway.

Love,

Byron

On the Edge of Something

Sunday, September 6, 2020
Cincinnati, Ohio

Dear Byron,

The past few days have been a blur. Don came through the surgery well, but it took about twice as long as anticipated. Apparently, his hernia wrapped around some fat nodules and things were a bit gnarly. So, he had fat removed too. Why couldn't that have happened to me?

Free liposuction.

Today is Sunday. We have already taken four walks. Yes, four. Unbelievable. The surgeon came out and took me into one of those "private rooms" in which they give you the update. Forever, prior to the surgery, people said to me—he shouldn't hike so far and so much. It is dangerous to walk around without this "thing" fixed.

But we did. High up. Into thin air. To summits.

So, I asked the doctor about this and if we had engaged in risky behavior. He said, "Maybe a little, but I support the hiking risk. This type of physical activity is what keeps one healthy."

Since we got home we have mostly been in our apartment, except for the walks and we did eat dinner out last night. Walking our city will always be of interest to me and will stick with me long after I live here. I often (yes, am morbid) wonder what scenes from life will play (in my brain) on my deathbed.

I know that I will remember being on the top of Kilimanjaro (Tanzania, Africa) and swimming across Alcatraz (San Francisco)—but I also think that I will think of Cincinnati's Fourth Street that takes me from childhood through now—and somehow, I always wind up there. I have been fortunate to travel and, truly, it is missed.

Yet with people losing so much—from life, to lives of close ones, to jobs and to a future—it is a privilege to miss travel. Today we walked to Findlay Market. The streets were crowded, the activity was high, there were some masks; there were many without. Boarded up store fronts seem to be multiplying. I am not sure that this city will escape an economic downturn—which is all but certain to arrive.

We are again, on the edge of something.

We walk through neighborhoods that are as they have always been—poor—hard-scrabble living, but real. And then we come upon gentrified blocks that are painted bright colors, with fencing and big windows. While the "new" blocks are "pretty" one thinks about what washed away with the old.

I won't be around to see how this all turns out. But, isn't that life?

To some extent, when one chooses to depart a place that has been central to one's story, it becomes similar to what it might be like to attend one's own funeral. The people, the places, the aromas, the memories—they rise to the surface. Yet, I know that it is time.

We talked with the kiddos this weekend. I am hopeful that some way, somehow we can see Nora in real life. Caroline is in the South on her own. She clearly is ready to make a move and I am hoping that my encouragement of Santa Fe works—so that she is near. I have decided to, yes, get on a plane in early October, and head to see her. COVID continues to take so much from each of us and, as selfish as it might be, I miss my daughters.

Simply, this is unimaginable—that one short year ago we lived on a small planet and, with a passport in hand, and a simple plan, we could journey to see folks—wherever they might be. And now here we are in this big and dangerous world—each trapped in our own thoughts in our own space.

One foot in front of the other … or as they say about hiking … the hardest steps to take are the first and the last.

Have a great evening.

Love,

Jennifer

Beer, Dr. Pepper, A Honey Bun

Monday, September 7, 2020
Cincinnati, Ohio

Dear Jennifer,

Welcome to Labor Day 2020, where we find official unemployment hovering around 9%, but we all know the true number is higher than that.

Usually, in Cincinnati, especially during presidential election years, Coney Island would be packed with people and the AFL-CIO would hold its big day of speeches. This is another sign of how COVID-19 has significantly disrupted our lives. Today, we went to a place I'll bet you have not gone to in fifteen years, if ever—the Tri-County Mall.

When we moved to Cincinnati in 2002, we lived near this mall and would go at least once a week just to get out of the house. Our favorite thing was to go to the pretzel place for lemonade and a pretzel. Usually, we would have one or two of Loren's friends in tow. It is astonishing how the landscape of retail has changed over the past eighteen years.

Jen, there were literally thousands of people at that mall on any given Saturday. Our purpose there Monday was to take Simone to the barbershop to get a haircut. Flatliners is the lone occupant of the mall's second floor in what once was the Food Court area. This is where we would go after working up an appetite from all the walking. Subway, two Asian-inspired restaurants, Arby's, Chick-Fil-A, and Gold Star were among the options.

Today, it is ghastly. All that's left in the interior of the mall is LensCrafters and Flatliners. A B.J.'s Brewhouse anchors the western entrance. Dillard's, Macy's, and Sears are no more. Simone even remembered tossing pennies into the fountain there and mentioned that memory today.

Remember when Walmart was killing mom-and-pop stores? Online shopping, led by Amazon, has killed malls, and I'm not so sure these spaces can be repurposed into anything usable. Manny Mayerson, who made all that money building malls near interstates all over the country, would be turning over in his grave, wouldn't he?

Meanwhile, with the click of a button, we can have our heart's desire delivered to our home, sometimes within twenty-four hours. My, what a time we live in.

An aside: I forgot to tell you the rest of the story shared by my angry aunt. When the rest of the family left the cemetery, a small group of the Texas contingent walked over to Uncle Bennie's open grave and dropped in a honey bun, a Dr. Pepper and some Miller beer. Those are three of the four things he loved most in the world.

Like the ancient Egyptians, I hope these Earthly goods make him happy in the afterlife.

Love,

Byron

Throw Ice Cream in My Grave

Tuesday, September 8, 2020
Cincinnati, Ohio

Dear Byron,

Election is less than two months away. Amazing.

So much hangs in the balance.

Re: Labor Day Picnic. For years Don has attended for the unions that he has represented. The greats have all spoken there. It is quite a scene. If not for COVID, certainly Biden or Harris would have been speakers—Ohio being a swing state. And you are right. Here we are … Labor Day with American workers without jobs and many thinking that our unemployment rate (over 8%) is OK.

We have normalized all of it.

I know the Tri-County (Springdale, Ohio) mall well. I grew up close by and spent many days walking the place. I fantasized at how glam it seemed to work in one of the (then cool) stores such as The Limited. (And now the owner of Limited Brands is tied to Jeffrey Epstein—Les Wexner, Limited Brands CEO. My mom went to Ohio State with him.) Back then, no one wanted to hire me. I was this ethnic looking kid. The girls with whom I went to school had blonde hair and were cheerleaders who were selected for those jobs. At some point, I realized that I wasn't the "type" and became a long-term camp counselor.

Ultimately, a much better move.

Speaking of ethnicity. Today made me grumpy. I have realized that I do much better when I stay in, rather than come face-to-face with the likes of human-kind. I become angry. Today I went for an eye exam. They asked me to fill out new paper work. It asked my "race" and "ethnicity." I selected "choose to not answer." The joke is that Jews shouldn't get on lists.

My mom, sister and I visited Auschwitz (Poland) in 2011. My sister (phone in hand) announced, there is not a "four-square check in here." I laughed and said, "I am not sure that checking in is a good idea." Billy Crystal (comedian) has famously joked that our tribe is best kept off lists.

Therefore, my ethnicity was none of their business. I then didn't answer the question about my medication. The receptionist said, "what medications are you on?" I said (as I was hot by this time) "I am not sure that is your business." She notated "refuses to answer." Then I felt badly and listed them off—all of those drugs required when one is fifty-seven—and I am a healthy one.

The doctor was terrific and clearly anti-POTUS and pro mask. I then felt like I had been a pill. There is something about walking around in the heat and seeing suburban folks without masks thinking that they defy COVID. It is upsetting.

I love that foods were thrown into your Uncle Bennie's open grave. That is some kind of hope. I have this fear of being placed in the ground and have asked for cremation. But, heck, if people would put ice cream in with me, I could be tempted to change my opinion. I want to believe in an afterlife. Truly.

Yet, it could be worse.

Here I am talking death again.

Such a Jewish thing.

It is always about food and dying.

The one time that I made the kids go with me to Yom Kippur services (coming up soon) I was on a fast. Nora kept saying loudly, "Aren't you hungry?" Clearly, I had not educated them properly.

Today I sent a note out to the family about "doing" something for Don's 70th in November. Instead of, "We would love to do something for Don," I got back a slew of how complicated everyone's lives are and how COVID makes them afraid. Don and I talked, and he said, "Tell them that I will wait to turn seventy until next year." As a good wife does, I followed suit—and now am hearing from the masses, "How will we see you guys?"

In the meantime, we bear the end of the seasonal heated weather.

Try to not let the news drag us down.

Listen to music.

Laugh a little.

And roll our eyes.

We won't let this &^%$#(* bring us down.

Love,

Jennifer

Dance With the Humiliated

Wednesday, September 9, 2020
Cincinnati, Ohio

Dear Jennifer,

I've been paying attention today to the comments of one of my favorite columnists, Thomas Friedmann, about the latest on President Trump.

Friedmann says Trump supporters feel humiliated and Joe Biden should reach out to them, maybe even spend a week on the road listening to them. This group consists of small-town White people with high school degrees who now feel persecuted. Trump is seizing on their fears in ads and rhetoric. This sickens me. I may be wrong, but I rarely feel empathy for anyone who does not make it when the whole system is geared toward their success. That said, I think it's a good idea, politically.

He would be doing what I have been asking Republicans to do for decades: Listen to disenfranchised Blacks and Hispanics who have always had centrist/conservative tendencies out of necessity and who may not feel comfortable with existing political parties.

Bob Woodward, in his new book *Rage*, is reporting more of what we already know about the president—that he is racist, heartless, and out for himself. The revelation that he knew the depth of the danger of the novel coronavirus in February and did not implement a strategy is absolutely sickening and grotesque.

CNN has been reporting about the book since mid-day. I think I will purchase this book because Woodward does his homework, and to get another perspective on Trump, who supposedly gave Woodward eighteen separate interviews.

Jen, I am not one to place my hope for happiness in politics, but can't remember a time when I have felt so passionately about unseating a politician as I feel about ousting the current president.

I have many friends who support the president, friends who I love and do not want to lose. For the life of me, I cannot understand where loyalty comes from. I have to respect their views as they respect mine, I suppose. And part of our American experiment is that it allows for civil disagreement.

But I don't remember it being this hard in the past.

Love,

Byron

Really, Nineteen Years?

Friday, September 11, 2020
Cincinnati, Ohio

My Dear Friend,

It was so great to see you in real life, in the flesh Thursday—and strange, too. I think that I am becoming awkward as we see most people from a distance. ZOOM is certainly a bit different than sitting across a table. I am so proud of all of the steps that you have taken for good health.

Re: the Bob Woodward book about Trump (*Rage*) … my thoughts are that people like us say "of course he knew" (about the severity of COVID) and his supporters really don't care—and don't believe he is capable of wrongdoing.

So, another September 11th with social media full of "remember" and the day that changed America. At the time, we thought that this was as bad as things could get. And it was rough. On September 11, 2001, I sat in Cincinnati in a conference room (in a Tuesday insufferable corporate staff meeting). We had the "giant" TV on (we were in the TV business). My boss, who generally was a great man said, "Turn this off. It doesn't pertain to us."

Shortly, in walked some of my coworkers (in town from NYC) in a "state." They immediately rented cars and hit the road bound for home. We had been together the night before. On September 10, 2001, Don and I received an award for our community activism. My friends attended. We had drinks, delicious food and hope.

Tuesday wrought a new reality.

It took my co-workers about four days to get into their city. When they arrived, it was tough to enter and see their own families.

As a nation, we pulled together. We walked in a dazed state, hugged others, ate comfort food, fought a common enemy. And years later, our cities came back and we, again, became fat and happy.

We behaved like Americans.

Nineteen years have passed. Our nation has been prosperous. In 2020 we are then hit by "this thing" and have never been farther apart. There is hate in our collective blood. There is no hugging, still much eating, too many drugs and drinking, lots of guns and we are poised for anarchy.

And people in their eighties (like my mother and my BFF Kathleen's father) have never been more frightened in their lives. And we have left a horrible mess for our children.

9/11 was not the end of life as we knew it. Today may well be.

I had lunch with my mom during which we both cried. She is sad about both the macro (state of the world and a possible Trump re-election) and the micro (her husband's aging challenges, her retirement and my moving). But to each of us the micro is what impacts us most.

My mother, who generally holds praise tightly said, "Jennifer, you have made good choices. You have a good husband and children. You have managed to keep it all together."

To me, that means something. I once sought praise about my career accomplishments. It is remarkable how little that seems to matter.

We have people in our own family who are truly lonely and unhappy. Some who can't seem to shake it. I try to explain (as politely as possible) that it troubles me when people who have the privileges that we have had can't find the beauty in each day. I have learned that it is a mentality. We can locate unhappiness or joy anywhere—it is dependent upon our own momentary choice.

You and I talked the other day about our own mutual scrappiness. Have I done life correctly? Who knows? Have I struggled? For sure. Have people had my back? For sure. And the same for you. While you, my friend, are the grandson of sharecroppers—I am the great and granddaughter of immigrants. My ancestry was a bit cushier and we were not forced across the Atlantic in shackles.

My own difficulty is suspect and nuanced.

The two of us figure out how to get out of bed and make each day better.

For me, it often doesn't take much. A good cookie. A pretty flower. The smile of a friend. A decent joke. An epic sunrise. Interesting clouds. I suspect the same is true for you. There are all kinds of reasons to hate, to be sad, to complain and to ask why me?

But more importantly, why not me?

Why not today?

I think I can.

Together, we can.

Or as a great profit once said: "Yes, we can."

Hope your Saturday is decent.

Love,

Jennifer

Advice for the "Queen"

Saturday, September 12, 2020
Cincinnati, Ohio

Dear Jennifer,

My Saturday was terrific. Thanks for asking.

Your Friday letter sort of broke my heart when you talked about Judy's winding down her career and that her husband is also fading. This is the circle of life, however painful. It never gets any easier. During the final years of my mother's life, when I had to leave her and return to Ohio, I often wondered if this was the final conversation I would have with her face-to-face. In 2012, four years before she died, I had her offer a message of hope to all of her three granddaughters. I also had her try to remember her loves. She did not have much to offer on that subject, but she did say that the father whom I knew, Buddy McCauley was always a fun person.

Seven videos of that moment remain on my phone and in the cloud to this day. When I want her to talk to me, I just push play. If it is what you choose, I hope you are able to have Judy do something similar before you leave the Midwest for the Mountain West for good.

Ironically, Judy wrote to ask my opinion on something that someone was asking her to co-sign on, and I thought, "Me, giving advice to the Queen?" Yikes. Then of course I said yes. Our families are intertwined.

It was great to see you Friday as well. You are right. I think the session was great. Your childhood friend the photographer certainly has a warm spirit.

Here's something novel and somewhat of a lost art amid COVID times and for us in general: Jill and I went out on a date Saturday night, sort of. It was actually a marriage seminar sponsored by our church just outside of Cincinnati near the mall recently talked about. Did you know there's this whole industry in the faith community that provides small group content, sermon outlines, and special seminars like the marriage one that we attended?

The event was broadcast live featuring marriage and relationship experts and fun, too. I had heard of the comedian, Michael Jr., but I had never seen him perform until last night. Today, I am a HUGE fan. He is clean and his comedy is what I would describe as cerebral. He actually broke down his approach to comedy to us. Interestingly, he has begun including audience participation at his gigs as a way to help people. He talked of one lady he asked to come on stage. She was deaf. A translator helped.

"Is there anything you need help with?" Jr. asked. She said "no" twice. Then she said she and her husband had not taken a vacation in years because they take care of their special-needs son and they could not afford to hire a nurse to accommodate their son. Michael Jr. then asked if there was a special-needs nurse in the audience. There was one from the balcony who came forth.

And there were tears.

This is why I am a fan, not just because of his comedy, but because of his humanity. You know, we talk and write a lot about what's wrong with the world, but if we are blessed to discover the good I hope we can take a moment to recognize it and illuminate it.

The organizers of the seminar are based in the Dallas area, and their execution is as tight as a drum. We can learn a lot from them. Those who have pivoted to an all-digital way of doing business during COVID will find success.

Our action steps:

- We need to work on effective communication, meaning we really need to hear what the other is saying before responding.
- Understand what makes your partner happy and seek to do more of those things (for me, this means folding more clothes and listening more).
- Make time to have more dates.

We are coming up on our silver anniversary. Marriage is tough. It is a choice. It takes a lot of work, and then more work. Your children will drive you batty and make you proud. You will hurt your spouse, though hopefully never maliciously, and there will be days they will do something that will give you the butterflies of yesterday.

At the end of the day, Jill is still the kindest person I know. She is a loyal, funny, and caring mom. And she is the one who I want on the front porch with me when things are slower than they are now. It has been quite a ride.

Love,

Byron

Byron and Ljillauna (Jill) McCauley.

Leaving It Behind Me

Sunday, September 13, 2020
Cincinnati, Ohio

Dear Jennifer,

I walked into my first newsroom as a professional reporter, albeit an internship, at my hometown newspaper, *The Times of Shreveport*. Fifteen years later I would become editorial page editor of *The Times*. Ironically, the reporter who trained me to cover the Bossier City Police Department would become my direct report.

My first journalism job as a college graduate was in 1987 when I became a state reporter for the *Arkansas Gazette*, which had won two Pulitzer Prizes for civil rights coverage, including the integration of Little Rock Central High School. I'm reflecting on this moment because I believe I may be on the cusp of leaving daily journalism for good. I don't count my proverbial chickens, but it is time. I'm reflective today because I may get some news tomorrow that will change the course of this final quarter of my life and career. If it comes to pass, you will be the first to know.

Meanwhile, I have done many things in journalism that give me a real sense of accomplishment. This year, I was part of a team that won the national Education Writers Association's top award for education coverage on the plight of teachers in America.

Just yesterday, I wrote about the state's oldest cemetery designated for Black people, which has fallen into disrepair and is unkempt. The church that manages it has a Go Fund Me solicitation that had fewer than ten donors who had raised only $1,100 since March. Today, more than forty people had given more than $3,500 over twenty-four hours. That's impact.

A funny story: Nearly thirty years ago, I was among the first journalists to trek to Bentonville, Arkansas. to report on the first-ever Walmart Supercenter. You had to be there. Walmart was famous for bringing in celebrities to tiny Bentonville. (For example, I once saw Lee Greenwood and Vanessa Williams while covering one of their annual meetings.)

Back then, the Black population in Bentonville was probably less than 1%, but on that day there were at least two Black men in town who did not live there: me and San Francisco wide receiver Jerry Rice. Turns out, Rice and Joe Montana had spent the morning in Walmart hawking a new sports drink, Powerade. And they had just left for the airport in a limousine. As Jerry left, I walked in. I figured Jerry and I didn't resemble each other, but we were both in our twenties, we were both wearing dark suits and we had a similar haircut—the high-top fade.

Children in the new Supercenter began to follow me through the store. Pretty soon, there were a dozen. I did not know Rice had already come and gone. So, imagine my amazement when they all began asking me for my autograph. "Mr. Rice, Jerry Rice!" They even followed me out to the phone booth that I used to file my story to the newsroom. I still chuckle about that day and I hope that I will be able to share that story with Jerry Rice someday.

Conversely, a few months later I walked into my neighborhood Walmart on a Saturday dressed in a denim jacket and jeans. I was with Vince, a former defensive lineman who was 6-foot-5, 290 pounds. Upon entering the automatic doors, I removed my sunglasses, placed them in a pocket, and slipped on my eyeglasses. No more than ten feet inside the door, still in the entryway, security guards pounced on me. Someone said they saw me "steal" something. And here I was the reporter who covers your company, I thought.

Even though it became clear that I had not taken anything, I received no apologies and was utterly humiliated. I left the store, almost in tears because I was so angry. I vowed never to visit a Walmart again. Sadly, I did not report the action to Walmart leadership I knew in Bentonville, which I still regret. That day served as a wake-up call that still stings. That was one of my first real experiences with what I believed was racial discrimination.

It would not be my last, but that incident colored the way I saw the world. And here we are today dealing with a country in the midst of a culture war and a pandemic at once.

Nevertheless, Jen, we can always hope for a better tomorrow. I may have rambled a bit, but I want to thank you for choosing to be my friend. You make my life better.

Love,

Byron

Losing Our Furry Friends

Monday, September 14, 2020
Cincinnati, Ohio

Dear Byron,

I love the marriage date and seminar that you two attended. I LOVE LOVE the power that your writing has had and the good that you are leveraging for the Black cemetery. A random man donates big $$$ for desperately needed improvements! Your voice and words are needed. You seriously may have positively altered the fate of its future.

One person truly makes a difference.

I woke up at 6:30 am to a text from Nora. They had to put their five-year old cat to sleep. His name was Siepie and he contracted a fatal form of cat COVID. Some would say, "He is only a cat." My girls and I are very attached to our kittens. The loss of any life is difficult. And putting an animal to sleep—is heartbreaking.

And again, whether it is joyous or tough news we sit on opposite sides of this planet and communicate through technology that our ancestors would have never imagined. I said, "I really miss you honey." She said, "At least I can see you on FaceTime."

Yes, at least there is FaceTime.

Moving across the time and space continuum.

You and I have talked about the concept re: life's regrets. Or paths not chosen. I am of this ilk that (in my gut) knows that things will never work out optimally for me. I have always been average:

1. Midwesterner (land of the average)

2. Mediocre student

3. Decent looking with an ability to "glam it up"

4. Good teeth (best quality)

5. Born into a good family

6. A quick wit

7. Uncoordinated and awkward but good endurance

8. Too ethnic for many

9. Loads of compassion

10. A long attention span

And extraordinarily well-traveled.

This indicates that I have half a chance. The reality is that I am willing to show up and stand up. I have learned that to ultimately count I have had to "work" for whatever it is—nothing came too easily. And maybe that is a secret blessing.

So, regrets. Somedays I wish that I had become a psychiatrist, but not smart or disciplined enough. Sometimes I wish that I moved West sooner, but I would have missed my family of birth. I truly regret that I worked too much and didn't spend more time with my daughters—yet I also know that my work enabled advantages to our lives.

I do know that I have made the most of each moment. We Jews don't believe that much comes after life. While I am not sure that I believe in God (yes, you heard that right). I do believe that the here-and-now is all of it. We have all pondered during COVID times. We were jerked back and slowed down.

There is something true in adjusting our pace.

Living as if all there is, is this life that one holds does make one grateful. Maybe I am becoming weirdly grateful for the life that I have had as well. And maybe, with what is happening to this nation, we recognize the bounty of what has been called the USA.

Truth: I was forced off the fast track at age forty-five. I also realized that I was ready. When one is on the fast track she never looks sideways, only straight ahead. She often creates a wake that throws others off balance. She believes too much in the conviction of her own words and actions. She thinks she is invincible.

Until she's not.

You and I chatted about plastic surgery today. My quick reaction is "bring it on and fix this face." Yet the other "me" says, I look like I have lived for a while. I have learned a few things, yet not nearly enough. The longer I live, the less I know. I have realized that I am willing to "let myself age."

But when I do check out, I hope that I still have these leg muscles.

Yep, again on death.

Just another Monday.

Love,

Jennifer

Goodbye Cincinnati

Wednesday, September 16, 2020
Cincinnati, Ohio

Dear Byron,

I often use "exercise" time to compose. I often wrote speeches for myself (in the day when I delivered), practiced employee terminations to appear decent and wrote prose. Today, I "wrote" a letter to Cincinnati. While this is out of order from all else, it might resonate.

Dear Cincinnati,

The moving truck arrives on November 20th. Our last ten days will be spent in an airbnb. The boxes will be pulled out of storage for what will most certainly be our final move to our last resting place. Yet, today do we really know what the nation will resemble (or who we will be) in two months.

This could be all for naught.

Don and I have moved together eight times. We have downsized more than once. It is clear, no offspring wants our stuff.

The time has come to say farewell. While I am not officially native as I was born in Canton, Ohio and my parents hailed from Charleston, West Virginia and Canton—you held me as one of your own. My family came to Cincinnati in the early 60s. My sister was born here, and we quickly moved to the burb known as "Wyoming, Ohio." Wyoming (where the earliest settlers arrived in 1805) is/was a placid, polite place and boasts some of the best public schools in the nation. My mother has lived in the same home there since 1970.

I have known two of my closest friends since we were toddlers. And yes, like any Cincinnatian knows, upon meeting anyone in "town" I quickly ask which high school they attended. In Cincinnati, high school is one's school, not university. My grown daughters attended my high school alma mater.

They believed it to be small and narrow.

While I have moved from Cincinnati three times—to Colorado, Michigan and Florida—I have always returned. I have lived in Cincinnati's great neighborhoods (Wyoming, Mt. Adams, Hyde Park, East Walnut Hills, Clifton and Downtown). Each is historic with its own story and classic architecture.

Cincinnati, you raised both my children and me well. You let us into decent schools, gave us meaningful employment, invited us to join boards, found good doctors, kept us safe and wrapped your luscious hills around our hearts. We are not one of the old or wealthy families, but we were included. We became close friends with several of your mayors and broke bread with power brokers in your state's capitol.

You accepted our outsider and otherness. I was never a committed Jew, which was apropos in Cincinnati, home of one of the oldest Reform Judaism communities in the nation. While I was never an insider, you invited me in close enough that I could make a difference. My daughters understood that on most days we would run across people whom we knew. They found this stifling.

I suspect (once they are older) they will recognize some value.

I was in a scandal as I became involved with my husband while he was married to another woman. I too was married to another man. I found two husbands here. While the rumor mill beat me up briefly, we also were accepted as Don and Jennifer Mooney.

My mother became an important community member. Most recently she was named "A Great Living Cincinnatian." This designation is only crowned upon those who have accomplished the most for our community.

I have been one of your harshest critics. I have resented you "not" moving forward with new ideas and being slow to execute. Yet somehow, I have understood that you are measured, steady and constant. You might be a bit boring, but always reliable. This is to be taken seriously.

These last months bring some tears and I find myself often choked up as I cross streets and structures with memories. This ranges from your Coliseum in which my dear friend Peter Bowes was trampled to death at the 1979 Who concert to the site of my daughter's wedding.

Cincinnati is where I took my first steps, had my first dates, smoked pot for the first time and eventually became a professional. When my daughters are my age, they will not have the panacea of memories and times have changed. My own daughters have left and become citizens of the world.

In recent years, my most treasured activity has been swimming across the Mighty Ohio (to Kentucky) and back. Or the body of water that we believe delineates the north from the south and slavery to freedom. In our last months we have chosen to live on her banks and often remark about what it might have been like all of those years ago.

Cincinnati, you are confused. Are you the most Southern City in the North or the most Northern City in the South. You speak a little funny. People often can't place you, but you can qualify for that flat "broadcast" voice when necessary. You have raised presidents and titans of industry. You have been in the national news for bigotry and racism.

At the same time, your natural beauty, appreciation for the arts and longevity is admirable.

The day comes quickly when we will pull out for the last time as residents. This has been my homeplace. We will often visit family and good friends. We will marvel at your changes and how you have remained the same. I imagine (if still on the planet) I will come back as a much older woman and reminisce about the old days.

Thanks for being in my life.

On to Taos, New Mexico. Take care of yourself. You are a good one.

Love always,

Jennifer

Caroline's Wedding at The Belle, Cincinnati, Ohio. Leigh (Jennifer's sister), Nora, Jennifer's Mom, Caroline, and Jennifer.

Goodbye Fourth Estate, Fare Thee Well

Thursday, September 17, 2020
Cincinnati, Ohio

Dear Jen,

I have had a mind shift. Too often, when we are dealing with untenable events or circumstances in our lives, our brains start to do weird things. Things like tell our inner being that you are not good enough. Tell yourself that you will never be able to do this or that. It's the small voice that can wreak havoc or prop you up.

For the past few years, it has not propped me up. I have fought with the voice in my head for years now. It all started when I was downsized from the most lucrative job I had ever held. I applied for 100 or more jobs, all over the country. I was a finalist for several. But nothing panned out. Along the way, we lost our dream home, we downsized to one car, and we stopped eating out. And then I had my health challenge. We began to pity ourselves because to us our problems had reached biblical rankings.

One day, I asked myself, "Why not us? Why not me?" Even through the fire, we never missed a meal. Sure, they were leaner, but we never missed a meal.

Fast forward to 2020. Be careful what you wish for. You might get a pandemic. Yet, today, I accepted the offer to leave my current organization and begin a marketing communications job with a venture-capital funder of seed-stage tech start-ups. Thank you, Jen, for your support and encouragement through all of this. Even in a pandemic and a significantly depressed economy,

I am leaving a struggling industry to an exciting opportunity, which is to help support and affirm dreams and dreamers. How cool is that?

Next, I will be working on a letter of resignation. I will be humble and thankful for what journalism and, specifically, my organization has provided. I also gave a lot of blood in twenty-two years with the company. Sadly, I don't have very much to show for it, financially, but I do have plenty of readers who I hope got joy from my work over the years.

I'm sure I will miss it for a little while but as one of my former TV anchor friends told me from Seattle, "Byron, the feeling passes quickly." He is an actor now and has not looked back in fifteen years.

And so here I go, Jen. For the third and final time I will leave journalism and my organization. This doesn't have to be as awkward as it seems. People move on every day, and they get replaced. I'm no different. Cincinnati has become my adopted hometown, and it is likely where I will die.

At the end of the day, I want to make a positive difference in the world, and there is more than one way to do that, right?

Love,

Byron

Mama Obama

Friday, September 18, 2020
Cincinnati, Ohio

Dear Byron,

I know that you are having a tough day. In your mind, you see yourself as a columnist and you have given that up to move to a new place on the continuum. It is always hard when we self-identify as or with something; a career designation, a spouse, a parent, a sibling, a community-member, a child and the picture morphs.

I also know that this is more challenging for men than for women. However, my eighty-one-year old mother is struggling as she departs being the head of an organization that she founded twenty-one years ago. She is the one, candidly, who taught me to not tie my identity into my career—that it would wreck me.

And yet, here she is.

But it might be different when you depart a place that you built. And one that truly impacted the planet and thousands of people.

Nothing I have done matches the significance of her own work.

Writing and being in the "media" does become a brand.

Trust me. You will be better for this. And you will still write.

Life today is about constant reinvention. I have been thinking through the times in which I have been the most immersed—learned, delivered value, experienced. It was generally not at the office. I had titles, received awards, had stellar performance evaluations. But I always knew that was for a "job" that I was doing, not for who I am. Focus on the "who you are part." What they say is true, "a good job doesn't love you back."

My thoughts have drifted to travel today. I wear a large klatch of beaded bracelets on my left arm. These were "sewn" onto me in the summers of 2016 and 2017 by a few Samburu Mamas (A Kenyan tribe). The bracelets are not able to be removed. They break and fall off slowly. Over the years, I have lost parts and someday they will be lost. It is remarkable that there are any remaining.

Last night a few strands broke free. To me, further breaking my tether to Kenya.

Kenya is a place to which I became deeply attached. I have traveled there a handful of times, first to Safari and later to work in villages among the "real" Kenyans. I ultimately spent time with Mama Obama (one of the President's grandmothers). She scolded me for wearing slacks.

She was-is a most delightful woman.

When one leaves Safari and White environment, one locates both a life that clings to age-old traditions and young people that hope for a future. While the Kenyans speak both English and Swahili, some only speak their native languages. A few tribes are still highly traditional with villages, plural wives, warriors, chiefs and little schooling for the children. When with these people, we westerners ponder:

1. Sadness that there is still genital mutilation (girls).
2. Sadness that the women seem to do all of the work.
3. Wonder at "who am I to judge?"
4. Wonder about "maybe these people are far happier" than we greedy Americans.
5. I surround myself with crafts from the mamas—with a solid place in my thoughts and heart.

Like any other place, Nairobi is a thriving (if chaotic) center of commerce. To be White or (mzungu) in East Africa is to stand out, to be looked at with curiosity, to have one's hair touched by children with giggles. Nairobi moves fast with (what appears) to be an incoherent plan, but at the same time is stunningly vibrant.

There is nothing as liberating as gazing across the savannah, a vastness of land, acacia trees, rolling hills and the occasional large animal. The Samburu live in mud huts with their protein eaten primarily from the goat. I was in a home on a Sunday. The wife spent the morning cooking (in her crude kitchen). I enjoyed a rice dish with pieces of "black" throughout. A co-traveler asked about this piece. We were told "goat intestines." I continued to chew.

Slowly.

Today I sit on my rooftop in the urban basin. I can see the Mighty Ohio and deep inside the two sports stadiums. The air is clearer than it has been in weeks. The smoke (that has blown in from the forest fires in the west) has abated, for now.

I am thinking of people on the other side of the planet. I am remembering what a privilege it has been to travel. I am remembering when I asked about poverty and hunger in Kenya being told by a native that, "Africa can feed herself." I felt ashamed for asking.

While Kenya is far different than our nation, her way of raising her people has worked for centuries. Yes, there are tribes who battle, mamas who are killed by lions, young people who want to journey to America and corrupt politicians, but there is also a deep history.

I have learned the most in places in which I was in the minority, where I didn't have a name, a title or a place. The best days are those in which I opened my mind and heart to what others have to teach. I listened.

You are moving to your next place. You are traveling.

This is all good.

Love,

Jennifer

Notorious RBG

Saturday, September 19, 2020
Cincinnati, Ohio

Dear Jen,

Ruth Bader Ginsburg died last night. This, we know. What has emerged today in politics borders on travesty. The president has promised he will nominate her replacement while Ginsburg's body was yet warm.

How quickly the Republicans forgot what they did to President Obama, when they blocked Obama's nominee, Merrick Garland, who was liked by both parties. Led by Sen. Mitch McConnell, the Republicans are hypocritical. Before, they decided principles (that the next president nominates a Supreme Court Justice) would guide them. Now, they have apparently thrown principles out of the window as the opportunity to name a successor to RBG is too great an opportunity. And, of course, Trump has no shame.

Trump has every right to nominate someone with a little more than a month before Election Day, but if he does, I hope voters will express their disapproval.

Enough of that.

I cannot believe you and Don were in Washington Park last evening when shots rang out. Jen, it's hard to figure where all of this violence in Cincinnati is coming from. I went over to Irving Street Wednesday to get a sense of what happened from people gathered around the street that dead-ends at the Colonial apartment complex, which has a history of violence. In January 2014, police reported thirty-six reports of "shots fired" on Irving. There were four killings there. That was when the community took action. With police, community leaders like Ozie Davis and apartment management, the bad element was reduced.

Now, as we mark the seventy-fourth homicide in our town this year, things have never been worse. The people who died at the apartment this week were executed.

A woman and two men were found dead, having suffered gunshots to the back of the head. Police said their bodies had been there for a while. I was also told the woman's young son discovered the bodies. The victims had no weapons and there were no signs of struggle.

No one knows what happened, but it occurs to me that some of the people that I interviewed might have had something to do with the killings, or at least had information about who is responsible.

We will probably be left to wonder for a long time. And I'm worried about the trauma any kid would experience upon discovering bodies that were in an active state of decomposition.

Jen, you and Don can feel thankful to be moving to the Mountain West, and particularly to your little town. It is imminently more peaceful, and the threat of experiencing random street violence is slim to none. I'm saddened that you guys found yourselves in such a dangerous situation last night during your urban hiking and dinner outing.

I have fancied myself as an urban dweller, but I know I am a rural/suburban person at heart. With every incident of violence that happens in Cincinnati, I want to seek refuge back to the suburbs or to the woods.

But here's the thing, Jen: That's a false sense of security, too, because I know that crime can happen anywhere. In fact, in our own former upscale neighborhood, the crime committed against our family was life-altering.

At the end of the day, we can just hope and pray for goodness and mercy to prevail.

Love,

Byron

She Doesn't Wear
High Heels Anymore

Sunday, September 20, 2020
Cincinnati, Ohio

Dear Byron,

We are in what is called by American Jews "the days of Awe." They start on the Jewish New Year (it was Friday) and last through Yom Kippur, the Day of Atonement. We are to think deeply about how we can be better people. I am a lapsed Jew. I do believe in the days of Awe these days. My father's family was from a serious conservative old-world sect. As a child, I went with him to Temple and fasted. My most vivid memory is when my paternal grandmother died. My father stood before his dresser (in boxer shorts) and recited the Jewish prayer for the dead each day for one year.

In my mind, I still hear the Hebrew words. Some of the only Hebrew words that I know.

These days of Awe are most strange. On this Jewish New Year, a shooting occurred fifty yards from Don and me as we walked in our city. I thought that the pop-pop-pop-pop-pop was firecrackers. I have never heard a handgun being fired. I saw people on either side looking at one another in disbelief. I heard someone call the police. Don said, "Let's get out of here." Minutes prior we were listening to a man play jazz and enjoying a drink.

We returned home to the news that RBG had died. By morning she was declared by Jews as the righteous. She died on the New Year, a day that only the best among us pass. Social media feeds are filled with her stories and politics. Will this open the moment for the presidential race? Will all of her work be forgotten?

I had lunch with my mom yesterday. We met in Wyoming at Gabby's. Gabby's is a small local joint with an old school Italian owner. They offer outdoor seating. The proprietor catered Caroline's rehearsal dinner. Crowds unnervingly packed Wyoming for an Octoberfest band. The environment was festive, upbeat, and scary.

COVID times.

My mother and I rapidly covered a range of topics that included your life changes, my sister, her retirement, Nora's cat dying, and shoes. Yes, shoes. My mother rivals the greats in her capacity to purchase stylish shoes. She is always in heels (high heels). My grandmother was also a fashionista, but not the original. The original was my great grandmother Rebecca—the legend says she was the most beautiful. Her photograph stood on my own grandmother's bureau until Grandma died at 104. My mom's parent's portraits sit on her bureau. I have a drawing of my mother (from 1951) at age twelve in our bedroom.

During the shoe conversation, my mom said, "I am not wearing high heels anymore." My feet are now in much better shape. I said, me neither. I let her know that our mutual handyman and family friend, Brian, commented recently on her shoe collection. I thought about my grandmother and how she was "turned out" until the last day of her life.

Looking like we have put forth effort matters in this clan.

It has occurred to me that this is a juncture point in both Black and Jewish America. While we have been systematically destroyed, we have always worn our "best" to the gallows. Our concerns have been about food. What is the recipe? What are we having for our next meal?

And about clothing. How do I look? Where did you purchase?

Good food and good clothing. It matters.

In even the poorest Kenyan villages, people came to the group meetings "dressed."

God help me when I show up to see my mother not "done up."

My mother got up to go to the ladies' room. After about ten minutes, I decided to go check on her. Beneath her stall, I observed four-inch wedge heels. Nope, these are not pumps, stilettos, or traditional heels, but darn those babies are high.

I laughed to myself. She is still wearing heels.

No matter what happens to any of us, we dress for the best.

Have a great Sunday.

Love,

Jennifer

Remembering Mother

Monday, September 21, 2020
Cincinnati, Ohio

Dear Jen,

I need to get out of my feelings.

I officially resigned today. I don't know what I'm supposed to feel. I'm excited about my next adventure, to be sure, but I can't help but feel a little bit tentative as I leave journalism for good. I am grateful for this next opportunity, and it's going to be amazing. The energy at the tech venture capital firm is infectious. The optimism is contagious.

And I shouldn't look back at a career that was. I still keep newspaper clippings from stories I wrote thirty years ago. A friend once told me to toss them out, that those heady days were never coming back. That is no more clear than today as I finally walk away from a business that left me a long time ago. I will miss phone calls from readers either mad, sad or inspired by the stories I found and told. I will miss the feeling of exhilaration of finding just the right word to tell the story.

This is a business. When I left, no one said, "What can we do to keep you?" This has happened in the past many times. But what do I expect? I chose to leave. I surrender with the hope of better days…

Yesterday, we celebrated what would have been my mother's 77th birthday. Mom died four years ago on the day before our 20th wedding anniversary. And so from now until the end of our time on Earth, our anniversary will also mark the anniversary of losing mom. When I say "we" I mean my aunt in Texas, immediate family and some cousins.

I had everyone call in on Zoom, expecting them to congregate together. Instead, four people in the same room called in from their phones, creating horrible audio. It reminded me of those commercials with older family members trying to navigate technology but mightily struggling.

Debra, whose zest for life and vigor is unmatched, had purchased a cake and a huge bag of Werther's Originals, which was Mom's favorite candy. Medicine and oxygen made her mouth dry, and Werther's candies provided a functional, sweet treat. This was the first time we all had gotten together since Mom's funeral. We sang the birthday song twice and we all shared memories. It is always a struggle for me when I'm around my aunts and we are discussing my mom. That's because she was their "mom" first. There is no story that I can tell about Mom that they can't best. It's not a competition, mind you, but it is frustrating.

Their memories of her are as vivid as yesterday. They knew her when she was fierce. She graduated from high school at sixteen and went to college at seventeen. Debra presented a picture of her in 1962. She was eighteen and beautiful! She could sew and cook and paint and figure things out. She was a terrific listener and giver of advice. She never raised her voice and always wore a smile, even when she was admonishing someone. The story that I told about Mom was about condoms. I hid some in a crevice in the wall when I was a teenager. She found them and left them there. And for all I know, they may still be there, because Lord knows I never used them.

The story was cringe-worthy and better left unmentioned. I always seem to go too far.

To a person, the rest of the stories had something to do with advice Mom gave them, a gift they received, and a gesture of unconditional love from her.

We all had a good time, and I hope we do it again next year. I'm still working through old feelings, and anytime there is an opportunity to remember and share I learn more about myself, about her and about others.

Family dynamics are complicated, but I wouldn't trade them.

Love,

Byron

In a Country of Mothers

Tuesday, September 22, 2020
Cincinnati, Ohio

Dear Byron,

I know that your resignation was bittersweet. Your life has been in putting words to paper and interaction with an engaged public. You have made a difference. I know that this is only the beginning of your influencing the public. The world of journalism has changed. It hurts. As one who has worked in the media business—what has happened to the world of media is ugly.

We seem to now have a cast of talking heads promoting themselves.

Yet, I also have hope that we now are able to also hear from the average citizen who speaks their own voice to communicate across multiple platforms.

Your new employer is fortunate to have hired you. You will be able to use your own learnings and business acumen to move forward entrepreneurs. And these big thinkers are the future.

Your mom sounds like an amazing woman. I love the image of her "Werther's Originals" and the mighty young woman who moved so fast and accomplished so much. Women like your mom built our nation. While we all mourn the death of RBG—and she certainly moved all women forward—it is the individual mother who has the greatest impact.

We each are a product of the mothering that we received. Your mom did good. She raised you.

Being a mother, myself, it is the most fulfilling, challenging and frightening role. One wonders what it is that will stick with their children long after they (the mom) is gone. One wonders how she has possibly ruined her children. I often replay scenes in my head and remember things that I said and cringe. And there are the times in which I witness my own children (adults really) and realize that they turned out quite well.

I have been hard on my own mother and she on hers. My grandmother (the fashion plate) was born in 1908 and died 104 years later. She was able to spend time with her great grandchildren. Nora "Esther" is named after Grandma Esther. Grandma was not educated. She was born of little means. Her role was raising her own daughters. She was an engaged and committed grandmother. My own mom describes her as a woman who (while she did much good) did not stand up for her own children when their father was angry.

I knew a different woman, a grandmother who had mellowed.

My own mother is an icon. She graduated from high school at sixteen and traveled across the country to attend the University of Colorado. She stayed for two years and then transferred to Ohio State, to be closer to home. She was a stay-at-home-mom for many years, consistent with people of her generation. While I was in middle school, she earned an M.A. and Ph.D. She went to work around that time, as she and my dad divorced, and he left her with nothing. Fortunately, her parents helped. I still remember (as a thirteen-year-old) sitting with them when they told us that we could stay in our home. While my grandfather had done well, he was a man of the depression era (who was born poor) and was very careful with any spending.

My mom, year by year, built a career and a name for herself. We were older and didn't need her at home. Once when my own girls were small, I said, "Mom, it is so hard to work and to raise kids at the same time. I witnessed you (as a mother) and all of the time that you spent with us and then later with a career. How did you do it?"

She simply said, "Jennifer, you were not supposed to do it all at once."

Today my mom is eighty-one. Her retirement is on November 9, from an organization that she founded—one designed to support moms and babies who are at risk. She is not at all certain that she is ready to step back. I have continued to say, "It is time. You have worked many years." It is clear that this is her calling. It came naturally. Her father was a pediatrician who believed that no sick baby should go out in the cold. She often went with him on house calls. She also explained that for doctors to best understand their patients (in this case, babies), observation of the home life was vital.

Her program "Every Child Succeeds" is about home visitation. Gramps would be proud. The sometimes-angry man who demanded so much of his eldest and brilliant daughter, Judy.

After RBG died, I said aloud, "Why did RBG wait? Obama could have filled her seat." Don received a text from my stepdaughter who said, "I think Judy waited, like RBG because, she was in the generation who had to wait until they were older to become what it was they were intended to be."

Yes, that's it.

Sometimes it's helpful when we have lessons in life in real time instead of in hindsight.

Talk soon.

Love,

Jennifer

Justice Denied

Wednesday, September 23, 2020
Cincinnati, Ohio

Dear Jennifer,

Jill and I were driving when Kentucky Attorney General and Breonna Taylor Special Prosecutor Daniel Cameron announced that there would be no charges directly related to Taylor's death.

At first, with all the legalese, it was difficult to figure out what the charges meant: one of the three officers in the shooting charged with wanton endangerment. As the day grew into night, it became clear that there would be no justice for the family of Taylor. On social media, people are apologizing to Taylor, saying her neighbors got justice before she did. Breonna died. But the charges reflect a police officer's reckless behavior in shooting up Taylor's apartment with the bullets piercing walls and traveling into the apartments of neighbors.

Two police officers in Louisville were shot tonight as protesters registered their dissatisfaction. That's not the answer. Breonna Taylor's death at the hands of police in March has represented a rallying cry and an example of over-policing that sent America into weeks of protests. Breonna's death came to light after the killing of George Floyd in Minneapolis.

I've been trying to make sense of the suddenness of it all. The fact that a new generation is protesting to call attention to police brutality saddens me, but policing needs to change. Some questions: How it is that Black people continue to be disproportionately arrested, jailed, and killed by law enforcement? Why does this happen now, even though modern-day police forces include those who have lived in a multiracial world, presumably with the opportunity to have a diverse set of friends? Why is it that police officers can execute "no-knock" warrants, especially in a place where children are endangered?

I have been a part of a grand jury. Grand juries are heavily influenced by the evidence and the influence of the prosecuting attorney. If the attorney wants to push forward on a case, they will sway the jury one way. If not, they will sway the jury another way. I blame Cameron for this outcome. I hope I'm wrong, but he is flying Mitch McConnell's flag and sees himself as the future of the Republican Party in Kentucky. He sees himself as a senator, and possibly a president, one day.

Meanwhile, the family of Breonna is left to mourn the loss of their daughter, sister, niece and cousin with no one apparently held accountable for her death. I have written about this case in my column. One person challenged me as to why I did not mention the fact that Breonna's boyfriend fired the first shot, which caused police to fire indiscriminately more than thirty times. My thought was that if someone is trying to break into my house and I have a legal firearm, I can't say that I wouldn't shoot, too.

The boyfriend fired low, so as not to hit organs or the head, according to Cameron. Again, this feels like justice denied, which has been the case so often for those on the receiving end of perceived injustice. The cards are always stacked against them—as they were stacked against Mamie Till, Michael Garner, Sandra Bland, Freddie Gray, Jacob Blake, Samuel DuBose, and a host of others.

Jen, this especially hurts because this is not representative of the America which I grew up loving and honoring. And this is why Michele Obama said she was finally proud of America after her husband was elected, because of our history of disregarding and, in fact, harming Black bodies and brains. The thanks she got was excoriation from tone-deaf conservatives.

We are friends, you and me. Authentically. We get each other. We appreciate each other's differences and respect them.

I often wonder what our America would be like if we simply embraced our differences and appreciated them—like Reagan and O'Neill, like Scalia and Ginsburg, like us. What if there had been no Jim Crow laws and if the powers that be were not dead set on maintaining White supremacy at all costs? Imagine the prosperity. Imagine the collective freedom. Imagine the size of the GDP and the economic tide lifting all boats.

We would have fewer people behind bars, needing government help, and more pursuing education and job creation. If we did not have this artificial construct of race, we would be able to live in harmony without fear of the "other." The money we would save on prisons and police forces and public assistance could be better served in other places.

I am beginning to sound Polly-Anna-ish, but when you think about it we have wasted so much on the wrong things as a direct result of the sins of the fathers.

Every time we lose a Sandra Bland or a Samuel DuBose or a Breonna Taylor under the same set of circumstances, it serves as a reminder of how recent our segregated past is. We continue to rip the scab off a sore that is 400 years deep. It will never heal.

Sadly,

Byron

Broken Dreams

Thursday, September 24, 2020
Cincinnati, Ohio

Dear Byron,

I am not sure that we will heal. I am not sure that a country that commits our crimes, for hundreds of years, gets beyond the pain. But maybe we recognize this and get along. Maybe we become better people. In these times of "hate" and forty percent of our public being OK with bigotry, I am afraid.

Yet I can't imagine how you and Jill truly feel, the parents of three daughters. My social feeds are full of friends crying and believing that their own lives have no value. My heart hurts.

I asked Don how bad he thought it could get with a second Trump term. He shook his head and said, "I never thought it could get this bad." I remember (when young) asking my own father if there ever could be a Holocaust here. He said never. "We have a system of checks and balances."

So much for that.

We live in frightening times. I believe that fifty years from now, 2020 will be looked upon as the time that the American Dream died. You and I and a random editor spent the other afternoon on the phone. I gathered that he believed that our thoughts on a fractured America were too lofty. That most people would not relate.

I disagree.

Our generation and our children now live in a country in which our greatest dreams and hopes are broken. To be sure, we are not the first generation for this to descend upon. But, much like Europe in the 30s and 40s, our way of life is threatened.

Our most basic freedoms.

I saw Martin Luther King, III interviewed last night. He said, "My father would not believe that we are fighting the same battles again." While he is on point, humans don't change. We seem to always revert to our own personal hierarchy of needs. And when people feel threatened, they battle. Sadly, some seem to believe that putting others down so that their own tribes may rise up, is an expeditious way to personal success.

Most individuals cannot grasp that making the "pie" larger nets greater results. The dog whistle that our president blows is calling out the worst in us. And every time I walk down a street, I look into people's eyes (above the mask) and wonder which side someone is on. Do they live with courage or fear? Hope, or have they given up?

Have their dreams died?

Some believe that the American Dream is about financial success. Some believe that one can become an American and become whatever one wants to be. To me, it has always been about freedom. It has been about equality. It has been about "huddled masses yearning to breathe free."

Our nation was born on weak footing. We were built by the hands of other humans (removed from their own lands) and beaten into submission. We removed humans who had lived here for thousands of years. We grabbed, we beat, we stole, we claimed it to be ours. We wrote a constitution for "one nation under God," yet we behaved as Godless souls.

Some of us came from people who were not slave owners, who were forced out of someplace else and believed that America, this United States, was better. But much of the USA's collective DNA is in "owning others." And somehow, we seemed to have gotten pretty far into "being better than our forefathers."

Yet how quickly that eroded. How fragile.

I am not sure what happens next. I am not sure how we make our children safe.

This, from one with Hope.

A big question in the world of psychology is, "Are people able to change?" I have wracked my brain with this question for decades. I fundamentally believe that humans are capable of learning and engaging in new behavior. And that we can be reformed.

But do we truly change? We are basically lazy. Change takes work. It takes constant reminders and vigilance. It becomes too easy to be swayed. To a great extent, once we are adults, it seems that we don't really change.

So, we live with the forty percent that believe what has happened to Breonna Taylor is OK and we link arms with our tribe in hopes of better days. I am not sure what else we do.

I close with this:

What is the American dream? The American dream is one big tent. One big tent. And on that big tent you have four basic promises: equal protection under the law, equal opportunity, equal access, and fair share. —Jesse Jackson

He would also say: "Keep Hope Alive."

Love,

Jennifer

Fierce Grace

Saturday, September 26, 2020
Cincinnati, Ohio

Dear Jennifer,

This letter is to you and about you.

A long time ago when I lived in Mississippi, a group of us got together in the home of a local psychologist and we discussed the tiny chapters of a book called *Jesus CEO*. The longest chapter in this book, by Laurie Beth Jones, is about three pages. It takes a moment in the Bible in which Jesus teaches a lesson and applies it to leadership in a modern world.

I still rely on the Bible today. I like all of the parts when Jesus showed righteous indignation.

I tell you this because at the end of our sessions together, we all wrote to one another the attributes we saw. To this day, it is one of the best exercises I have ever done with others. It is truly a gift when you get to hear positive truths about yourself from others. Sometimes the perceptions are familiar. Other times they may surprise you.

So, Jen, here it goes. This is all that I see in you and have also learned from you.

You are fierce. This is perhaps the one trait about you from which I benefit the most. I have lost some of my ferocity. You helped me find it again. Even when I was having second thoughts about whether we should write to each other like this, you took the idea and ran with it, producing our very first letter. I fiddled about, wondering whether the idea was pretentious. You went with it, and here we are. You employ the same ferocity when you are pitching something for a client or finding a different way to do something if you encounter a roadblock. So, with apologies to Jesus, I sometimes find myself asking, "WWJD?" What Would Jennifer Do? Increasingly, the answer is, "She would slay these fools." So, I slay.

You offer grace. So, Jen, you were close to the C-Suite in your corporate career. You traveled about the world and met and influenced very important people, including presidential candidates, movie stars, and famous artists. I know you had to be tough in these environments sometimes. You had to be decisive. Sometimes, yes, you had to be ruthless. But I have seen you offer grace so many times, including to me. This is a great gift to others who may not meet your expectations right then and there. But, your extension of grace encourages others to move forward. I thank you for that.

You are a terrific mom and wife. In these times, I even hesitate to say this. Women choose not to marry and choose not to have children. Being a wife and mother is a choice and a gift. I have a great example in Jill, who faithfully develops our three daughters and me as well. You do the same. You take care of Don and you counsel your daughters through life. I have come to know them as great people through you. Having been married twenty-five years and raising three children, I know how difficult a job this is. I admire the way you prioritize your family as you do life with others. This a gift and an example to others.

You are kind and generous. We need more people in the world who exhibit these traits. How do I know this? Because so many people are willing to help you accomplish things without question. This is a sign that you have treated others well over your lifetime. It's important that we build bridges, not walls, as one of my dear friends signs at the end of her emails. I try to do this, too, though I don't know how well. It is my nature to be kind and generous with my time and talent and treasure. But I struggle, honestly, with how to process hurt. I have grown less forgiving as I have gotten older. And I guess this is to be expected. No one wants to be a whipping boy! But I could do better.

You respect people and you listen well. Jen, in our business, we have to be able to listen well to the ideas of people, whether those ideas align with the things we believe or not. We have to learn to navigate even the most contentious relationships, because, frankly, our roles in serving others work being neutral. Even so, it's a good habit. I have seen you respect those who may not deserve it, and I have seen you root for those who don't have a huge cheering section. Again, this is a great gift.

I'm going to stop here, but there is much more. I just wanted to take this moment to praise the traits that help me every day.

I close with Robert Burns:

> O, wad some Power the giftie gie us To see oursels as others see us! It wad frae monie a blunder free us, An' foolish notion.

Love,

Byron

High Road

Sunday, September 27, 2020
Cincinnati, Ohio

Dear Byron,

Happy Sunday. As we get closer to the election, I feel as if I am waiting for the world to end. Through my eyes, I see everything as if it is about to disappear. I am truly concerned that we will face another Trump term. They know how to steal this election.

On a happier note, thanks so much for your over-the-top words about me. I truly hope that I am that woman. I most certainly have bad qualities; envy, vanity, sometimes extreme dislike and maybe manipulative. People wear me down. But I do try to be "better."

My mother and I walked 1.2 miles through the city center to eat outside on Main Street. It was her first time downtown since the pandemic. I showed her the many closed storefronts (not to be reopened) and she shook her head. It is clear that her greatest concern is what will happen to this nation.

We sat on the street outside at restaurant LouVino with a crowd inside. An elderly man came to our table (with his cane and shopping bags) and asked us about the quality of the food. I let him know that it was my second time in one week and that it was worth his try. Yes, we have been eating out and outside. To me, it's important that we support local businesses (to the extent that we can). People make major pronouncements, they put their names on sides of buildings to demonstrate their wealth, they showcase their designer possessions, yet they say, "I am not risking going out to eat during COVID times."

So, order in. It matters.

It makes all of the difference.

Later the same man came back. My mother was in the ladies' room. He said, "Do people think that she looks like RBG? I couldn't stop lookin'." I laughed. "Yes, all of the time."

When out (which is not often) I note the smallest interactions between humans. People are starved. I also note the crazy and nasty behavior which comes when one is wearing a Biden–Harris shirt and walking in Northern Kentucky. I like to believe that people are pushed, sad, scared and that the hate that they spew is not representative of humankind.

But I am not so sure. Not certain at all.

My daily mantra is "stay on the high road." It takes reminding. Lots of self-talk. I am convinced that how we each speak to ourselves is our personal inflection point. The mind is powerful. Many of my own accomplishments (be they career, weight-loss, climbing a mountain, swimming a channel or even prudent parenting) have been mind-over-matter. A certainty that we can only provide for ourselves.

The change and the will come from the inside.

Last night Don and I again hiked 1.5 urban miles to eat on a sidewalk at Restaurant Salazar. We lamented the cold weather coming and that possibly Ohio had another month of life in the outdoors. I said, "I don't want to think about what happens to these places next." We sit on the brink of harsh reality.

We wandered to the sound of music in Washington Park. Aaron Copland performed on a giant screen. Couples sat in white circles drawn on the grass. At first glance, a dystopian socially distanced scene with heads moving to the music and each in their own world. After a crowd scanning, I noted this same location was fifty yards from the shooting that we "heard" about ten days ago.

And now, contented faces, living in our normal. This is America.

Today, on the hike to eat brunch outside at Allyn's (on the East end). Soaking up the last of whatever now might be.

Have a great Sunday.

Love,

Jennifer

Fierce, Not Frightened

Wednesday, September 30, 2020
Cincinnati, Ohio

My Dear Friend,

I have been on this planet for fifty-seven-and-a-half (or so) years. For the first time, I truly feel it moving beneath my feet. I see it on the faces of our fellow humans. I see on-air news people aging before my eyes. I feel time mutually moving too quickly and too slowly. There are days that I wish to be over sixty-five to have all of the "benefits" that one earns at that age. Yet I pull back and think, why do I want to rush any of this?

In my world, we only get to go on the ride once.

I also love life and have never thought of it as an endurance activity; but all that we have and to be cherished. Your writing about Lea at age 107 is beautiful. There is much to be learned from one who has prevailed across time and circumstance. My own grandmother lived to 104. I remember (when turning forty) I made a "big deal" about aging. She said "that's nothing." What she valued most was people, and a good outfit came in as a close second. She also loved sweets, yet (when we visited her for the last time) when we brought her hand made chocolates, she still lamented that "she shouldn't overdo it."

Simply, she lived as one who valued her own health and life, not as a path to death. I wish that I had asked more questions. I wish that I had listened harder. Over the years, I felt as if I knew Grandma Esther. And I knew that she valued me, her oldest granddaughter.

She would be surprised at today's turn of events. Her generation believed in humankind and in the promise that we call America. They believed that their offspring would live better lives, would be better people, would be smarter. She would have never anticipated that a dictator would be our president.

The likes of Hitler were a warning, a horrible memory, a lesson. Not to be repeated. And never on our land.

I had a phone call with Titus on Friday. He worked in our call center (in my business center) and often stopped in to talk with me. We spoke of life, marriage, the world and sometimes work. He's moved forward and is a minister in Owensboro, Kentucky. He called looking for advice on some work (in his community) that he wishes to launch. Titus, a Black man, seeks to work with other churches to bring unity to all citizens; no matter their politics.

Unite, not divide.

He brought me to tears. He said "Jennifer, I don't think you know how much you did for me. The talks that we had meant so much. And the time that you learned that my job was in jeopardy and you saved it. And then you told me that if someone asks me to pass the salt, always pass the salt with the pepper."

I laughed and cried. I loved this man and remembered our talks—but not in the detail that he had. He thanked me profusely for my time and I said, "Titus, after all of these years, what you have said to me means more than you know."

Titus has neighbors who support Trump. Most of them. Yet he still believes in Hope and Unity.

Last night's first presidential debate was an exercise in rubbernecking. I couldn't look away. I watched Joe Biden, the good man that he is, fumble and seem old. I watched Trump spew hatred and not denounce White supremacy. It is certainly a sad time.

It was more like an argument in which the listener is able to hear nothing.

There is no time for sadness. We need to be fierce and not frightened.

A woman, my grandma, raised poor and lived through the 20th century with successful offspring. A man, Titus, from Lincoln Heights, Ohio is able to become a leader with a vast following. Your woman, Lea, who still has hope.

I close with a favorite quote by Maya Angelou: "I've learned that people will forget what you said, people will forget what you did, but people will never forget how you made them feel."

Love,

Jennifer

We, The People

Dear Jennifer,

That was lyrical. Thank you. Be fierce. I will.

Tonight was my going-away gathering at Karikkin Spirits Company. Let's meet there before you and Don head out west. They have a great patio area, and they have cocktails that I think you will like. Genuinely, I enjoyed it. Everyone is pulling together and doing the best they can. I appreciated the gesture. They didn't have to do it, and I appreciate that.

Allow me to chime in on the debate between the president and the former vice president. I've never in more than thirty years in media experienced such a horrible moment in politics. Trump showed his basest tendencies as a bully, not honoring debate rules and going in the gutter to expose Joe Biden's son's drug issues. How did we get here? When did we get here? Will we ever recover?

Yes, of course, we will. I am sure of it. Fact is, we have been placing too much stake in what our politicians are telling us and not betting on the ingenuity of Americans to solve our own problems.

Jen, tonight so many people said so many nice things about me. Loren and Kevin were there, and it was good for them to hear others' thoughts. I am "fatherly," "brilliant," "an amazing storyteller," "kind," "patient," "a good listener," "always helpful," "have a smile that lights up the room." One of my dear friends, Randy Tucker, said he aspires to be like me. That was the highest compliment. I even received an MVP trophy from Anne Saker, who told everyone I was the reason our team won first place for the diversity of our Storytellers speakers throughout the whole company.

And then I think about your and Titus' relationship. Often, we do not grasp the depth and breadth of our impact on others. Clearly, your impact on Titus was invaluable. Because you cared about him, he could better care for others. And now look at him, a big-time racial healer in the faith community. Never doubt how the power of the universe can and will use you, even when you have no idea what's going on.

Thank you for sharing Titus with me. This is how we are called to live our life—in service of others, helping them the best we can while we can.

This is indeed the kind of spirit that makes America great and good. No dog whistle, mud-slinging, or immature leadership—on both sides—can change that.

I think We, the People, need to find our voice again. Right now.

Love,

Byron

Byron and his eldest daughter, Loren.

The Long Road Home

Friday, October 2, 2020
Cincinnati, Ohio

Dear Byron,

The planet is spinning. Now TRUMP has COVID.

I am exhausted.

I went to Columbus (our state capital) on Wednesday and Thursday. My farewell tour to our homeland continues. The goal: to spend time with my cousin Louise and to see an old friend and boss from 1987 (who was the field director for then Secretary of State, now U.S. Senator of Ohio Sherrod Brown). I traveled I-71 North two hours through the cornfields and back. Unbelievably, I sometimes made that trip twice per week.

My first days on the road were in working for Sherrod Brown. I ran a large part of his territory. Today, I am often asked if I know that boyish senator, who always stands up for the left, from Ohio. I chuckle to myself. I know the man well.

And he is truly a good man.

In the old days I was often meeting with lawmakers and "educating" leaders in the hallowed halls of the State House and State Senate. This time, I arrived in a "dead" city in which Louise and I might have been the only guests. We stayed in a high-rise hotel, one that has walls that have seen me through decades. This is when my "expense account" paid for accommodations. I never would have anticipated choosing to pay (out of my own pocket) to sleep in what are now a Sheraton's beds.

Louise had never been inside the Capitol. I asked the guard if we were permitted in—during the time of COVID. He said that "you have a few minutes until we close." In those moments we were able to see a special display that commemorated Lincoln's days lying in state. The viewing included the American Flag that flew during those days and a lock of Lincoln's hair. Yes, that's right.

Did a staffer cut this while Lincoln was in repose? Honestly, a bit creepy.

I am the eldest of the eight grandchildren of Esther and Jack Basman. Louise is the third and four years behind me. We look alike, sound similar and resemble our grandmother. We arrived with our bags full of dark "getting colder" clothing, tasteful and funky jewelry and decent handbags. Our grandmother would have approved. We were practical, yet stylish.

We would be able to go the distance.

Louise is a therapist. Louise, our cousin Becky and I all have advanced degrees in psychology. We are the eldest in each of our families. We each have a strong sense of responsibility and an intense desire to figure these people (from whom we have spawn) out. Our grandparents were good to us. They were generous with their life lessons, their love, their time and their money. They told us that we could be and do whatever we wanted. They loved us unconditionally.

We also know that our mothers, and their children had a much different life experience.

While our grandparents were born and raised poor, they became well-to-do and important members of their Charleston, West Virginia Society. They were humble and not pretentious.

They valued hard work, family loyalty and yes, beauty.

We were to "get ourselves together" and have a profession.

As we have aged, we learned that Grandpa was very tough on his daughters. While they each had their own experience, the theme is that he was feared, and that "mother" did not stand up to him. The word is that he mellowed by the time that we came along.

Over food and drinks, because in Jewish life, there is always food involved, we discussed our kin. Food, with an "I shouldn't, and I need to fit into a certain dress" is a recognized retort. It was thanks to my grandfather that I am most at home in the Mountain West. His favorite pastime was the quiet on a fast-moving mountain stream, in wading boots, with organized fishing lures, catching dinner. A deer head (from 1962 in Cheyenne, Wyoming.) hangs on our wall.

He taught me about risk-taking and adventure. He survived two small plane crashes and knew both Jonas Salk and Albert Sabin. He was the 100th member of the American Academy of Pediatrics. He founded hospitals and started the State and Maternal Care Section for the State of West Virginia. Decades later, his eldest, Judy, my mother, started her own program to care for children of at-risk mothers. Like Gramps she became known, highly regarded and award-winning. Like grandma, she did it in heels and beautiful fabrics.

And at age eighty-one, she continues to excel.

As I sit across the table from her for Saturday lunches, I often feel "less than." While I know that she is proud of me, she is not an effusive woman. Likely this has made me soar, made me reach, made me fierce, made me strong.

Maybe this desire to impress our parents and seek their approval engendered excellence. I have climbed, I now seek the quiet of the mountains.

I am the offspring of people who had vision. People who loved their family intensely and people who never took no for an answer. Like you, my people knew that few would "stick up for us" and that our sheer ingenuity and tenacity would open doors. We were not special, we were average. We were fortunate.

The trip to Columbus provided some closure. Goodbye to a place that once meant so much—with stakes so high, whether it was the state capital-Ohio, necessary for "becoming president" or one in which I just needed to secure a few votes for my employer.

On October 1, it was a different place. One where I would say "Goodbye" to Ohio and to a friend and cousin (whom I'd likely see on her visits to New Mexico). The City was quiet. COVID has shut down businesses. It was not the vibrant, lively place that it used to be while the legislature was in session.

It was a set of buildings in which I remembered and smiled that the next stage of my journey was imminent. My grandfather used to say (a la Thomas Wolfe) "You can never go home again."

Dr. Basman, I disagree. For me, home is where the heart is. I am with all of you today and all days.

Have a great weekend.

Love,

Jennifer

I Hate Your Ugly Ways

Saturday, October 3, 2020
Cincinnati, Ohio

Dear Jennifer,

You are right. President Trump has COVID-19 and is currently in Walter Reed Memorial Hospital in Washington, D.C. Stew on that a moment. It was fresh and surreal as we drove up Interstate 71 to our meeting Friday.

Having had a day or so for all of it to sink in, I'm still trying to process this new reality. Jen, out of all the things that have happened during this administration, this takes the cake. I need to confess: I wanted him to contract it for one day, make a complete recovery, and possibly gain empathy for others who have suffered and died from COVID-19. But I do not wish permanent bad health on anyone, especially the leader of the free world. Trump has willfully ignored all safety protocols during the pandemic and has mocked those who sought to wear masks and practice social distancing.

Every time I saw him make fun of someone, regarding COVID, I couldn't help but think about our sweet Etta, who died of cardiac arrest (complications from COVID) with no family around, and about Bennie Jr., who thought he had licked COVID, only to go into cardiac arrest and die in an ambulance on his way to a local emergency room.

He has been the Great Disrupter during his entire presidency, and I hope this health scare will lead to changes in the way he governs, though I doubt it. I wish him a speedy recovery, but I also hope this serves as a lesson for him to be more compassionate to others. As I told you and our hosts in Wilmington, it is my moral duty to love our president, even as I find him completely insufferable.

I thought this might be a good time to share the column that was spiked 14 months ago in the *Enquirer* by the editor. I still mean it:

Dear President Trump,

Welcome back to Cincinnati. We've missed you. Well, not really, because you are ubiquitous. You are always with us on the news and social media. But it's good to see you press the flesh, so to speak.

The family trotted me out again to draft you a quick note. They wanted me to share some concerns and observations since your last visit. But first, I need to share a memory that my cousin brought up last week.

"Do you guys remember when Donald Trump was cool?"

Everyone nodded their heads in affirmation.

"I mean, this dude had money, women, cars and swagger. I kinda wanted to be like Trump, or at least have what he had," my cousin said.

Truth is, many of us did when we were younger. You represented what we thought was the American Dream. You hung out with heads of state, movie stars, and pro athletes. You built hotels and casinos and rode in limos. Champagne and caviar all day long.

Hard stop.

You were gaslighting all of us, and it hurts. You burst our bubble, starting with the $85,000 full-page newspaper ad urging the execution of five black kids accused of raping a Central Park jogger. And even when it was found that they were railroaded into a confession and exonerated on DNA evidence, you never took it back or apologized. We got to know more about you and learned that your family business denied black people housing in your apartment buildings.

There's more. And I'm trying to hold on to my Mama's advice, which mirrors my religious teaching. She would say, "Baby, remember, don't hate the person. You can hate what the person does, but never hate the person." It's another version of loving the sinner, hating the sin.

So, I love you, Mr. President.

I just hate your ugly ways.

Your public behavior seems completely controlled by the id, which is the only component of our personality that we all have at birth. The id is the "psychic energy derived from instinctual needs and drives," according to Merriam-Webster.

America Lost and Found in Letters

I hate the way you segregate and rank Americans based on their zip code, rather than highlighting their God-given potential. For example, the attack on Baltimore and Congressman Elijah Cummings the other day. You made an anchorman weep, talking about how rat-infested his city is and how it's not fit for human beings to live in Baltimore. You like to use the word, "infestation" when talking about these issues.

You are a counter puncher. I get that, but isn't there a better way to make the point as the leader of the free world? History has taught us that such comparisons can be the first steps to something more sinister.

I hate it that you won't publicly take responsibility for Russian involvement in our elections process and that you don't seem to care that they are at it again, along with other countries. Voting integrity is the bedrock of our democracy. What does it say to Americans when their leader refuses to fight against the threat of election tampering by foreign governments?

I hate it when you call journalism "fake news" and the "enemy of the people." Five of our colleagues in Annapolis, Maryland died last year at the hands of a person with a powerful weapon who stormed their newsroom. I'm not saying you are responsible. I'm just saying you need to remember that our duty to report about our government and its actions are secured by the U.S. Constitution. And news gatherers and editors go home to partners, children, and dogs they have to walk every day.

(By the way, have you ever thought about getting a dog?)

I hate it that you are playing de facto secretary of state, relying more on charm than years of learned international diplomacy. The dysfunction of this approach is most obvious in your relationship with North Korean dictator Kim Jong Un. North Korea returned Cincinnati's Otto Warmbier to his family in a comatose state. He died a week later. "He tells me that he didn't know about it and I will take him at his word," you said.

Kim continues to flout economic sanctions by importing Rolls Royces and good liquor. Just this week, the country launched two short-range missiles. And you two exchange love letters.

I hate it that my cousins and much of my extended family don't admire you anymore. None of us want to be you anymore. They think you are racist because you do not readily condemn racist behavior. They hear your words dehu-

manizing black and brown people all the time. They look at your Cabinet and see fewer minorities and women than the past four presidential administrations.

I hate it that I feel like you are content with evangelizing to 40% of Americans with a separatist message, instead of painting a sweeping vision. America as the shining city on a hill. America with low unemployment and rising wages. Opportunities for young people to grow businesses and start families. An America that leads the world in innovation. Immigration as a historic core value that made our country great. Neighbors helping neighbors.

Mama said I have to love you, Mr. President. But not your ugly ways.

And, now, look at us, Jen. This guy has completely succeeded in wrecking our democracy. That was a good column.

Now, back to your Forrest Gump life. It never ceases to amaze me how many experiences you have had, both in politics and in corporate America. We are similar in that way, and I think it's a testament to our grit. Your time with Sherrod Brown must have been pretty exciting. He remains one of my favorite Ohio politicians. I mean, he gets it. He truly understands what common citizens deal with on a daily basis and earnestly seeks to help. He also reads everything.

Last month, when I wrote about the Black cemetery in Madisonville in need of restoration, he had his director of communications to contact me about it, and she reminded me about legislation he sponsored Sen. Lamar Alexander (R-Tenn.) to help fund the restoration of Black cemeteries nationwide. He has also written me personal notes over the years. Not only is that good PR, but it's also an easy way to reach constituents through journalists. For politicians, having an EQ is important; Brown is an example of this. Trump is not.

Thanks for listening.

Love,

Byron

Measure for Measure

Monday, October 5, 2020
Cincinnati, Ohio

Dear Byron,

Life continues to be on fast-forward. We are now in the midst of the Trump Administration COVID count. It is clear to me that since we first started to write to one another (6/6/20) we have been on a long farewell to the life and the nation that we assumed to know. We waved to the life that we lived and the inherent expectations. Namely that our children would have a healthy future.

This has been more than a mere pivot.

Your tribe and mine are accustomed to making "something" with "nothing" and navigating charged waters. Somehow we are both hopeful. While we know much has been lost, we know that learning is found.

One step in front of the other.

It is your first day of school. The first day of the new gig. First days of work are always loaded. These days I guess it is a hello on video and hours on a new payroll. When I first saw the futuristic video via phone (in TomorrowLand, Disneyland, Anaheim, early '70s) I never thought that it would be instead of being with other humans.

With the rare exception, (you on FRIDAY!) I almost never see real people. Where is one supposed to wear all of these outfits? I have thought much about the working world—mainly at the experience upon which my own children currently embark.

They have a unique form of anxiety.

I sit today, working, from our place in the high tower overlooking the Ohio River in a sports bra and shorts. I remember the hope and promise about the workplace. I expected it all to be significant. And then I realized that it was as dysfunctional as most families. Before that time though, I found it heady.

In my corporate days I was often in NYC and on Capitol Hill. The days in "the city that doesn't sleep" was filled with staying in Warner Brothers' favorite hotel. There were five course dinners with TV chefs, self-important meetings on high floors and the contemplation of something that was called the internet. I remember the first personal interactive device called the Blackberry and thought that my thumbs could never move fast enough.

This felt like the center of the universe. Like Thomas Wolfe wrote in *The Bonfire of the Vanities*,

"There it was, the Rome, the Paris, the London of the twentieth century, the city of ambition, the dense magnetic rock, the irresistible destination of all those who insist on being where things are happening—and he was among the victors!"

Life felt like that, if only for a moment.

And then there was Capitol Hill. I was mesmerized by the sightings of the "greats" (or so I thought) and seeing the late Senator Kennedy testifying on the floor. To me, Washington was the city of the grey suit, the overworked, the too serious and the no life.

In my twenties this "life" was magic. These are places and times that our children will not likely experience. We live in the world of an unimagined future.

At the same time, they will have interesting times to call their own.

You and I talked recently about careers on the downside. With few exceptions, when one passes fifty (and especially today) we become more expendable. I have learned (as a consultant) that my "history" is of some value. Don and I joke that on many days our work is on less important matters than upon which we endeavored in our thirties. The good news; it doesn't matter so much to us anymore.

We learn that being the most titled or wealthiest person in the graveyard is not an aspiration. I do not have the stamina that was once a core part of my being. While I am known for my high energy (and good teeth), it is not what it once was. I also know that I seem to have the physical energy for exercise, but my mental patience for garbage has diminished. I am also longer on wisdom.

To today, we have a president (in his mid-seventies) with COVID who apparently says he "finally gets it" and a running mate who is healthy, but older. I often wonder how these men or the eighty-year old Speaker of the House manages these challenges. I do know that I would take the older Biden (as I know that his core is about integrity and decency) over Trump at any age.

As humans age we seem to be an extreme version of our younger selves. And Biden has always been a good man.

It is in these times that we take the measure of the man. Who was he? Who is he? With whom will he surround himself? Who can we trust?

Or maybe Shakespeare said it best in "Measure for Measure."

Trump
To have a giant's strength, but it is tyrannous
To use it like a giant.

Biden
What's mine is yours and what is yours is mine.

You are one of the good ones.
I am honored to call you friend.

Hope Jill packed your lunch today.

Love,

Jennifer

Covidiot

Tuesday, October 6, 2020
Cincinnati, Ohio

Dear Jennifer,

I am humbled by the response I have been receiving since I announced I was leaving daily journalism to take a marketing position at the tech investment firm.

It's true that you rarely get the chance to learn what people truly think about you, but I have the pleasure of seeing that through their words. Thank you for posting on Facebook. It means the world to me. In my farewell column, I talked about being kinder to one another as civility in America has taken a holiday.

Oddly enough, the president contracted COVID-19, and another police officer has been arrested for shooting an unarmed Black man, this time in Texas. Officer Shaun Lucas shot and killed Jonathan Price Saturday in an East Texas convenience store. The circumstances have become all too familiar. We began writing, partly in response to the death of George Floyd this past summer. And now, another one. Jen, I have no expectation that this will end.

Some will argue that Price should have obeyed police commands, but it seems that he was playing the role of peacemaker and sought to leave the scene. No matter what, that's a poor excuse to be killed that day by a cop.

Back to Trump and civility. I thought he would emerge from Walter Reed, having received the best therapeutics, as a kinder, gentler person. I thought he would share lessons of how it feels to suffer from COVID. I thought he would have empathy for the families of victims of COVID-19, more than 200,000. But instead, he emerges from a helicopter, climbs stairs to the second floor of the White House and can barely catch his breath as he staged a photo opp.

And he followed up by taping a statement encouraging people to "not be afraid of COVID" and to "not let it dominate your life." Talk about tone deaf.

In contrast, former Vice President Biden today gave a real speech at Gettysburg that encouraged Americans to be kind, to listen to and heed the science and to wear our masks. To me, the choice could not be more clear, Jen. Trump's actions over the past few days are insufferable, disgraceful and unpresidential.

It's time for him to go. I heard his former communications director on a news talk show say he was a COVIDIOT. I found it humorous and appropriate.

Love,

Byron

Swimming Across

Wednesday, October 7, 2020
Cincinnati, Ohio

Dear Byron,

Another day, another COVID count of The White House staff. While I have felt that POTUS is evil, I now believe that his drug cocktail has caused even more mania. Our nation is hanging by a thread. It also seems that Biden-Harris may succeed.

Just in time. I continue to seek momentary escapes.

Water matters to me. Drinking it and submerging in it. I feel free when swimming. You and I have extensively discussed the plight of Black America and swimming. I had thought that youngsters were not permitted into public pools and learning to swim was not an option. While this was sadly the case until recently, I have also learned from a current read, *Wandering in Strange Lands* by Morgan Jenkins, that the relationship embedded in American Black DNA is traced back to a negative association with water. This dates back to slave ships.

The Gullah people, the very early enslaved, apparently have become adept at "all things" water as they live on the sea islands. Tomorrow I head south to see my Caroline and we will spend the weekend on the islands. Before they were "developed" (and for centuries) they were exclusively home to the Gullah. They have kept customs from West Africa alive and vital.

I've learned that access to swimming is a privilege. Immersing in water creates buoyancy, lightness, a quiet place to think and a refuge. Yesterday, at forty-six degrees, my friend Kathleen and I submerged in an outdoor pool. Stroke after stroke reminded me of how this simple, but complex activity has carried me through time. I trust my own body most, without question, in the water.

America Lost and Found in Letters

Andrew Grove, Holocaust Survivor and Intel Founder, scribed *Swimming Across*. A lifelong swimmer.

He was a good student who excelled at chemistry which he was studying at the University of Budapest when the Hungarian uprising of 1956 persuaded him to "swim across" the border and emigrate to the West.

And then there is the Mighty Ohio. The water that so many crossed to get to the Ohio-side for freedom. While a long-time Cincinnatian, I have only lived on the river, once. I have learned that (as I depart from this place) I would have missed an entire life chapter without being near her.

On morning walks, one notes vast activity—be it the barges or the other walkers. I am reminded that this is the artery of commerce. When squinting, I can almost envision what life would have been like hundreds of years ago, with traders on the banks, merchants buying fruit and vegetables and the enslaved fleeing in the dark of night. It is novel that one can stand on the Cincinnati side and be in Kentucky by merely crossing a bridge. The seven hills of Cincinnati are proximate as is the bend that leads further south.

This place will serve people, beyond us, for hundreds of years hence.

Today, I noted the Cincinnati Bengals posing for a photo in street clothes (or workout attire). I thought about taking a photograph—but being a non-sports fan, I find the water itself of the greatest interest. Most days, people are fishing, "port of Cincinnati" boats pass and occasionally an old model steamship.

I think of what Mark Twain said about this place "that things happen ten years later here." As a young person we seek speed and to grow up. As an older human, we wish for life to slow down.

Our world is on fast forward. Each week is now an "old month or so" in news coverage.

I wonder what the former enslaved and Andrew Grove thought as they crossed water to freedom. Because water makes one think about the dangers, the possibilities, the hopes the dreams.

Let's pray that we all land well.

Have a peaceful day.

Love,

Jennifer

A New Hope

Thursday, October 8, 2020
Cincinnati, Ohio

Dear Jennifer,

I have almost completed my first week in my new role. I have been drinking from a hose. My new workplace is located on the fourth floor of a renovated building that once housed Cincinnati's flagship Sears department store. Jen, everyone loved Sears. It was the original retailer where you could buy everything from a fan belt to an air conditioner to a pair of Toughskins denim jeans.

I jokingly imagine that my desk, which is in a corner with two walls of glass and a huge concrete pillar, is in the exact spot where ladies once purchased their dresses.

Three things that I have learned:

1. There is life after daily journalism, although I miss interacting with the readers of my column. Four years of producing two-to-three weekly columns has made for a rhythmic discourse between my words and theirs.
2. There is true optimism out here in America in ways that I did not expect, regarding to the economy.
3. The people in and around CincyTech and the VC world are really smart. I'm happy to be a part of this ecosystem.

For the better part of twenty years, I have developed mastery in my trade. I have always been the voice of reason and consistent change, and I sat at the seat of power in my various roles leading editorial pages throughout America. That life has been waning for a while now, but now that I'm away from it, I can appreciate that influence and popularity that life provided. I feel secure and satisfied that I have moved on to greener pastures, so to speak.

The optimism that I feel from my new team is exemplified by a whip-smart CEO with a team of other brainiacs, including my boss, who truly believe in the transformational power of economic opportunity and success. These folks have their fingers on the pulse of the economy, and the kinds of businesses they invest in (life science and tech) have fared well during the COVID-19 epidemic. One of the thirty companies in its portfolio will have some news related to a drug that will play a role in slowing the pandemic. This is exciting stuff!

I have worked with plenty of smart people. I think this bunch may be the smartest. This may be because of their focus on business concepts that are not as familiar to me. Or it might be because I'm still new. But I like being a part of a team that thinks big, takes calculated risks and remains optimistic.

This is one of Cincinnati's secrets, and I want to change that. I want to make sure that people beyond Southwest Ohio know about the impact of CincyTech, but most of all I would like to see some of the companies in the portfolio emerge as the next LinkedIn or perhaps even FaceBook, and we have a few that fit the model.

Enjoy the Sea Islands!

Love,

Byron

Lost to Be Found

Friday, October 9, 2020
Hilton Head Island

Dear Friend,

So happy that your first week delivered. It was time.
Time for appreciation of your talent and time for you to expand.
My day was a bit different.
At around 6:30 p.m., once "off the water" I noted this text.
"Hi, this is Andy from Outdoor Augusta checking to see if Y'all were doing OK out there. It's been a little bit of time. If Y'all end up going down river I do have a boat out so we can come to get Y'all."
The day started at 4:15 a.m., when I rose to catch two flights to Augusta, Georgia. My goal, to see my Caroline. It had been seven months. She lives alone, and I am her mom. All advised against travel.
I did it anyway.
I was in three airports: Cincinnati, Atlanta and Augusta. Not crowded, but definitely people on the move. Everyone masked, most shops closed. I arrived at Caroline's in North Augusta, technically South Carolina, with Georgia up the street. Great to be together again. My oldest independent girl.
She planned for us to enter the Savannah River to kayak. My reading has been focused on the South and slavery. The Savannah River conjures images of those times. It is a hauntingly beautiful spot high on Spanish moss, old trees and the high and warm southern sun. Her friend joined the journey. We set out in three boats.
I cannot help but to ask questions. It has driven my children (and husband) crazy. I want to learn about people, their attitudes, hopes, dreams, bias, and

true self. So, I did it again, questioning her poor friend. He came to Augusta for the military base. He is intelligent, speaks Farsi and is an expert on Iran. He comes from Texas. During the cross examination it became clear that he thinks Trump is OK and he agrees with his positions on the Middle East. As the mom (in this situation) I determined that (during this tranquil day on the river) I would be polite and not make him wonder why he wasn't the one doing the questioning.

I kept my mind open and did not profess my love for Biden-Harris.

I saw a twenty-nine-year-old who believed in the promise of America and our safety in the wide world. I saw not a Trump "supporter," but one who is intent on protecting what we are allegedly about. I saw his own hope for a safe future. And a guy who is good to my daughter. He has brought company to her during a hard time in her own life. I also witnessed a young man desperate for the unity of a broken nation. Much like Titus's desire to align his neighbors—left and right—this White boy from the South has the same hopes and dreams.

The river delivers.

You and I have talked about your own life spent on rivers. The appreciation for these waterways that connect the commerce, life and the people of our nation is intense. One understands the foreword movement of our people.

These moments of glory on a perfect day led to our laying back on our kayaks, eyes closed, silent.

And that is when the mistake happened. We were about three hours in (and close to our turn off) and floated far downstream. We sat up and kept paddling with the assumption that the turn off was just ahead when Caroline said, "I have never been on this part of the river before."

I said "I guess that we need to turn around." Caroline said, "We can't paddle upstream." I said, "We have no choice."

This was at 4:00 pm. We launched at noon.

We asked a fisherman how far to the turn-off. He said, "Just a ways up there." We were also out of water. Jennifer, the "great adventurer" had not thought through the water situation. I had risen early and was tired.

Not smart.

With a waning but hot sun, we paddled.

And paddled.

And paddled.

The young ones complained, and I said "Hey, I am the old lady."

At some point I fell far behind. My arms and shoulders ached. The current was fierce. While going under a bridge, I was sucked far back three times. I wondered if I should hop out and simply pull my boat and swim it.

I felt the phones ringing and beeping in my dry bag and could not answer for fear that it would move me backwards. I knew that folks were looking for us. I had left Don's number as my emergency contact.

I had "Amazing Grace" stuck in my head and kept on repeat

Amazing Grace, how sweet the sound
That saved a wretch like me
I once was lost, but now am found
Was blind but now I see

While I know that the song's intent is not about an old woman lost on the Savannah River, I was simply thinking about being lost. I was also grateful for this long afternoon, in which my daughter was a small dot far ahead, with no news coverage, no vitriol and an acceptance of a young man who thought so much differently.

I felt hope. I dug in hard. I pulled the fast-moving water and I smiled.

Traveling upstream is something that comes to me naturally.

It is said that we remember best the times that went wrong. It is one of my stepfathers most favorite concepts. My daughter reminded me of a time in Northern India in which we had to "flee" as we were close to a terrorist incident. While we laughed about it, there was nothing funny at the time.

And it is a time to remember.

One memory connects to another. Different time, different continent.

We pulled into the dock hours later sunburned and smiling. I unpacked our wet phones and found troubled messages from Don. They had called him. And the message from our kayak man. He asked if I wanted a drink. I joked "a vodka tonic." He handed me water.

Sometimes we have to get lost to find ourselves. My body hurts and my mind hopes.

A day on the river offers some answers.
Keeping hope alive.

Love,

Jennifer

Fire in the Sky

Saturday, October 10, 2020
Cincinnati, Ohio

Dear Jennifer,

Your heartsong is the call of the water, whether swimming or canoeing. To me, that is brave.

Mine is the transition from summer to fall, when the trees become elevated fields of fire meeting the horizon.

Where I come from in Northwest Louisiana, there is fertile ground for farming pine trees. If I had to guess, I would bet that the nation's largest consumer goods maker, Cincinnati-based Procter & Gamble, has long-term leases with several timber farmers there, who offer a ready supply of pulp wood used to create Charmin and Bounty. Down there, people use their needles as mulch.

Pine trees are useful but could be considered boring if you like the way leaves change colors this time of year. They look the same all the time in my part of the country. Green with flaky brownish-grey bark.

This is October, when leafy hardwoods display their glory.

My grandmother must have intuitively known this when she planted one sampling sweet gum tree about sixty feet outside her front door. By the time I was twelve years old, the sapling had grown large enough to provide ample shade, and shed the prickly balls that seemed more of a nuisance than anything. The shedding of these balls (which were really seed pods) signaled that summer was ending and fall was on the way. (I just learned that Tamiflu was derived from the inside of these balls, and that you could make tea using them as an elixir!)

No tree is more beautiful in the fall than the sweet gum. Its leaves are the color of sunrise and sunset: red, yellow, orange, and auburn. In October, they sometimes look like they are on fire. I came to love that tree in "Mama's" yard. Sometimes she would sit underneath its shade and creak back and forth on her metal gliding couch. Plus, sweet gum hardwood makes pretty furniture. Shorter days equals less sunlight, which means less energy for leaves. With less energy, leaves begin to break down and yield their fall majesty—first yellow, then orange, then red for a little while if we are lucky.

When we moved to the Midwest years ago, a Louisiana Tech classmate of mine, Paula Goodnight, lived in Maineville with her husband and three daughters. They have since moved to Tennessee. She remembered my love of the colors of fall, and told me how the hardwoods here made for a beautiful fall show. Since you have been out of town, it's like the leaves transformed overnight. I'm going to drive through downtown Mariemont tomorrow, because the town's main drag reflects the essence of fall, even rivaling the hardwoods of some New England towns.

My neighbors who live four houses down raked leaves in their front yard today. Overnight, leaves from two ancient oaks fell, leaving a yellow floor canopy. The same canopy has taken over my backyard from the oak tree in my neighbor's backyard. On Arnsby Place, trees on either side of the street seem to be bowing to one another, as if to pay a compliment to the other's fresh face of make-up. "Darling, you look mahvelous. No, Darling. YOU look mahvelous!"

Jen, you and I know the unusual stress the other experienced this week, with your travel and my starting a new job and the news you and I received from up north. Here's the thing: You and I are two of the most optimistic people I know, and we will move through this next phase.

To me, fall signals a time to plan and contemplate how we will emerge when the days grow longer again. This year, it is marred by COVID-19 and American uncertainty. Now is the time for us to lean in on each other, Jen. Stronger, together!

Meanwhile, we've got two weeks to enjoy the show before the trees reveal their grey nakedness. Let's enjoy it while it lasts.

Love,

Byron

Land of Cotton

Monday, October 12, 2020
North Augusta, South Carolina

Dear Byron,

I too love the beauty of fall. Once the leaves start to die, I have pretty wicked allergic reactions—part of life. The time in the South has been good in that I have gotten to see Caroline after so many long months.

COVID has taken much from so many.

I had wanted to visit Gullah sites, and all was closed. However, just driving around reminds us of the old and deadly times for the enslaved. Markers everywhere that name plantations. You, being from the South, are likely accustomed to this. I am not. I worked in Tallahassee much and was on a constant quest to understand this little place, thirty-five miles from more plantations than anywhere in the nation and the site of throwing elections.

Once, while having dinner with a group of educated folks I mentioned The Civil War. I was quickly told it was to be named "The War of Northern Aggression." I was also asked by Black people about my apparent goodness for Black Americans. I was told that they didn't hear that much from White people.

We spent the weekend on the coast. These are the islands where the Gullah settled (once free) and where they still maintain their customs. At the same time, I am also reading *Cane River,* one of Oprah's favorites (about Creoles). I am wondering if you know the Louisiana spot. It is a nonfiction family story of women who came up in the area starting in the 1700s.

We can sit in Cincinnati and sort of pretend that not much "bad" happened there. We paint ourselves as the "good guys." We now seem to vote mostly blue. We say that we care about Black Lives Matter. We are also the place that is nationally known for race problems and other bigotry. We are not so great.

It is eerie (to me) to see wide fields of cotton and wonder about history and at the same time (in the lane across) to pass a large and noisy Trump parade. Loud and proud with flags galore.

Caroline and I did what we do best: exercise, eat, drink a little, sit on the beach and do some outlet shopping. While I would like to know more about the thoughts inside my eldest's head, I am glad to just be together. I am grateful that she has turned into a fine young woman who loves her family and cooks meals for her old mama.

I know that she rolls her eyes when I run to swim in the Atlantic—half wondering if I am nuts or sane. She has never asked for much and is thankful when we offer a hand. I remember well being twenty-eight years old and believing that I had forever. She was born when I was almost twenty-nine. I thought that I was old and wise.

I knew that I loved that little baby fiercely. Not until now did I know how much.

I would have never expected her to come to the South. Like many women before her, she came for a man. They split; she stayed. I am hopeful that someday we will live closer to each other. It seems possible.

The weekend was spent in view of ancient American memories—that are still only skin deep. At the same time, it was filled with my own. The leaves are slowly changing here, but not yet putting on the northern show. I return to the North this afternoon.

These are the times that we remember. Our memories are ultimately all that we've got.

See you soon.

Love,

Jennifer

Not a Cult,
But Loyal Followers

Tuesday, October 13, 2020
Cincinnati, Ohio

Dear Jennifer,

I once watched "American Horror Story," the terrifying series on FX that has redefined the genre on television. I don't watch it anymore, but the writing, acting and filming are superb. It attracts big stars, too, like Stevie Nicks, Angela Bassett, Kathy Bates, and Jessica Lange.

The last season I watched was about a cult, which followed a local politician who wielded absolute power over his followers and used the classic "us versus them" approach to campaigning. He would inspire an "insta riot," where groups of his followers would gather quickly to incite a riot and sometimes kill people in the process. Then, as quickly as the riot appeared, it dissipated at the cult leader/politician's command. By no means am I comparing our current commander in chief to an overt killer, but I'm troubled by the latest developments today from President Trump's rally in Florida.

Despite testing positive for COVID-19, this insufferable president is holding open-air rallies, and his cultish following is risking their lives in worship of Trump. One lady was quoted as saying, "I don't care if I die" from COVID.

Days earlier, it was learned that a Michigan militia group had plans to kidnap and kill Governor Gretchen Widmer, and also had their sights set on Virginia governor Ralph Northam. Both are Democrats and have been targets of Trump.

How do you make a logical argument against such illogical behavior? "When did we get so stupid?" Jill asked. I wondered the same thing.

I have been of two minds about the 2020 presidential election. On one hand, I believe Joe Biden will win the presidency, but only if the turnout is high and there is no fraud. But I also believe Trump can win when I see rabid supporters disregarding their own health and well-being just to be near him. If I were still writing a column, I would encourage people to get out of their homes, register and vote. I would outline the things we stand to lose if we continue down the path of Trump, which leads to a dead end. There are no plans. No vision. No America shining on a hill. For him, there are only made-up personal grievances to continue to fuel.

You know, we've talked about our true-blue Republican friends. Some have turned away from Trump; others have doubled down in their support. I will never understand how that can happen, but it does. For example, take the Supreme Court Justice nominee, Judge Amy Barrett. She is no RBG, but she does not appear to be the bogeyman, either. I'll bet her neighbors and friends adore her. She represents the best of what America has to offer, or at least that's how many people around the country likely think.

Yet, she is a Trump nominee. And I have friends who truly love the pick—friends that I love dearly. Judge Barrett almost seems moderate in her answers to questions from the Senate judiciary committee. And if the Democrats don't watch it with their questioning, they will be accused of playing politics with this nominee.

At the end of the day, I just hope we can come together as a nation and heal. I saw a news report from Texas in an area where 128,000 people came out to vote on day one. "We are voting for peace and tranquility," said a Black voter who appeared to be retired.

Four years of divisiveness is enough. We need real change.

Love,

Byron

Hope, Interrupted

Time Often Solves
What Reason Can't

Thursday, October 15, 2020
Cincinnati, Ohio

My Dear Friend,

As we head through the slowest (almost in slow motion) time in America, we must take solace in what matters. In some ways we pray for this election to be over. In the same way that I do not wish my own life away, I am not so eager for November 3 to pass. We often spend our time contemplating what lies ahead. This exercise invalidates the living now part.

I want to live now.

I have come to the part of the journey for which we have planned. I am going to be surprised when we pull out of Hamilton County for our western life—that we actually do make it to that time. In the now, I have enjoyed my last days in this place that has been my home. Once, years ago, I complained endlessly to our then mayor about this place. About our conservatism, our narrow-mindedness and that certain families controlled all. He laughed and said, "I call this place my home."

This has been my home.

What I notice are the simple things: the brilliant fall that we've had, the deep and enduring friendships, the Midwest predictability, the "knowing" what's next that we do so well, the steadiness and the "puritan work ethic." I'm being asked by many why leave here? And I wonder if I have gotten this whole thing wrong.

I do know that I seek a life separate and apart of what we have known. I did not plan for the feelings of sadness.

In July 2013 my mother, the girls and I traveled to Northern India to a region called Ladakh on the Tibetan plateau. This is a place of miracle and wonder. I have since said that if I were a good enough human, I would be a Buddhist. We were in the middle of the high temples, the deities, the monks, the nuns and the disciples of the Dalai Lama. We spent the weeks at very high altitude (always over 17.5K) and visited ethereal sites.

On July 6, 2013 we attended a festival in honor of the birth of the Dalai Lama. It was dancing, singing and prayer for the life of the man, their leader, their spirit, their soul. We were asked if we would like an audience with his "top" disciple. (Our guide was connected.) Within moments we were seated in a chamber on oriental rugs, cross legged and offered tea. My daughters smiled and looked left to right, left to right as we drank our tea. We became aware of how difficult it is to sit straight with legs crossed. In walked a solemn and smiling Lama who sat at our head. He regaled us with stories. My mother proceeded to ask him deep and meaningful questions.

We listened.

I piped up.

I asked, "What advice do you have for the children of America?"

He said, "It is simple: eat more vegetables" and he grinned and laughed.

Not deep, not on its face meaningful, yet so simple.

Eat more vegetables.

Today we sit in a complex time. We want the future, but we pine for the past. The Buddhist culture has their personal view of time.

"In most schools of Buddhism, it is understood that the way we experience time—as flowing from past to present to future—is an illusion.... These are past, present, future, and timeless time. This is sometimes expressed as 'the "three times and timeless time."'"

These learned people believe in knowledge, kindness, a simple life and nature's beauty. They are not tied to their material possessions. They have deep faith.

For me, the time has come. This includes being open to what is next.

It is about being free, free thinking and here and now, wherever that may be.

Love,

Jennifer

Political Free Agents

Friday, October 16, 2020
Cincinnati, Ohio

Dear Jennifer,

In June 2016, Jack & Jill of America hosted a President's Summit at the Marriott Rivercenter in Covington. There were 400 women, including my wife, Jill, who is an officer in the local chapter. The Jack & Jill event coincided with the Bunbury Music Festival, whose June 4 headliner was one O'Shea Jackson. The world knows him as Ice Cube. Cube was staying at the Rivercenter, too, and his whole family traveled with him: his wife, his children and his father.

Jill and one of her friends encountered Cube and his father over breakfast, and Jill, ever the servant-leader, made Dad a breakfast plate and took pictures with the family. Hereafter, I will use Jackson's legal name.

Jackson is ubiquitous because of his proposed "Contract with Black America" plan that President Trump ended up including as part of his "Platinum" stimulus plan. I say it's a political ploy to gain Black voters. Jackson has taken major criticism for "partnering" with Trump, but Jackson denies currying favor with any party, just embracing those who are willing to listen to his plan and take action. Among other things, the Contract proposes to eliminate income taxes for the descendants of slaves in America.

Oddly, Jackson said the Biden campaign seemed lukewarm about talking about the plan, at least until after the election. I get that. After all, you and I both know about the importance of staying on message. Eleventh-hour muddling would be a mistake. (Note: Jackson's plan has been in the works for at least six months.)

Trump's people listened, Jackson said. But that's because they don't have a plan. For years, Black voters have said they feel they are taken for granted by Democrats and ignored in recent years by Republicans. This situation reminds me of that, but only a little bit. To be sure, I feel like the Trump administration has been openly hostile to "The Blacks," as he calls us. I recently had a conversation with an opinion writer about Black people and their commitment to the Democratic Party. Our conclusion: Jackson has a point, essentially that Black people should be free agents, but his timing is wrong and Trump has shown he is not an honest broker.

For years he's used famous Black men (Kanye West, Don King, Mike Tyson) in transactional ways. But his disdain for non-famous ones is apparent.

This is why I cannot understand why any "minority" Trump has stomped on would entertain the thought of working with Trump, who has shown nothing but disdain toward minorities both during his presidency and his business practices.

I think Trump's people are playing chess to Jackson's checkers, and Jackson is showing his political naivete. You mentioned earlier that for the first time you feel like Biden will be our next president. I have remained skeptical, but because of the high voter turnout in places like Georgia, where people have stood in line for hours, I'm feeling more confident of a Biden-Harris outcome.

Meanwhile, Republican lawmakers have grown brave, and some are beginning to jump off the Trump train. Problem is, they may land in a briar patch in the middle of nowhere. The damage has been done and they allowed it.

Nebraska's junior senator Ben Sasse said he believes there will be a Republican "bloodbath" during the coming election, as did others, including middling Texas Sen. Ted Cruz. Even Trump sycophant Sen. Lindsay Graham is hedging, wondering out loud if Trump will lose the presidency. We will look back on these days in the future having understood them better with the wisdom of time.

I have no sympathy for any of them who allowed the indecency of Trumpism to flourish all these years. Let the chips fall where they may.

Finally, if there is anything to Jackson's plan, I hope he gets a hearing.

Love,

Byron

Turn Turn Turn

Sunday, October 18, 2020
Cincinnati, Ohio

Dear Byron,

It is that time. It is when the late summer turns to cold fall quickly. While there might be some more epic, blue sky, warmish temps and full bloom of the trees left, days are dark and winter beckons. People are standing in line to vote, to be heard, with a shred of optimism and hope for the future.

I voted last week. It was a quick transaction, yet a long ballot. I fed it through the machine and prayed that we were turning a corner. The hopeful part of me says that our country is learning, and we will come out better people.

We can only hope.

I loved hearing about CUBE. I think that some celebs have become co-opted by a mesmerizing man. Trump does seem to cast a spell over many. I was hesitant to ever compare him to Hitler, yet they are similar. If Trump were honest he might even admit loudly that Hitler was a role model.

Princess Ivanka Trump came to our town the other day. Her initial appearance was to be a short walk from our building. If she had turned up here, my friend Kathleen and I planned to mask up and witness the strange phenomenon that we are helpless to understand. Yet she went to a wealthier neighborhood and only those with invites could attend. How Trumpian.

Family has been heavy on my mind. What is a family? I grew up in a traditional family that became blended when my mom remarried. My dad also remarried. While I visited their home in Arizona with some regularity, we ultimately were estranged. When he died, I sent my stepmother a letter to thank her for taking care of him. It came back, unopened, "return to sender." This was decades ago. I sometimes Google her and wonder how life has turned out.

My mom and her husband have been married for over thirty-six years. Through their marriage I have six step siblings. We went to an outside distant dinner at my stepsisters the other evening. She took great care for the safety of the older crowd. This was likely our last time together before our departure. No one could understand our desire to leave this town. The hosts live blocks from where they were raised.

A permanent journey out of this zip code is something that (I have learned) does not occur to many Midwesterners. To be sure, this is one of the great cities with reliable people, solid friendships, a stable economy and predictability.

And yet we will leave, to something a bit known, but not like this location.

Don and I created another blended family. Almost three decades ago we merged and created a new unit. The years have been kind to us. Our semblance of different personalities, but generally similar values has treated one another with respect. As I evaluate my lifelong relationships, be they with friends or family members, I recognize that I have cobbled together a motley crew.

I am a mom, a stepmom, a sister, a daughter, a stepdaughter, a wife, an ex-wife and a friend.

They all matter to me. While they say that blood is the thickest, I know for sure that we can go deep, shallow, serious, intense, fun and funny with any and all in our lives.

While the nation is sometimes hopeless, we must still hold onto the memories and those with whom we have created them.

Love,

Jennifer

Blood Is Thicker

Monday, October 19, 2020
Cincinnati, Ohio

Dear Jennifer,

Mom found Wilson Pete Jr.'s phone number and address in one of the black, hardbound alumni booklets published by Grambling State University as a way to raise money and, in my case, if you needed to find your Daddy.

Surely, she had looked him up before. What an odd name, one that was about as foreign to me as an Asian or Russian one to a sixteen-year-old: PETE, Wilson, Conoco, construction eng. It gave the home address and phone number. Was he still there? He probably wasn't. I felt my heart racing as I dialed the unfamiliar area code. What do I say to him?

"Hello, this is Pete!" Everyone called him by his last name.

"Mr. Pete, you probably don't know me, but my name is Byron McCauley. Versia Williams is my mother. You knew her in Grambling."

"Of course, I know who you are."

I did not realize I was holding my breath until I needed to talk.

"I'm doing fine. How are you doing?"

Silence. *Get it together, Byron.*

"In a way, I've been waiting on this call. I had been waiting to hear from you," he said.

I didn't know what to make of that. *I mean, I was a kid. And they were the adults. And I just found out you exist.*

We eventually got around to agreeing that I would come for a visit. He would send me a bus ticket, and I would ride for four hours to the south-western tip of Louisiana—Lake Charles—to finally see a male in my family who looked like me. It was dark when I arrived, but I recognized a man who looked like me. I grew weak in the knees, filled with excitement and fear at the same time. I could not look at him enough. I stayed with them for two days.

I had a brother, Greg, who was two years my junior. He was a high school freshman with a really tall girlfriend. And I met Etta, Pete's sweet wife, who died this year of COVID-19. And I met my grandmother, Ruth Franklin, a 4-foot-11 ball of energy with a Cajun accent and enough shoes to marvel Emelda Marcos. She died of complications from Alzheimer's in 1999 weighing seventy-five pounds.

I learned of her penchant for fashion during her comical funeral. "You mess up, I dress up!" was her most well-known phrase, which was directed toward her husband. I met a slew of uncles, aunts and cousins. They all knew about me and showered me with good wishes. A whole other family in a whole other city.

I have seen him five times since then. Once when he and several family members drove to my home in Shreveport, La. fleeing a hurricane. Once when we lived in Mobile, Alabama, and we met Pete and Etta at a Mississippi casino. Once when Loren was born. Once at my brother, Greg's house in Indiana. And once during his 60th birthday party, when I drove there from Shreveport.

We talk about every two weeks now. It's hard to fill in forty years, so we are more like buddies. But I can truly say I love him. He is probably the most optimistic person I know, besides maybe Tony Robbins. This year, he has suffered a lifetime of tragedy: losing his wife, getting COVID, having his home destroyed by a hurricane and fleeing two hurricanes to higher ground. He is currently homeless, though not destitute. It's going to take a lot to re-build at seventy-nine while mourning your mate of fifty-one years.

His birthday was Friday. Someone posted a picture of him on social media sitting behind a big bowl of gumbo, French bread and a bottle of red wine. He looked just like he did in 1981, the first time I laid eyes on him. His hair and beard have gone from brown to white.

We spoke on the phone. Small talk, mostly. He asked about the girls and Jill and the job. "Always go with God," he said. That's what Etta used to say.

No pity party for Pete. No sir. He remains thankful to see the light of day every day.

I think Mom died angry at him. She could never understand why I wanted to have a relationship with someone who never really acknowledged my existence. After all, it was she who returned to my hometown in shame, having gotten pregnant in college—about the worst thing that could happen to a poor country girl with no job and now no chance of a future. Her hope was interrupted.

But not only did she survive, she thrived. My very existence serves as the reason that I am not a proponent of abortion, though I don't feel I have a right to personally judge anyone who makes that legal choice. Life is complicated. Mom is gone. And Pete's blood runs through my veins. I forgave him, and I better understand my mother, by and by.

Love,

Byron

The Universe Is Right

Tuesday, October 20, 2020
Cincinnati, Ohio

Dear Byron,

And the constant pelt of rain continues. In a downtown high rise, it is most visible on the windows. The election is two weeks from today. People wait in lines, adorned with rain gear, and vote. The momentum appears equal to 2008. In 2008 I lived in Winter Park, Florida and waited outside of my neighborhood library to vote early. There were concessions sold including liquor.

Only in Florida.

Central Florida was a slice of time for which I am (in hindsight) grateful. At the time we left, our departure was swift, and I focused on moving North. I value the learnings from this strangest of all places. For a time, we became Floridians. This included:

1. Hurricane survival (four times).
2. Losing a roof in a hurricane.
3. Being robbed by people working on one's home (ours).
4. Recovering our family silver, lawn mower and my jewelry in a pawn shop.
5. Daughter staying out (at age fourteen) with another mom who took her to a bar until 2 a.m.
6. A tree in front of our home falling on a passing car (twice).

And I could continue.

Of course, I read the books by *Miami Herald* Journalist Carl Hiaasen:

> *The Florida in my novels is not as seedy as the real Florida. It's hard to stay ahead of the curve. Every time I write a scene that I think is the sickest thing I have ever dreamed up, it is surpassed by something that happens in real life.*

You really cannot make it up. We were there when the astronaut drove from Orlando to Houston in astronaut diapers (so that she did not need to stop) to confront members of her love triangle. Classic Florida.

> *In 2007 Lisa Nowak, a former mission specialist who'd once flown on a NASA space shuttle, drove 14 hours and more than 900 miles from Houston to Orlando and attacked Colleen Shipman, her perceived rival for the affections of another astronaut, Bill Oefelein, in an airport parking lot. To avoid bathroom breaks on her hurried drive to meet Shipman's arriving flight from Texas, Nowak told police she wore an adult diaper, a detail later disputed by her attorney.* (People Magazine, October 3, 2019)

I likely saved my skin and the futures of our daughters by moving North. 2008–2020 and we stand in line.

We watch the poll numbers. Don compares polls. We are on edge. We refuse to believe that we will live four more years in a Trumpian America. I have eaten one half tray of gluten free, sugar free, low carb brownies. Healthier than normal, but still dessert food.

I am not a religious woman. I do believe in Karma and the Universe. Controversially, I think that if our nation maintains the current level of hate, we have not learned our lesson and Mother Nature will continue to make her presence known.

Through whatever happens, we must continue to hope—to hope that we can mutually repair a troubled country.

I was in Rwanda in 2016. Rwanda was then twenty-two years from their genocide. We visited the sites, we interacted with the people, we saw the rebirth of a most torn nation. We "heard" people praise their own government.

We saw prosperity in the streets. We witnessed people rise (in the dark), place their goods on their heads and walk miles to jobs, schools and church. We witnessed peace.

We can do this.

We must.

As a great man who was elected in 2008 said,

"Yes, we can."

Love,

Jennifer

Haves, Have Nots, Haves

Wednesday, October 21, 2020
Cincinnati, Ohio

Dear Jennifer,

Guilty pleasure: I love Carl Hiaasen's books. Such fun. He is my connection to the Florida underbelly, so I can write about "A Florida man…." with authority.

Jen, I can relate to deep poverty. I can also relate to astonishing wealth. By proxy as a journalist, I have seen both. I have interviewed Sam Walton, the scion of Walmart, once the richest man in the world. And I have talked to people whose only possession were the clothes on their back, and perhaps in a trash bag.

The poverty I know firsthand. The wealth I primarily know as an observer. I'd like to think that I am not a respecter of persons, but we show deference to the wealthy in America. Marketers send you stuff according to your zip code. For instance, we once owned a house in a wealthy subdivision. We were house rich, and cash poor, so while we had some disposable income, I suspect we paid a higher percentage of cash on hand to the mortgage company in this particular neighborhood than most. We lived the dream for ten years and then fell on some hard times during the Great Recession.

While there, we received offers in the mail to test drive luxury cars, attend high-end catered events with famous chefs (and also invest in a particular fund), be an active member of the community foundation and join this or that racquet or golf club. The zip code lied on our behalf.

Growing up where I did, poverty was generally a shoulder away. As in, the child who sat beside me on Buddy's bus route waited to be picked up every morning down the hill from her parents' house with no running water or heat. Thank God for school-provided breakfast, because I'm sure that relieved many hunger pangs—still does to this day. My family is comfortable only because I have been gainfully employed for most of my adult life, so we reside somewhere in the middle, and we have a tight budget like many American families.

This past week, I had a chance to golf at a venerable old Cincinnati club where no Jews or Blacks were allowed fifty years ago. And I lunched at another club surrounded by fluffy mums and colors, and leafy canopies. And I contrast this with an afternoon three years ago, on the coldest day of the year, when I interviewed some of our homeless population living under the interstate downtown. They spoke of the city's failure to keep portable toilets from freezing over and overflowing that night, where the low would be two degrees.

My mom would always say, "There but by the grace of God go I."

Dunne put it another way:

Each man's death diminishes me,
For I am involved in mankind.
Therefore, send not to know
For whom the bell tolls,
It tolls for thee.

Being involved in mankind is a burden sometimes. This is especially true today, during COVID, racial unrest and a leader who appears mad at times (meaning, not angry).

All I could do is highlight the plight of those folks under the interstate. But, like Oscar Schindler in Nazi Germany, I felt badly for not being able to do more. And I experience cognitive dissonance when I leave that environment and go to my warm home, go to a club, drive a fancy car, or even grill a steak.

Paradoxical America, I suppose.

I remain involved in mankind.

Love,

Byron

The In-Between Times

Thursday, October 22, 2020
Cincinnati, Ohio

Dear Byron,

We are in a state of suspension. The season cannot decide what it wants to be. The leaves are brilliant, the rain falls, the temperatures range from the high forties to eighty. The polls appear to favor Biden, but we remember 2016. COVID is rising. We have guarded hope for 2021.

Today's is my little sister's 54th birthday. While our relationship has included some disagreement, she is my only sibling. I wish for her to find only happiness. It is time for peace. Both at home and on the planet.

And she truly is one of the most entertaining people.

This morning's walk on the river was filled with both magic and fear. The fog was slow to lift. I thought of your time recently at two country clubs, both of whom would not have admitted either of our tribes. You mentioned that there doesn't seem to be poverty in these places. At the same time, the groups of people experiencing homelessness (along the river) have increased.

Our economy isn't going to recover soon. The greed of ALL politicians has resulted in no further help for the people of this prosperous nation. I am sad.

My communications consultancy was designed to give voice to the voiceless. This has included homelessness, addiction and infant mortality. The increase of people on the street displays the short path from warmth, work and home to a cold pavement.

I witnessed a younger couple. She was wearing a hoodie that said, "Micro aggression for racism." They had a load of belongings in decent backpacks and luggage. They were well-groomed, White and could be mistaken for friends of my children. One wonders what had happened; drugs, falling out with family, job loss—any and all?

These are the in-between times.

At the same time, the question of what and where is home is central to me. I was reared to believe that home was a static place to which we could return. This was consistent for many in our generation, be it the family farm or the home in Cincinnati.

It seems that home can be anywhere our people reside. My own tribe was kicked from one homeland to another for thousands of years. I asked my grandmother once, "Where did we actually come from?" She said, "It's hard to say. We went from one place to another." I have learned we are from Spain, Portugal, Poland, Russia, Germany and England. I am not a blue blood. Not even close.

To folks my mom's age, I am certain that the luxury of one place, across a lifetime, is something of which their ancestors would revere.

My life has been spent with a primary place in Cincinnati and a heart that moved often, both across town and across states. The movers arrive in less than one month to cross our country's interior and land in what has become our chosen homeland. New Mexico was the place to which many Jews fled during the Spanish Inquisition. They understood the climate, the land and the culture. They were called Crypto Jews and also became Catholic. Today many of their names such as "Rael" were "Israel," etc.

I do not believe that my connection is accidental.

Don and I traveled to Ireland several times. Don saw folks on the street to whom he could be related. For me, wherever I travel, people immediately speak the native language to me. With my darker complexion and lighter eyes, I look like I could be both from anywhere and nowhere. That is where this "mongrel" tribe of mine benefits.

In Ireland, they knew that I was not one of them.

I am in between places for a few brief weeks.

My goodbye to the Queen City is long. I will return, as a visitor.

To me, home is where the heart is.

Love,

Jennifer

Dance Like a Ginger

Friday, October 23, 2020
Cincinnati, Ohio

Dear Jennifer,

I feel your angst during this "in between time." We rise, work, worry, find joy where we can and do it all over again, but with masks and abundant caution. Today, we are living like Ginger Rogers danced. She did everything Fred Astaire did, and she did it backwards.

Today, I am tired, though not necessarily in a physical sense. This is the kind of tiredness that happens to your brain when it's on overload. That does happen sometimes, and I need to learn to be OK with it. However, the over-achiever-perfectionist-woo in me frets over things. In an effort to hold things close to the vest, I probably do not do myself any favors, health-wise. So every day this week at 3 p.m., I have taken a twenty-four-minute walk around the neighborhood before returning to work. It helped. It was also refreshing, though 77 degrees in late October feels a bit weird. Jen, I think you and others warned me about "project creep," the thing that can sabotage production on a new job. I'm there, I'm afraid, but I aim to remedy that this week.

Meanwhile, life goes on. I, too, am anxious for two primary reasons: 1) the election, of course, and 2) COVID.

Our staff had plans for an outing at a local golf-party place in an adjacent county. We received word from the lieutenant governor's office that COVID cases had spiked and that we were advised not to hold the event. The event was canceled. Workplaces should protect their employees and not exacerbate any health issues. On the other hand, tonight we went to the art museum overlooking the city to a diverse event featuring a prominent Black artist,

Hank Willis Thomas with a sought-after traveling exhibit and also art from Cincinnati-native artists.

This was unusual for our town, as you know. The venerable old art museum (founded in 1881) with Rembrandts, Renoirs, Picassos and centuries-old artifacts from all over the world exhibiting contemporary art by young, Black artists? It was brilliant. Jill and I met the newish executive director of the museum, Cameron Kitchin, at Felicia's house. He formerly held a similar role at the Pink Palace Museum in Memphis, which holds a special place in Jill's heart, because it played host to many a field trip. Literally, the museum was housed in a pink "castle" that once was the private home of the founder of the Piggly Wiggly chain of grocery stores. He began building it in the 1920s, but had to file for bankruptcy in a New York Stock Exchange dispute. He never finished construction on the house, and it became public property.

Cameron was there tonight, professorial in a bow tie and a tweed jacket, as was Felicia looking cute in some shiny pants from Banana Republic. Many people there you would have recognized, either because you know them, personally, or you have seen them around town. TV news anchors, young entrepreneurs staking their claim on a piece of Cincinnati.

On particularly stressful days, I once made my way from downtown to the museum, ate some tomato soup in the café and "art bathed." I would return to work refreshed and whole. And tonight a whole new generation became exposed to one of our city's great treasures, possibly for the first time ever.

Cameron told me that he didn't give a second thought about saying "yes" to the proposal of having the local art exhibit piggyback on the Hank Willis Thomas exhibit. I wrote about a young entrepreneur named Ricardo Grant, co-founder of Paloozanoire, who initially intended to rent a warehouse to showcase local and native artists during his lifestyle event. Then COVID hit. But he was not deterred. The Greater Cincinnati Foundation stepped in, as did ArtsWave, which has a new commitment to diversity programming.

All those efforts culminated in a slam dunk event and weeks-long installation, adding some new color to our grand museum on the hill.

When we talk of hope, this is what it looks like. Old welcoming new. Black and White together. Social change often starts with the artists, doesn't it?

As we all learn to live like Ginger danced in this new normal, I think we will all be better for it, learning new things and doing them in new ways.

Love,

Byron

Was I Much Older Then?

Saturday, October 24, 2020
Cincinnati, Ohio

Dear Byron,

The exhibit sounds incredible. And a gathering of a diverse cross section of people at the Cincinnati Art Museum on the hill. Mission critical work.

Black & Brown Faces responds to the need for creative expression and dialogue to promote openness, health and wellness in communities of color and in our society.

That place has been a constant in my own life as well—from taking painting classes there (as a youngster) to many school field trips, to the adult stop-ins, and I too love their café.

Last summer (when Nora and Erwann were in town) we toured all of the local art installations which culminated in Chicago and a visit to The Chicago Art Institute. Erwann, raised in Europe, is accustomed to "the masters." He said (while in Chicago), "The American artist collection is great. Why don't the U.S. Museums focus on American Art and eliminate the lesser European works that are shown in the states?"

We have an abundance of American artists and, to me, he had a point.

I have not been to any gatherings (except to hear music from a far distance) since pre-COVID.

I too am fatigued. I continue to bake more brownies. They are "a bit healthy," but still chocolate. Pick your poison, right?

This week was a whirlwind of final sightings of friends, work, election fear and general anxiety. Between the election and the move, there is this long and drawn out display. I had dinner (outside on a terrace near our Tyler Davidson Fountain Square) with two old and forever friends. It was (maybe) one of the final pleasant nights outside. We talked of shared history, our futures and fears for our children. Ambulances zoomed by repeatedly.

Loudly. We wondered if it was a drill. Were people hurt? Blaring noises are the dystopian sounds in our Midwestern City. I wore my Ohio for Biden-Harris mask. I have had it on constantly for the past few days. I am often stopped and asked where one can be obtained. There is the occasional dirty look, but it is outpaced by hopeful glances and questions.

I saw my mother today outside (in chilly weather). Our Saturday ritual will halt shortly, initially due to weather and then I will be gone. She is planning her time post-retirement. She explained how women in her generation (born in the later 1930s) generally never thought about a career. I explained how my generation generally did while raising children simultaneously.

We "had it all" and the price was high.

We talked of Gloria Steinem and women's rights. We women have only come so far. Pay is still out of balance, women still are not given many chances and choices. I am also weary of "fighting the system."

Whether it is bigotry, lack of equality or an intransient old guard—does this "battle" continue ad infinitum?

We also recently sat with friends who have children in the same age range as our own. We all agreed that this is, in fact, the first generation that will not do as well (financially) as we have. Yet all agree that this generation has different values.

Perhaps they are healthier.

They do not seem to live in a fantasy about the dream of America. They do not hold our nation out to be something "great." They merely want to live their lives. They do not seem to obsess about home ownership and "new stuff." They spend what they have and not more.

Perhaps they have outsmarted us.

They do not want to be tied down to much of anything. My mom explained her dream (as was my grandfather's dream) of her family all living together (in separate homes) on one large piece of land. I understand the sentiment. To know that we are all together for the benefit of one another.

But I also know the wanderlust. The desire to be part of the greater world. The desire to be brave, original and insightful. About three years ago I spent time in small Kenyan Villages. Many tribal families live on one estate. The Mama lives in the larger home with the family members through cousins and mass offspring build their own places.

While this all seems idyllic, it is much more so for the families of boys. The brides move onto their husband's estates. This dream of a family plot is nonexistent to a family of all girls (ours).

And one wonders what is a family?

For our children the questions of what and who is family, what does gender mean, "what you are?" (based on skin color) and from where you hail—these are questions of an older age. Our children are not fixated on covering these basics.

They seek a modest living and life experiences.

They are the future. They are the largest voting bloc in this presidential election.

They have learned from us and primarily how not to be, but how to live.

Love,

Jennifer

Growing Little Women

Sunday, October 25, 2020
Cincinnati, Ohio

Dear Jennifer,

Funny, Jen. My dream is to live on lots of land joined by relatives. The challenge is making enough income to sustain the lifestyle where we have such land, free and clear. (Provided that I get to choose the relatives who would want to share the land with me.) Some of them, I think are best left to themselves.

We have satellite radio. It was tuned on the jazz channel today and a song by Helen Reddy from 1974 played. This was my opportunity to share a story about her with Simone and Laila, fifteen and thirteen. Helen Reddy, I told them, was most famous for her song, "I Am Woman," which became an anthem in the 1970s as part of the women's liberation movement.

"Didn't she say, 'I am woman, hear me roar?'" Jill asked.

"Yes," I said.

I elaborated. My mother loved the song. It was all over the radio as women were finally getting equal rights with men.

"You guys should find the song on YouTube. You might like it," I said.

"We still don't have equal rights, Dad," said Simone, fifteen. "We don't get paid the same as men and we are not treated like men in the workplace."

This, from the "shy" daughter of the family. Her words made me proud. Jill and I have managed to raise some strong and very opinionated young ladies who I believe will find their place in America and make a difference in society. They are enlightened, learned and not afraid to say what's on their mind.

Their eldest sister, Loren, twenty-three, is the most opinionated of them all, with her minor in African-American literature and her nouveau militancy. Loren grew up in the suburbs and attended one of Cincinnati's famous private Catholic girls schools. She was a prime candidate for falling into the comfortable middle that our city and region cultivates. But at Loyola University-Chicago, she found her tribe, joined a sorority, traveled abroad and became enlightened about injustices and systemic racism.

She has even founded a social justice group based in uber-red Butler County with some of her "woke" childhood mates. I'm glad she has found herself. I'm proud of her. I see Loren's younger sisters learning from her and learning to make their voices heard. Simone is particularly well-read. She has probably read 800 books of all types. So, she has a ton of primary knowledge from which to draw.

Interestingly, Simone's observations about women and their state in America were disheartening. We are on the cusp of possibly electing our first Black female vice president, and women are game-changers in so many areas, but Simone is right. Women still lag behind in wages, in corporate leadership and in so many other areas. As Judy said, women of her generation didn't expect to have careers. And, as you said, women of your generation were not meant to hold down full-time jobs AND raise children at the same time. I think of you with two little girls and your high-octane communications leadership role in Florida.

Our generation expected women to be superwomen. It was unrealistic, but so many did it anyway. But you are right. Our children won't do what our generation did. Neither Simone nor Laila say they will birth their own children. Simone wants to adopt. Loren may have one child. None of them want mortgages or cars. Simone is seeking to drive a used Subaru "because of their safety ratings." I've wanted a Porsche 911 since I was fourteen years old when I saw the one our local pro golfer, Hal Sutton drove. I still want it.

Simone and Laila hung out with friends Saturday in a new suburban out-door shopping center. Laila takes urban hikes and bikes with her girlfriends in the neighborhood, an eclectic and diverse bunch. I love their little lives.

It means that as much as we struggle and fret and wonder if we are being good parents, we are doing something right. And all we can do is the best that we can.

Love,

Byron

The Big Things
Aren't Done for Money

Monday, October 26, 2020
Cincinnati, Ohio

Dear Byron,

I contend that our children may have surpassed us in what matters most: good sense, decent values and quality of life. Our generation (whether we admit to it or not) was on a quest that involved money. I think we believed that having it could mitigate the challenges of living.

We didn't calculate that the living was what mattered.

Our offspring watched us ascend the ladder, get the awards, plan the trips, book the summer programs, pay the people who helped to make our home run. In some cases (some of us) even paid people to essentially raise the children.

We felt that there would always be time. We didn't understand that monetization of that which is spent away from our children we would never get back.

No return. We paid a steep price.

We are one week from the most significant election in our lifetime. The incumbent has made the worship of money and stuff foremost. And he has spent our hard-earned toil to finance his empire. And whether we voted for him, or not, we have been cogs in the wheels that have moved the USA to today. We were enablers.

Someday historians will pinpoint the inflection point and the turns that carved the pathway to today.

The times in our lives that have likely impacted us most are those in which we were surrounded by love, our version of beauty and peace. They were not sitting at a desk in an office. They were not in a boardroom. They were not at an awards ceremony.

My life has included people with too much (more than any human needs) and many with barely enough. I have been with families in Sub-Saharan Africa with little more than a small dirt home, the clothing on their backs and an accurate sense of time without a watch. They often see us westerners with our pricey gear and fancy sunglasses and most certainly wonder how these things might improve their lives.

Truthfully, I have had more stuff and money than many. I spent the first few decade's acquiring and have since been unloading what now seems to be a barrier from a simpler life. My thesis was entitled "Soul, Purpose and Meaning in Individuals and Organizations." Money is not what essentially motivates humans. Ultimately it is about what delivers upon purpose and meaning.

Our children understand.

Some now lament that COVID is here to teach us.

I too believe that a large plot surrounded by family could be blissful. Yet it raises more questions than answers. Who is in the family? What if someone's dreams are yonder? Who is responsible for the fruit and vegetables? Who makes the rules?

And if we have raised our children well, we have prepared them to be part of what lies on the other side of the picket fence and that they have the nerve, bravery and wherewithal to see for themselves. I have thought lately lots about my late best friend Lori. Our mothers met at Ohio State and we met when we were toddlers. While, over the course of our lives, we often resided in different locations, we had an unbreakable bond. She never had children. She often asked if I worried about my grown girls.

I simply said that "I have the confidence to know that they have good values and they are decent humans with sound judgment."

She smiled and said, "that's so good."

Our girls were raised to venture out.

Lori, who liked Bernie Sanders before the rest of us ever heard his name, would be most surprised by the state of this country. She had hope. When I went dark, she told me about new music. When I was frightened, she told me what her psychic said. When she was on her deathbed, she told me that she was not afraid.

She would now likely say money could not have extended her life. A fence around all of us wouldn't have kept the monsters away. She would have reminded me that the ultimate value is in the living.

I'm keeping hope alive.

Love,

Jennifer

Democracy Restored?

Dear Jennifer,

Hang in there. In one week, we will elect a whole slew of people, including a president, who have asked us for our votes since before we began writing to each other. Here is what I know for sure. In the thirty years in journalism since I have been paying attention to elections, I don't think the mudslinging has gotten any worse. There's just more of it everywhere. And because our television media market straddles two states, we get a double dose. So, for instance, we know that Mitch McConnell must be beholden to the Chinese government because his Chinese-born wife's family owns a shipping company that does a lot of business in their native land.

And we know that his opponent, Amy McGrath, is too liberal for Kentucky. We know that Steve Chabot is somehow "shady" because he paid his son's company to build a "clunky" website and that the FBI is investigating his office for some missing funds. And we know that his opponent, Kate Schroder, will raise your taxes as much as $65,000, which is higher than the average wage of most Americans. President Trump would have you think Joe Biden is headed to the grave, based on the doctored images of Biden in his ads. And Trump? Well, he has done himself no favors with his response to the pandemic, and Biden is stopping short of calling him a killer.

In the 1991 Louisiana gubernatorial election, white supremacist David Duke made the run-off against three-time governor Edwin Edwards, a fast-talking populist purported to love gambling and women. He had been indicted more than a few times and eventually was found guilty of racketeering in 2001. During the 1991 race a popular bumper sticker made the rounds: "Vote for the crook. It's important."

Four years ago, I lived and worked in New Haven, Connecticut. My apartment was one block away from the New Haven green, close enough for me to see the green. And if I wanted to hear what was going on below, I just opened my fourth-floor window. On a warm April afternoon on the green, Democratic presidential candidate Bernie Sanders held a rally before more than 2000 people. I raised my window and listened while calling my eldest daughter, a Bernie fan, to share the moment. That man really knew how to move an audience, and his supporters seemed as loyal to him as Trump's audience is to him.

That day, he pointed over toward the old campus of Yale a block away, pointing out its $24 billion endowment in a city where 36% of children live in poverty. He slammed tax breaks for "millionaires and billionaires." Sanders mostly talked about the staggering economic gulf between the haves and the have-nots. During the current administration, it has been reported that the global billionaires' wealth increased 27.5% during the height of the pandemic in 2020. In that regard, Bernie was right. But he lost the Democratic nomination to Hillary Clinton, who lost the presidency to Trump and his peculiar brand of personality politics.

Here we are four years later, a world away from 2016. I was one of the people who knew we were going to celebrate our first woman president in Hillary Clinton, though I was not particularly concerned at the prospect of that person being Hillary Clinton. I did, however, change my political affiliation in New Haven to vote against Trump. I returned to Cincinnati before getting a chance to vote as a registered Democrat for the first time in gosh knows how long.

But in 2020, I will be voting for Joe Biden and Kamala Harris. I won't be voting a straight Democratic ticket, but I do think our country has been fractured by Trump and we need a person with a unifying message and intent in the White House. We need, dare I say, some normalcy. For that, I would welcome paying more taxes for the good of the many. I would welcome a gradual move to clean energy to sustain the only planet we have. I would welcome political debate that didn't begin and end with degrading and dehumanizing those who do not share your views.

America Lost and Found in Letters

Occasionally, I post a picture of the late great Thomas "Tip" O'Neill and President Reagan heartily laughing. They were political rivals, but they were friends when the day was done. Biden served with both of them. He remembers when different political beliefs did not mean you disliked a person. It just meant you disagreed on certain issues. We must get back to that, Jennifer, so that we can begin to heal as a nation and take back our democracy.

Love,

Byron

All Politics Is Local

Wednesday, October 28, 2020
Cincinnati, Ohio

My Dear Friend,

And again, we align. I adored Tip O'Neill. His book *Man of the House* (1987) may have been the one to me that made me starry-eyed about politicians (as I was for many years).

Now, not so much.

"All Politics is Local" may be the best phrase ever.

Beginning in 1988 I spent time on Capitol Hill and was mesmerized by what seemed to be men and women who loved their country. We have since learned that not to be entirely true then or ever. To be sure, many join the field for the right reasons and then add power, money, position and the individual morphs into someone else altogether. I ultimately spent some time with Chris Matthews (former on-air NBC personality, writer and chief of staff to O'Neill.) Like many, Chris got into some trouble and has not been heard from since.

The mostly men of yore often could weave a good story, orate a moving speech and bring people to their feet. In recent days, we have witnessed Barack Obama on the trail. He has reminded us what great leadership looks like.

I miss our former Congressman John Boehner (another Speaker of the House-Congressional District 8, OHIO) who, while knowing that I was not a Republican, helped me on countless occasions. He was forthright, honest and had a sense of humor about himself and the system. He made mistakes—there was a recorded cell phone conversation in which he was caught making out of school comments. He often wept from the dais and, knowing John, I knew that was for real.

I now walk on pedestrian ground. My favorite audiences are longtime friends and people who knew me when I was young. Today, for the fourth week in a row, my friend Kathleen and I swam outside (in October in the Midwest). We swam our laps and ultimately took to the kickboards and crossed the long side of the pool again and again. Or at least until we had sort of solved the challenges of our aging skin and the best low-carb recipes.

Kathleen is that friend who goes back to toddlerhood. We were not the popular or brainy girls, but we both had lots of heart. Our relationship started in pink ballet slippers when we were only four. We have participated in each other's weddings, pledged the same sorority, double-dated and baked for each other.

Today we unwittingly played the Cincinnati Game. This big city and small town. Between the two of us we generally know:

1. To whom each person mentioned is related.
2. To whom each person has been or will be married.
3. The status of the mentioned person's children.
4. If the mentioned has had "work" done.
5. If the person is worth mentioning at all.

Some call this gossip. We call it catching up.

Swimming is our favorite pastime. We crossed Alcatraz together and wax poetic about crossings such as The English Channel and Catalina Island. We have matching wetsuits. We both agree that the one place in which we have the most confidence in the capabilities of our own bodies is in the water.

Our relationship is about deep love and relentless trust.

The days click by. Now less than one week until the election. About one month until we head on the road to our own manifest destiny.

I am thinking about an epic song penned by Taos singer-songwriter Jennifer Peterson.

It is called *HOME:*

A baby is crying.
a woman's heart bleeds.

a man, he is dying.
blood runs to the sea.

and will we know by the end of the hour,
who is a hero and who is a coward?

we will sing out in the words of our mothers.
we will find solace in the arms of our brothers.

Who is the hero and who is the coward?

I am keeping hope alive.

Love,

Jennifer

Hope Has Always Been

Thursday, October 29, 2020
Cincinnati, Ohio

Dear Jen,

I'm just trying to find balance right now. I'm half-listening to the news. Sadly, I did not realize that police in Philadelphia had shot and killed another Black man. He seemed mentally ill and wielded a knife. Why would the police not have tased him, though? Argh!

Balance.

Breathe.

Repeat.

I'm looking for hope wherever I can find it. A few years back, a friend of mine had a seizure in his luxury sedan on U.S. 50 while driving home to his Anderson Township home. He is 6-foot-3 and weighs 240. He and his wife have an MBA. He is Brown, originally from Guyana. Hamilton County Sheriff's deputies trailed him when they noticed him driving erratically. He was out of it and had no idea what was happening. He ran up on curbs and off the side of the road and finally came to a stop.

Deputies bashed in his window and proceeded to beat the holy hell out of him. Broken bones and internal injuries. He told me he thought he was about to die. But a state trooper made it to the call. He pulled away deputies and assessed the medical emergency. It took nearly ten years, but the county offered a settlement that should help him live.

He found hope in this predicament. The state trooper was his guardian angel. Otherwise he would have been another Black man resisting and dying at the hands of officers in need of more training.

Hope in the form of a state trooper. A law enforcement officer. The thin line between life and death was simply recognition of someone else's humanity.

I have been so fortunate in Cincinnati. I have got to meet and tell many stories of hope.

The man who himself suffered from brain aneurysms standing outside with a sandwich board pleading for a kidney for his wife. Just yesterday, he posted on social media that they are almost ready for a transplant.

The parents who lost their child to suicide founding a national organization to help children serve as peers to other kids who are being bullied.

The federal appeals court judge who invited me into his home upon my arrival and assured me that someone would always have my back in this town. And around that table was a prominent pastor, the head of a civil rights organization, minority owners of the Cincinnati Reds. What he did was allow me to be free in this town, to become what I became.

The 107-year-old woman who told me to tell others to be kind. And to not say bad things about each other.

The former youth pastor with a plethora of health issues who nearly lost his life and everything making a comeback with a barbecue truck. And training kids to help him, creating jobs and instilling values.

Members of a local church telling me to spread the word about all the nourishment they had to give away. And then later thanking me because I did and the needy told them how they found out about it.

The coffee shop owner who hired hard-to-employ citizens with criminal records, in recovery or just down on their luck. She treated everyone who entered her shop with dignity and respect. And offered them free coffee and breakfast.

There is hope everywhere we look, Jen. And if we look hard enough, stories of hope will eventually serve as a counterbalance to the bad things that happen everyday.

Meanwhile, balance, breathe, repeat.

Love,

Byron

Packing and Hiding

Friday, October 30, 2020
Cincinnati, Ohio

My Dear Friend,

It is another one of those gloomy Midwest days. The rain is constant and teeming. Don is again working at the Board of Elections on voter protection. I am packing boxes. I have this gig down. We have moved too many times.

Today has been dark. We are five days from the election. The talking heads are busy connecting the dots. We mere mortals keep our fingers crossed and pray. Our fellow Americans have shown themselves. Another Black man killed in Philadelphia, Walter Wallace. Shooting by law enforcement seems to have gone the way of all shootings, we barely hear it anymore.

What has become of us?

I should be working on clients. Yet I pack boxes. I have a constant thread of emails from a man with whom I worked for many years. He too is packing boxes to move from Colorado to Jackson Hole. Like us, trying to distance himself from the noise.

I have moved many times in my life:

Canton, Ohio to Cincinnati (as an infant)
Twice in Cincinnati (Kenwood, Wyoming twice)
College in Michigan
Life in Colorado
Move back to Cincinnati
Move to Winter Park, Florida and back

In at various times: Cincinnati Hyde Park, Mt Adams, Hyde Park, East Walnut Hills, Hyde Park, Clifton, Florida, Clifton, Wyoming, Clifton, Downtown

Taos

Many times with Don. I have worked from home for the last three so I have been the chief packer. We have given away items, and acquired more, given away again. I have likely repacked the same items that I have never used.

I have thought of all of the homes that we have shared. While doing life in less places might have been easier and less costly, I learned a little more about living and left a piece of myself in each place. Our photo albums are full of memories. I recall in vivid detail the view from each bed in which I slept. There are some items that move from place to place; an afghan that my Aunt Robin made for me when I went to college, a wooden trunk that my stepfather built for college that says August 22, 1981 on a brass closure, cowboy boots that I have worn for twenty years and family photographs.

As a Jew, born post-Holocaust, we learned how people lived and died in Europe from the 1930s until the end of the war. Often those who did not get out, prior to round up, found hiding places. These were often in their own homes or in the homes with others who were willing to protect them. This included basements, attics, inside walls, in barns, sheds and closets. They were fed and cared for by non-Jews willing to take risks. Each time I have moved (into a home) I have looked and identified the hiding places. When one asks fellow Jews about hiding, one usually gets this sort of answer, "Yes, and my mom always had extra snacks for us (in her purse)." We were raised to be prepared to move quickly and to not be hungry.

Most people cannot relate to this type of strange planning.

Today is filled with wonder. Wonder about what America will be one week from today. Wonder about what this Queen City will be like decades from today.

I took a breather and walked along the river in the drizzle. A bright rain slicker ahead was worn by our former mayor, Roxanne. We chatted (from six feet apart) about life during these unique times. She said, "It is odd to say this as a former official, but I really do not know what can be done." We shook our heads. We both knew one another when we were on the way up. Now, two women on a bleak day, in Cincinnati's front yard. Heads spinning.

My old friend, Dan, popped into my email on a strange day. A non-Cincinnatian, he valued his time here. When he left he simply said:

"I am leaving a big piece of myself in Cincinnati."

Me too, Dan.

I close with Johnny Cash:

"I plan to crawl outside these walls and close my eyes and see, and fall into the heart and arms of those who wait for me.

I cannot move a mountain now. I can no longer run..."

Love,

Jennifer

Hope, Interrupted

Halloween 2020

Saturday, October 31, 2020
Cincinnati, Ohio

Dear Jen,

We found hope in Halloween 2020.

We have done Halloween with our children in seven neighborhoods starting with a three-year-old Loren McCauley as a Disney Princess. We have done a church-oriented, non-scary Halloween in parking lots from the trunks of our cars. We've gone to haunted houses and to the big amusement park's scary event.

We have done Halloween in other neighborhoods with other families. In one old neighborhood with wide boulevards named after U.S. presidents, our neighbors warned us: "Buy extra candy. The whole city comes to our street." Sure enough, no fewer than 150 kids came through between 6-9 p.m. We drew the line at the bearded twenty-something "kid" who rang the doorbell after bedtime. He was spooky without a costume.

This year was different, and we knew it would be. All over the country, citizens had been warned not to celebrate Halloween in the traditional way. The coronavirus can live on candy wrappers and in the air and on your front porch if you do not social distance.

America has reported more than nine million cases of COVID-19. More than 200,000 have died as of today. Our freedom-loving citizens clearly have not been abiding by the rules intended to keep us safe. In some cases, perhaps they followed all the rules and still contracted the virus. And surely others must feel invincible. So, I expected Halloween 2020 to be a corona fest, children walking shoulder to shoulder and breathing one another's germs.

Corona-covered candy sharing. It wasn't that in my neighborhood. Jill reported that two trick-or-treaters stopped by to retrieve our COVID-safe candy placed on a table at the end of the driveway. That was compared to about thirty last year.

Turns out, looks like some of us *can* abide by the rules. Finding hope in Halloween 2020. The local public school district apparently has less hope in what its students would do over the weekend. My daughter's sewing teacher required students to take home all of their equipment over the weekend—just in case. Our county was on the cusp of turning purple—the worst category of COVID infections. If kids didn't abide by the rules, I suppose teachers figured that the number of cases would increase and schools would close.

We have been confidentially advised to prepare for our kids to be home for the rest of the year after the Thanksgiving break in anticipation of an increase of virus cases. Actually, that's OK with me because of the age of our children, but I have great empathy for those parents who will struggle to homeschool their children and have to juggle jobs at the same time. I know Don probably knows more than any of us the perils of our school system. I will tell you that I am not satisfied so far with the level of digital instruction. One of my daughter's teachers has not mastered it, and it's the students who are losing.

In any case, Jen, I'm going to keep hope alive. I leave you with the words of Helen Keller: "Optimism is the faith that leads to achievement. Nothing can be done without hope and confidence."

Love,

Byron

Half Past Autumn

Tuesday, November 3, 2020
Election Day
Cincinnati, Ohio

To My Dear Friend Byron,

America Votes.

We have both voted.

We wait.

It is election day.

Much hangs in the balance.

While the past six months have had challenges, the next six may be more problematic. COVID's on the rise. The economy's on edge. Black men are still being shot with hands up. Violence post-election is all but guaranteed.

So much has happened with so little progress made. Or so it seems. Historians will look back and name the inflection points. We are living in it. We cannot yet see the forest.

Yet I continue to be hopeful.

Hopeful that our fellow Americans will unite and not divide.

Through our windows, situated on the mighty Ohio, we see the five bridges that connect Ohio to Kentucky. In a mere few weeks, the freight elevators will move our worldly goods to a truck, bound for New Mexico. In many ways, this is the day for which I have lived. In others, it has come too fast.

The living goes fast.

It is that time in my life. I am officially older, well past "middle" age with the heart and mind of a thirty-four-year-old and a body that wishes to still pursue adventure. The late photographer Gordon Parks would call it half-past autumn.

Step by step. Breath after breath.

Our writing took me to places that I often pushed aside. It wrought painful and compelling memories. It let me into your life. It is a good thing. It is my hope that people find a method to move forward positively be it through action, writing, peaceful protests or simply good thoughts.

We ARE all in this together.

Or as the late music legend Prince said, "Dearly beloved, we are gathered here today to get through this thing called life."

Six months have provided a myriad of learnings.

What I've Learned:

1. Underlying health matters. We will each be afflicted with something, be it COVID or another ailment. Taking care of one's self daily makes all the difference.
2. People can know and connect with one another, even virtually. Our writing has been an act of getting to deeply know and understand another human.
3. History repeats itself. We don't learn well. We don't listen.
4. Our great republic is a fragile place.
5. Cats make great companions.
6. Stevia and monk fruit make a superior sugar substitute.
7. We should never take one day for granted. Tomorrow we may be shut away from our mundane, but essential activities. Tomorrow we may not be.
8. Take the risk.
9. The planet is not as evolved as we might have assumed.
10. Being at home is a good thing.
11. I make really good cookies.
12. Time is our most vital asset.

My thinking about our country, the one that we love, has been continual. Many days I shake my head. Many days I see the beauty in our land and our fellow Americans. Woody Guthrie had it right:

This Land is Your Land 1949

This land is your land, and this land is my land
From California to the New York Island
From the Redwood Forest, to the Gulf stream waters
This land was made for you and me

So today, November 3, 2020, on this first Tuesday after the first Monday in November (designated by our Congress in 1845), our nation votes. Together we will elect a president with the hope that all votes are counted and that our system has the integrity sought in our constitution.

We may not know the outcome today, tomorrow and maybe not until sometime ahead. We will still encounter one another on our streets and across our lands—filled with the diversity of opinion that we are known worldwide to embrace.

In this Great United States of America,
In sickness and in health,
For better or worse, and
Richer or poorer.
One nation under God.
Indivisible.
With liberty and justice for all.

Hope, not fear.
I am Keeping Hope Alive.

I am heading out for another late season swim with my forever friend. We will take the plunge into warm water and exit to cooler air. It will remind each of us that we have known one another for well over fifty years.

Love to you and your family, today and all days,

Jennifer

Never Surrender

Tuesday, November 3, 2020
Election Day
Cincinnati, Ohio

We are as sick as our secrets. —Jennifer Lewis, American actress

Dear Jennifer,

Four years ago, in the middle of October, I drove home from Connecticut for good.

The majesty of fall in the Northeast is unmatched. The reds, oranges and yellows were just a little bit brighter. And each mile was more beautiful than the last. I had moved less than a year earlier to do the good work of education reform in Connecticut, where the divide between the haves and the have-nots is sinful. The divide manifests most dramatically in the schools. The fortunate send their kids to elite prep schools like Taft and Choate, and those same students often matriculate into the Ivies, or their close approximates.

I worked for a group that sought more equitable funding for schools in the state, primarily through legislative lobbying. The founders of this organization were the founders of the company that manufactured OxyContin, and now they find themselves in legal dire straits. Strange bedfellows, indeed.

I was not expecting to be back home so soon, but here I was. Prior to Election Day, a friend and I were interviewed by a European television reporter about the Republican candidate, Donald Trump, whose unorthodox style had caught fire in the USA. Both of us had come out publicly as "Never Trumpers." Our next president would be Hillary Clinton. When it was apparent that Trump would win, I wrote that we should not worry.

We are America and our democratic republic will stand. A friend angrily responded, "Do you understand what just happened?"

His anger was not out of place.

Four years later, Trump is choking out our democracy. He has defined deviancy down so completely that I do not recognize the country that I love. A pandemic has gripped our nation, and his leadership botched the public health response. He has even picked a fight with the man instrumental in getting America through the AIDS-HIV crisis.

Over the years, even through our warts—and there are many—we strive to right historical wrongs and seek to create a better future. Some of the same people who elected Trump elected our first Black president. And now I feel the races have never been further apart, with a leader who splits us further with incendiary rhetoric.

Yet, we must hold onto hope, Jen. You have helped me refresh and renew over these past six months. Knowing that you are there counting on me to share my thoughts and feelings helped me immensely. I, too, have released secrets, and allowed myself to heal through words. More than anything, I believe in the healing power of communication. I hope people gain insight and understanding about us, our friendship and even about themselves in these pages.

And no matter who wins the presidential election tonight, we are all living in the only place we know of that harbors human life. Every human being on our planet faces a common enemy in the coronavirus. Even something as meaningful as a presidential election takes a backseat to what we all face.

Yes, buildings are boarded up because people fear the worst. After all, a spring and summer of protests and violence have primed us for what may be coming. I'm alarmed at reports that there is little ammunition to be found for sale in stores. Survivalists have stocked hefty supplies of food. Our civilization seems as tenuous as it has been in my lifetime.

Even so, we move forward in hope not fear, my friend.

Hope, never fear.

All the Best,

Byron

Epilogue: Hope Found

January 20, 2021
12:27 pm Mountain Time
Taos, New Mexico

Dear Byron,

On January 20, 2009, I returned to Cincinnati after my stint in Florida. This was the inauguration of Barack Obama. (Inauguration Day has stood on this date since 1937.) We had credentials to attend the convention, but instead, were in the middle of a family move. The one that would bring our family to ground in my hometown, Cincinnati.

It was in the suburb called Wyoming that my young daughters would finish high school, that I would reinvent myself and move forward. I was forty-five years old. The odds were likely against my career as I had peaked young. My daughters were to attend a school in which they knew few people. They were fresh off the beach, eating Cuban food for breakfast on Sundays and a temperate climate.

I was hopeful.

The next twelve years would include living near my mother, being present for the birth of grandchildren, two daughters graduating from college, graduate school, four marriages, one daughter moving to the other side of the world and the election of a near-fascist.

Like most families, we packed lots in, often wide-eyed and blurry from the fast pace.

Today, we inaugurated President Biden and Vice President Harris. I am a proud stepmama as Don's second daughter will again return to The White House (she worked for Biden last time). The news coverage showed a

America Lost and Found in Letters

diverse America, many with tears in their eyes as we sat on the edge of our seats worried about violent protesters. The collective exhalation of American breath seemed palpable.

We are hopeful. We know how close the nation came to catastrophe.

Today, we know that even in our darkest moments, optimism and hope won. Yes, we are still ravaged by COVID with possibly more than 500K Americans dead. The vaccine is slow to be deployed. While I have witnessed friends bearing their shoulders to a syringe (on social media), we are somewhere further down the list.

Sadly, I have also witnessed privileged people force their way in line while many who work the front lines wait. America continues to be unfair to many.

Our daughter, Caroline, is a Georgia voter.

In the middle of this month's chaos, we saw Georgia elect a Black man and a Jewish man. Another historic moment. People just like us. Yes, we have a place in the world, in this nation. While hope was interrupted, faith, belief and what our founding fathers may have envisioned held true.

And, then twelve hours later, a sedition occurred. Trump sat in the White House watching TV while his thugs stormed our capitol and sent our general assembly to shelter in place. Republican Senator Mitch McConnell cried, on the Senate floor, as he begged his colleagues to approve the Electoral College votes.

Hours before, a woman was shot, and thousands broke windows (our taxpayer-funded windows), barged in and sat in Nancy Pelosi's office chair. CNN's Anderson Cooper asked, "Is there a conscience? Will Trump stop this?" We learned that both the vice president and speaker of the House could have been assassinated. We all sat, front-faced, by our televisions rapt in a nation that we did not recognize.

This, too, is our America.

Our nation is built on stronger stuff.

We are ensconced in our new homeplace, Taos, New Mexico. While people are less likely to get sick here, people are more likely to wind up dead (when infected) than in Ohio. We take to the trail most days, either skiing, in hiking boots with spikes or snowshoes. Exercise matters to us. We see some friends at late afternoon bonfires. We speak of hope—with the pulsing fear of the many Americans who have a different vision of America. Some of us have been vaccinated, but not enough for comfort.

You and I put our pens down on November 3. We believed that hope would prevail resulting in a unified nation. We are not there. We do know that our offspring have a fresh world view. They don't see race, creed, religion and differences between their fellow citizens. They simply want to earn a fair wage, breathe clean air and be free to express their First Amendment rights.

Like our cohort, there are outliers—but, for the first time, they appear to be better humans—mostly realistic people who value life more than wealth and privilege.

The time that you and I have committed to one another made us dig deep. We examined the arc of our lives, the promises, the regrets, the happy, the sad, the memories and the laughter. We confirmed that we are mortal and temporary. We, like many Americans, thought about death. In a conversation that my mother and I had, I asked where she wanted her cremains to be spread. She is a world traveler. I expected a faraway place.

She simply said, "Charleston, with my parents."

COVID has hurt our people but it hasn't broken our faith. And as a musician friend (who has had very few gigs in the past year) said last night "It has been a gift, too. It gave me time. For forty-five years, I have hustled, and I got to rest and recharge."

His new music dropped last week.

The days ahead will not be easy. There will not be a "normal" world. Our President has a historic list of challenges. Joe Biden has struggled. His life has been a thread of loss and hope. And, he is the right man at the right time. He knows endurance.

I have often ended my letters with other people's words. For me, music has often been the soundtrack of my days. While I have no musical talent, am tone deaf, with no rhythm, tunes have carried me through. I have learned that many (in our generation) have this experience.

While I was not a Bee Gees fan during their highpoints, I recently learned how they stayed relevant across the course of decades. This scrappy

Australian bunch, with their sound grounded in R & B, seemed to influence diverse audiences and wrote music for many of our greats. While all but one brother is dead, their words from the 70s sound like today:

Whether you're a brother or whether you're a mother
You're stayin' alive, stayin' alive
Feel the city breakin' and everybody shakin'
And we're stayin' alive, stayin' alive
Ah, ha, ha, ha, stayin' alive, stayin' alive

Well now, I get low and I get high
And if I can't get either, I really try
Got the wings of Heaven on my shoes
I'm a dancin' man and I just can't lose

You know it's alright, it's okay
I'll live to see another day
We can try to understand….

This is now. This is today. A side bonus is that if one sings these lyrics, the time lapsed is about long enough to wash our hands effectively (twenty seconds) and beat the coronavirus.

Today is a new day.

With deference to Reverend Jesse Louis Jackson,

We Kept Hope Alive.

Hope was interrupted.

But not lost.

Never lost.

Thank you for being a friend.

Love,

Jennifer

January 30, 2021
Noon, EST
Cincinnati, Ohio

Dear Jennifer,

Only you could give the world a Bee Gees earworm in the end. Now, where is my polyester three-piece suit (with bell bottoms)?

I'm writing these words ten days after Inauguration Day for a variety of reasons, but the primary reason is because I was waiting for the other shoe to drop. I'm wondering if I should continue to believe that the Biden-Harris campaign truly was victorious and that they will be ultimately given the opportunity to govern. I remain hopeful but also traumatized, though not in the way our elected officials surely must be.

I was not there that day in the Capitol when domestic terrorists went looking for elected officials to presumably capture and kill. But, I remain stunned all these days later that an insurrection prompted by a president happened, and that few responsible for what can only be described as an act of terrorism seem to have been held accountable.

For a few hours, my hope in so many things was restored. On Inauguration Day, I watched a young lady in a yellow designer coat dazzle the world with her poetic prose. Amanda Gorman is going places. I watched Garth Brooks (one of my all-time favorites), elbow bump and hug the Obamas, Bushes, and the Bidens after singing at the inauguration. We all watched Vermont Senator Bernie Sanders sit socially distanced with homemade mitten-covered hands. And by the end of the day we saw a photo of the moment go viral on social media because of its sheer authenticity. This was so Bernie.

I saw a powerful array of fireworks over the Washington Monument while a pretty pop star with a big voice sang her song, "Fireworks," to a hopeful America.

I watched Congress get back to work, and work into the wee hours after a scare for the ages. They voted to impeach a president for a second time. I saw footage, horrible footage, of a young police officer screaming in pain because he was trapped against a doorway and being crushed by a mob of hundreds. I saw a woman pulled from a crowd. She had been trampled, and she died. I watched a Capitol police officer lure dozens of interlopers away from the Senate chambers, possibly saving lives.

Surreal. In my America.

I, too, see COVID numbers rise daily. A friend forwarded a picture of a group of nine of us from last year. At least two of the men in the picture have been sickened by COVID-19.

These are the times in which we live, Jennifer. Some would say there is not much hope to be found, considering the condition of our heart and health. I beg to differ, as do you. We know what hope looks like. We have lived it in these pages: overcoming career displacement, health challenges, racism, sexism, anti-Semitism and many other of life's pot bunkers.

Hope is a friend bringing food to a family whose patriarch recovers from a long hospital stay. It is masking up and loading boxes of food into the cars of appreciative strangers. It is looking into their proud eyes and thinking, "*this too shall pass*." Hope is sometimes agreeing to disagree and remaining friends because you are better together than estranged. Hope is believing that although America seems as if it is tearing apart at the seams, we know that there are better days ahead.

Yes, our America is "built on stronger stuff."

We were prompted to begin writing to each other because we felt there was an inflection point happening, civilly, politically, and healthwise in our country. Our feelings turned out to be prophetic in many ways, and I believe we successfully addressed them in these pages.

There is plenty more to write about, and that may be another project for another day. Your daughters are grown and interspersed around the country and around the world. At this moment, I have two who need to finish high

Hope, Interrupted

school and another college graduate who is learning life lessons fast. But my deepest hope is that America collectively gets it together and remembers its glimmer—that it remains a star on the hill to light the path for the world. We are not perfect, no. Not even close. We have teetered much too close to anarchy than I ever wish to see again.

For generations, people have migrated to our country for the promise of freedom and the pursuit of happiness. America's promise must remain true for me, the son of surviving African slaves, and for you, the daughter of surviving Jews. We represent our ancestors' wildest dreams—hope, interrupted, then found!

Those same Bee Gees—brothers Maurice, Barry and Robin Gibb—sang and wrote and recorded *Too Much Heaven*:

Nobody gets too much heaven no more
It's much harder to come by
I'm waiting in line
Nobody gets too much love anymore
It's as high as a mountain
And harder to climb

Indeed, heaven (hope) is hard to come by these days, but I'm waiting in line.

Thanks for being my friend.

Love,

Byron